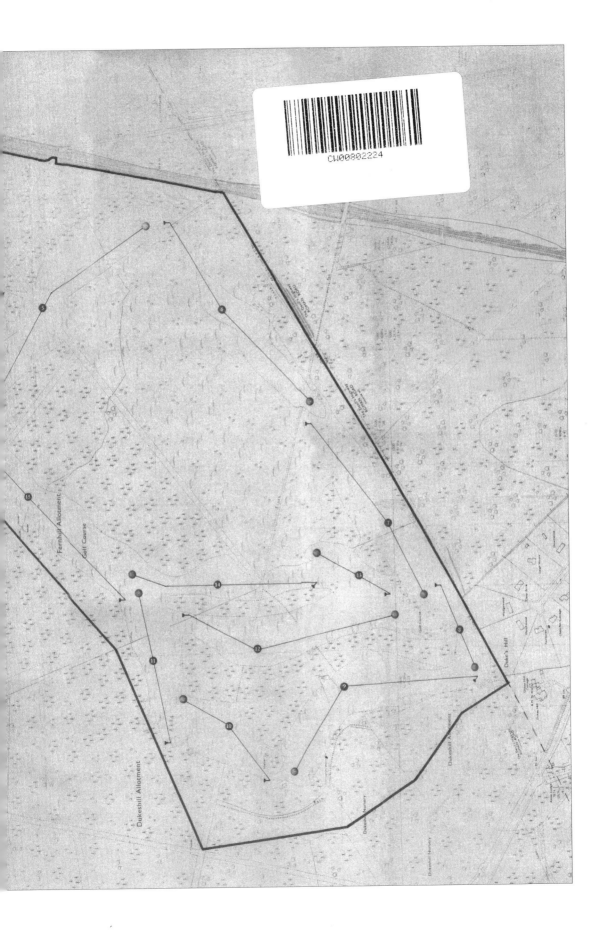

Fernhill Allotment

Golf Course

Dukeshill Allotment

Dukeshill Allotment

Duke's Hill

5

6

15

7

8

9

10

11

12

13

14

SWINLEY SPECIAL

ONE HUNDRED YEARS OF HARRY COLT'S *LEAST BAD COURSE*

SWINLEY SPECIAL

ONE HUNDRED YEARS OF
HARRY COLT'S *LEAST BAD COURSE*

NICHOLAS COURTNEY

2008

Published by
PHILLIMORE & CO. LTD
Chichester, West Sussex, England
www.phillimore.co.uk

ISBN 978-1-86077-481-2

Printed and bound in Great Britain
by Cambridge University Press

For Vanessa

Contents

FOREWORD BY
HRH THE DUKE OF EDINBURGH, KG, KT

The Swinley Forest area was added to the Windsor Great Park by King George III in 1782. It was subsequently handed over to the Commissioners for the Crown Estate in 1810. Since I have the honour to enjoy the title of Ranger of Windsor Great Park, I think I can claim to be the honorary landlord of the Swinley Forest Golf Club. I am also, of course, an Honorary Member of the Club, in spite of the fact that I have never taken up the game!

For all these reasons I am delighted to have this opportunity to congratulate the Club on achieving its centenary. It is usually the founders of great institutions who tend to get all the credit for the success of their ventures. However, this ignores the part played by the succession of Chairmen, members of Committees and Secretaries, whose contribution has ensured their continuing success over the years. In the case of Swinley Forest Golf Club, it has ensured that the Club is presently ranked among the hundred best courses in the world.

Author's Acknowledgements

To thank individually each person who has made the writing of this book so enjoyable would be reminiscent of some best supporting actress at the Oscars ceremony and therefore definitely 'not Swinley', but in the words of the regimental sergeant major, 'You knows who you are!'

ILLUSTRATION CREDITS AND ACKNOWLEDGEMENTS

Reproduced by gracious permission of Her Majesty The Queen (The Royal Collection © 2007): 49, 52, 101, 123.

Author's photographs: frontispiece, 6, 18, 27, 33, 63-4, 67, 92, 94, 100, 110-12; Aird, Sir John Bt: 73-6, 103; Alvingham, The Lord: 72; Arsenal Football Club: 107; Barings Bank (reproduced by courtesy of): 60; Bateman, Mrs Kitty: 77-8; Brabazon, The Lord: (reproduced by courtesy of): 71; Bridgeman Art Library, 120-1; C. Hoare and Co. (reproduced by courtesy of): 50; Calvin, William: 68; Courtney, Vanessa: 108, author photo on jacket; The Crown Estates (reproduced by courtesy of): front endpaper; Derby (licence granted by courtesy of The Rt Hon.The Earl of Derby, 2008): 1, 2, 3, 20, 31; Dunmore, The Countess of (reproduced by courtesy of): 34; Edgeworth, Anthony: 57, 98; Fernhill Artisans: 59; Foster, Richard: 114; Getty Images: 38, 40, 51, 61, 65, 85; Gibbs, Sir Roger: 96; Golf Illustrated: 99; Government Art Collection (by courtesy of the artist's estate/Bridgeman Art Library): 35; Graham, Miss Angela: 84; Gullane Golf Club (reproduced by courtesy of): 42; Harrison, Mrs Hazel: 66; Hawtree/Hamilton Golf and Country Club, Ontario: 43; Heywood, Mrs Shirley: 70; Hughes Onslow, Mrs Fergus: 95; Illustrated Sports and Dramatic News: 32; Jaipur, Rajmata of (reproduced by courtesy of): 116; Legouix, Geoffrey: 23; Macdonald, Alaister: 58; Meoli, George: 113; Moore, Michael: 69; National Portrait Gallery: 25, 81; Parker, Bob: 87; Phil Sheldon Golf Picture Library: 8, 10, 12, 45; Popperphoto: 83; Stafford, Mrs Elizabeth (by courtesy of): 55; Stoke Poges Golf Club: 88; Sunningdale Golf Club: 5, 9, 13, 48; Swinley Forest Golf Club: 7, 11, 19, 24, 16, 41, 62, 93, 102, 104-5, 109, 115, 117-118, 120; The Tate Gallery: 30; The Times: 54, 90; Truett, Philip (reproduced by courtesy of): 14, 15, 17, 21, 106; Walton Heath Golf Club (reproduced by courtesy of): 28, 47; Wellesley-Smith, Roger: 79; Wilmot-Sitwell, Peter: 97; Windsor and Royal Borough Museum: 124.

1   *Edward George Villiers Stanley, 17th Earl of Derby, painted in Court Dress with the sash of a Knight of the Order of the Garter by Sir John Lavery, 1915. From the very beginning he adopted Swinley Forest Golf Club as his own fiefdom for the benefit of his friends and family.*

Introduction

The moment he drove off the first tee Lord Stanley knew that this round of golf was a mistake. But he had been serving in South Africa for the last year, latterly as Private Secretary to the Commander-in-Chief Lord Roberts, 'Good Old Bobs', had been cooped up in the troop ship Canada for the last three-and-a-half weeks, and now needed some time for himself. He had missed his game as he worked tirelessly as Chief Press Censor, monitoring the reports of the progress of the Boer War. The campaign had opened badly, but with the arrival of Roberts the fortunes of the British had changed dramatically, and the Field Marshal returned to a hero's welcome and his Investiture with the Order of the Garter by Queen Victoria, along with an earldom.

For this, Lord Stanley, who was due to be presented to the Queen at the same time, had driven straight to Coworth Park, one of his father's houses near Sunningdale in Berkshire. There he had spent the night with his wife, always known as the Lady Alice, the daughter of the 7th Duke of Manchester, and their three children. The next morning, 2 January 1901, was as bright and sunny as a January day can be. The park, with its low, sweeping cedars of Lebanon and grazing white cattle, was far removed from the scorched veldt and the dark waters of the Atlantic he had endured over the last year. It was then that Edward George Villiers Stanley decided that there was just enough time to play a round on the links at Sunningdale, a mere five minutes away from the house, change into his uniform, and be at Windsor Castle with plenty of time to spare before the ceremony.

And so it was that he found himself playing his second shot from the middle of the fairway, nearly 200 yards from the tee. As is so often the case after a long absence, he was playing far above his game. Always prone to slice the ball, this first, uncharacteristically good drive gave him great heart, and by the time he was on the green in three and holed in two he had totally forgotten his appointment. Playing near perfect golf, his good form continued from hole to hole. By the time he had reached the tenth, the farthest from the clubhouse, he had bettered his best personal score by a dozen shots. Neither he nor his old caddie could believe his performance. It was then that disaster struck. The course had been virtually deserted, but without his usual zigzags up the fairway and the constant search for lost balls that characterised his game in the past, he had caught up with a four playing ahead.

Lord Stanley's mistake was to send his caddie to ask the quartet if he could play through as he was in a desperate hurry. The message that came back was terse. His lordship would have to wait for all of them to play out the hole, and then he was welcome to go through. It was then that Lord Stanley remembered his duty, one that posed a dreadful dilemma. To leave then would be to deny himself the pleasure of a really decent score; to wait for the four to finish the hole would make his timing critical at best, disastrous at worst. It did not, however, take much to convince himself that he should stay. Had he not spent a year abroad, giving up a wife, children and a promising political career to return to his regiment to serve his country? This would be just reward. And so he stayed, and waited. And waited. And waited. Stanley willed the four men forward. He nervously looked at his hunter as the minutes ticked by.

At last he was waved through. Lord Stanley played the remaining seven holes like a man possessed. Never very athletic, he now almost ran from shot to shot, his elderly caddie puffing as he struggled to keep up with the punishing pace. That he had bettered his personal best by ten shots at the end did nothing to dispel the agony that he might be late for one of the most important occasions of his whole life. He cursed himself for his selfishness, his rank stupidity, something that was totally out of character. The chauffeur, seeing his master's obvious distress, had brought the motor car round to the 18th green and in minutes had him back at Coworth. Likewise, his valet had him into his uniform—that of a colonel of the Grenadier Guards—in a flash and he was out on the road again, heading at break-neck speed for Windsor.

There was an aura of grandeur as the Knights of the Garter, resplendent in their robes and regalia, processed into the Garter Throne Room, part of the Royal Apartments at Windsor Castle. They formed up at the far end around the low dais, with its simple chair under the rich Canopy of State emblazoned with the arms of Queen Victoria. Set into the walls were portraits of all the sovereigns, from George I to the Queen, all wearing their Garter Robes. The portrait of the Prince Consort KG hung over the fireplace surmounted by carved festoons by Grinling Gibbons. Waiting to enter the chamber from the long corridor outside, Lord Roberts of Kandahar VC, wearing the undress uniform of a Field Marshal and with his right arm in a sling, was standing with his military secretary, Lieutenant Colonel Cowan. Clearly, Roberts was not amused that his Private Secretary was missing. But just as a pair of footmen opened the heavy doors Lord Stanley slipped into his place beside Cowan, and the three slow-marched into the chamber and up to the dais where by then the Queen was seated.

In later life the Earl of Derby, as Lord Stanley became on the death of his father eight years later, could recall little of the Investiture and nothing of the moment when he himself was presented to the Queen, such was his unbounded relief at his narrow escape. Frequently he would recall, only too well and with much horror, his audience after the ceremony. Just as he entered the Grand Reception Room the Queen's Private Secretary waylaid him, saying that Her Majesty wanted a word with him. Lord Stanley's heart sank, but he followed the man through the throng of guests to where the Queen was seated. Though less than five feet tall, she and her full dress completely filled the chair like some vast, black blancmange. Stanley gave an involuntary Coburg neck-bow, and as their eyes met she addressed him. Her voice was faint.

'Lord Stanley. I noticed that you were late. You very nearly did not make it to the Investiture. Pray, what was the reason?'

'Your Majesty', began Stanley. 'I have to admit that I was on the links and was held up by four men playing ahead of me.'

The Queen lifted her pince-nez and eyed him with disdain.

'Really, Lord Stanley', she replied icily, 'I would have thought someone in your position would have had a golf course of their very own.'

With that she waved him away. It was the first time Stanley had ever met the Queen, although his second audience came just four days later when he accepted Lord Salisbury's invitation to become Financial Secretary to the War Office. Just two weeks after that the Queen died at Osborne House on the Isle of Wight. But her rebuke lived on, and nearly ten years later her reproof was to come true as Lord Derby, as he had by then become, was instrumental in the founding of Swinley Forest Golf Club for the benefit of himself, his family and his friends.

This part of the story of the origins of Swinley Forest Golf Club is oft repeated, and through this constant repetition has become the accepted truth. But it is, sadly, apocryphal. The facts simply do not bear out the events as recounted. It is true that Lord Derby was presented to Queen Victoria on those dates, but Lord Roberts' Investiture with the Order of the Garter and his appointment to the War Office took place at Osborne House, not Windsor Castle, thus far from Sunningdale. It would be unthinkable then, as today, to be late for a meeting with the Sovereign, and it would have been totally impossible for someone like Lord Derby, who habitually 'put service before self',[1] to be caught up on the golf course rather than do his duty. Nor was there even a golf course at that time. Queen Victoria died on 20 January 1901. A year before, almost to the day, the first committee met to form the Sunningdale Golf Club, which obviously appealed to Lord Stanley as he was among the first to pay the five guineas entrance fee to join as an ordinary member, although he declined the offer to become a bondholder. It was to be another nine months after the death of the Queen before Willie Park's links were ready for play.

2 *The imposing figure of Lord Stanley in the uniform of the Grenadier Guards.*

It is remarkable that this particular legend has persisted for so long, but as with all legends there has to have been a grain of truth somewhere for it to spawn in the first place and survive. It is far more likely that the remark was made by Edward VII in some casual conversation with Lord Stanley. Stanley's father, the 16th Earl of Derby, was the King's exact contemporary. At Eton he was conscripted to spend time with the young Prince of Wales, both at Windsor and then on educational walking holidays in the Lake District and on the Continent. Although they were never really close friends, the King often stayed at Knowsley, the Derby's seat in Lancashire. Memorably, he was staying there in 1900 when his horse Ambush II won the Grand National. More often Lord Stanley found himself in the King's company, partially through his wife Alice, an Extra Lady of the Bedchamber to Queen Alexandra. The King and Stanley shared a love of racing. As owners they frequently met at race meetings or were included in the same house parties, such as at Quidenham, near Newmarket, as guests of the King's ADC, the 8th Earl of Albemarle.

It is known that at that time Lord Stanley was becoming increasingly disaffected by the growing number of members being enrolled at Sunningdale, so it is perfectly feasible that he related the incident of the foursome to the King, only to receive the famous reply, 'I would have thought someone in your position would have had their own links!' This bluff remark would have been quite in character. Although Edward VII did not especially care for golf, he had been Captain of the Royal and Ancient in 1863. He did, however, play on the Continent, at one time taking lessons from the Grand Duke Michael of Russia, possibly a mistake as 'he was a delightful old gentleman, but probably one of the worst golfers in Europe. In spite of this, he loved his game'.[2] As Prince of Wales and later Edward VII he was captain of many clubs, among them Marienbad and Biarritz. In line with many of the larger landowners—the likes of the Duke of Bedford at Woburn, Alice de Rothschild at Waddesdon Manor, the Duke of Devonshire at Chatsworth, and the Trotters of Mortonhall, Edinburgh—he had nine-hole courses laid out on both of his private estates of Sandringham and Balmoral, as well as at Windsor, but these courses were more for his family and guests, the Royal Household and servants than for his own amusement. Had the King's words really struck, Lord Stanley, particularly when he inherited on the death of his father, could easily have built his own golf course.

Known as 'the King of Lancashire' with over 56,000 acres, Lord Derby was one of the richest men in the country. It was said of him that he owned eight houses but lived in none of them; when it was suggested that he should abandon Derby House (his London residence in Stratford Place just north of Oxford Street, the present Oriental Club) as they so rarely used it, he dismissed the idea saying: 'Well, Lady Derby must have somewhere to change when she comes up from Coworth to go to a play!' In fact with his Parliamentary career Lord Derby spent much of his year at Coworth, near Sunningdale. With its 260-acre park it was more than

3   *The Countess of Derby painted by Sir John Lavery, 1912.*

enough for a private 18-hole golf course—today there are two polo grounds and three stick-and-ball practice areas.

Lord Alvingham, a Swinley member since 1946, recalled his father saying that the reason Lord Derby left Sunningdale to found Swinley was that he could not take the gambling, both in the clubhouse and on the course. Sunningdale then, as now, had the reputation as a high-rolling club. As early as 1902 the bridge stakes were limited to ten shillings a hundred, a massive sum considering this was auction bridge with higher scoring than today's contract bridge. Although one of the most successful owners of his day, Lord Derby never bet on any of his horses, and positively disliked all forms of gambling. In his youth he had found himself in 'financial difficulties' from a 'great betting scrape which had worried him more than any other episode in his whole life'.[3] He wrote a begging letter to 'Nunky', his uncle, the 15th Earl of Derby, who reluctantly bailed him out, probably with a promise never to gamble again. He had also seen first-hand, when in Australia, how gambling had ruined the career of Captain the Viscount Deerhurst, ADC to Lord Loch, Governor of Victoria. Deerhurst refused to pay a Sydney bookie, who promptly thumped him. Later, in 1890, Deerhurst, a lieutenant in the Worcestershire Regiment, had accrued 'unsecured debts of £10,746 with assets at £559 ... the Official Receiver states that the insolvency appears to have been brought on by unjustifiable extravagance in living and losses by betting and gambling'.[4] Creditors were eventually paid off at 10s. in the pound, with the remainder held over until he inherited the Coventry estates. It was a salutary lesson for Lord Derby and, most likely through his influence and dislike of gambling, card-play at Swinley was banned from the very beginning. The matter has often been raised over the years, and only comparatively recently was the rule rescinded. Even now there is no bridge and no backgammon—as the past chairman, Peter Hill-Wood, said: 'I doubt that there is a single pack of cards at Swinley.' Unlike Sunningdale, where there is a card room for bridge and backgammon, with large wagers taken on rounds of golf, the members of Swinley tend not to bet on their game—it has been said that at Swinley they play for the love of the game, at The Berkshire for a golf ball, for very high stakes at Sunningdale, and for each other's wives at Wentworth!

Another theory why Lord Derby was disenchanted with Sunningdale was their attitude to women. Lady Stanley became a keen golfer, yet under the original rule 4 she could not even set foot in Sunningdale, as women 'be not allowed to play over the links'.[5] A little later the rule was relaxed and women could

4 *Lady Stanley, always known as the Lady Alice, did much to further the cause of women players at Swinley during the formation of the Club.*

be 'introduced by a member to play on any day except Saturdays and Sundays, competition days and public holidays … A Match in which a lady is playing must allow an ordinary two-ball match to pass'.[6] In addition, women were only allowed into the dining room for tea after four o'clock on a Sunday. In 1903 Lord Stanley's 'application regarding Ladies playing on Sunday afternoon was refused'.[7] Yet if the question of playing with his wife whenever they wanted was really an issue, would he not have brought the matter up again, particularly when he was Captain of Sunningdale in 1905 or serving for many years as an active member of the committee? He cannot have been too averse to life at Sunningdale, with its rising membership, gambling and treatment of women, as he remained a member there to his dying day.

And so, contrary to all belief, the founding of Swinley Forest Golf Club does not lie with the Earl of Derby. But if it was not Lord Derby, then who?

CHAPTER 1

'You can bring in the drinks now, Johnson, we have finished our meeting.' The butler shuffled off and returned with a decanter of whisky and three glasses for his master, Sir Hubert Henry Longman Bt, and his two guests, Alexander Rutland Davey and Harry Shapland Colt. Johnson set the tray down in the library of Lavershot Hall, a commodious red-brick house on the edge of Windlesham right on the Surrey-Berkshire border, then drew the heavy velvet curtains against the late autumn dusk. Bookcases lined the walls from floor to ceiling. Many of the works on the shelves had been published by Longman, Green & Co., of which Sir Hubert was a fifth-generation director. In pride of place was the run of their *The Badminton Library of Sports and Pastimes*; the volume on golf, one of Sir Hubert's passions, was his personal contribution to the series. The three men felt that they had earned their whisky. And so they had, for their meeting had been highly successful. What they had done that afternoon was to inaugurate the Fernhill Golf Club—soon to change its name to the Swinley Forest Golf Club—on part of the nearby Earlywood Farm. It was Friday 15 October 1909.

But the story officially began just five months before, at the May committee meeting of the Sunningdale Golf Club. As usual, the chairman, Sir Hubert Longman, sat at the head of the long oak table. He had been one of the key founding members of the Club and had been unanimously elected Captain for the first two years, 1900 and 1901. Along either side were the other members of the committee—the Earl of Derby, Major Evelyn Lucas, W.G. Rigden, and Tom A. Roberts, who, with his brother George, had been instrumental in setting up the Club in the first place. Henry A. Trotter had sent his apologies for his absence. At the other end of the table sat Harry Colt, the Club secretary, sitting bolt upright and taking notes to write up the minutes later. The meeting followed the usual pattern—the previous minutes were adopted, le Comte de Lolaign, the Belgian minister, was elected an honorary member for his time in England, and the admission of Service members was put to the vote. They discussed the perennial problem of their dipsomaniac professional, Jack White, winner of The Open in 1904, who was returning from a 'drying-out' session with a Dr Bruce. This was followed by a debate on some aspect of the caddie's house. Then came item 10, later to appear in Colt's meticulous hand in the minutes as:

5 *Item 10, the first mention of Swinley Forest Golf Club written in Colt's meticulous hand in the Sunningdale Golf Club's minutes, May 1909.*

[Transcript:

The Secretary and Earlywood Links.

The sec[r] mentioned to the meeting that he had been consulted by Mr Davey with a view to laying out a course at Earlywood, Windlesham & with regard to the establishment of a Club and that he desired owing to the close proximity of the proposed course to Sunningdale in the first place to lay the matter before the Committee.

The Committee unanimously resolved that there was not the least objection to the sec[r] accepting the work in question and in their opinion the new Club would be a help to Sunningdale and not a detriment.[1]]

It is significant that the vote was unanimous, for had any luminaries at that meeting of the Sunningdale committee, in particular Lord Derby, Sir Hubert Longman or Evelyn Lucas, been involved in the project at that time, it would have been unethical for them to have given their approval of the new club.

From the very beginning the committee and members of Sunningdale had recognised their great good fortune in having Colt as their secretary. He had been appointed in July 1901, shortly before the course was open for play. As a qualified solicitor, a former Captain of the Cambridge Varsity team, the winner of two Jubilee Vases (in 1891 off a handicap of 2 and as a scratch player in 1893) and a Founder Member of the Royal and Ancient Rules of Golf Committee, Colt's credentials far

6   *Lavershot Hall, Windlesham, home of the publisher Sir Hubert Longman. It was here that he, Harry Colt and Alexander Davey met on Friday 15 October 1909 for the inauguration of the Fernhill Golf Club, later to change its name to Swinley Forest Golf Club.*

outshone those of the other 434 applicants who applied for the post. He also knew the pitfalls of running a new club, having been honorary secretary at Rye for three years beginning in 1895. He also had experience as a golf course architect, having been partially instrumental in the design and construction of Rye. With that and his experience and knowledge of green-keeping the committee of Sunningdale recognised that Colt would be of inestimable value to them during the final stages of Willie Park's construction of the new course. As *Golf Illustrated* wrote: 'Both Mr Colt and the Club are to be congratulated on the appointment which is an excellent one in every way.'[2] The article was accompanied by a rare image of Colt, who always disliked having his photograph taken. He began at an annual salary of £150 that rose to £200 a year later, then to £300 and 'drinks at cost price'. By January 1904 Harry Colt had proved himself so invaluable to Sunningdale, and had become so well entrenched, that he could virtually set his own agenda. The committee and membership indulged him to the full. Whenever he was away from Sunningdale, either competing in all the major tournaments throughout the country or advising other clubs on how best to improve their course (as with his fine-tuning of the new Alwoodley in Yorkshire), they invariably granted him leave of absence. Slowly his reputation grew. Commissions for new courses followed and by 1907/8 he was working on Kingsthorpe in Northamptonshire, the Forest Course at Le Touquet and Stoke Poges in Buckinghamshire. He had taken on a pupil, a man called Aylmer, to assist him and cover for his long absences. At the same time that Earlywood was proposed, he was working on Newquay in Cornwall, Denham, Dun Laoghaire outside Dublin, and the Northamptonshire Country Golf Club.

The committee of Sunningdale can only have been delighted that Colt was to work on the new course at Windlesham, as at least it would keep him at home to fulfil his position as their secretary. For Harry Colt it was a God-given opportunity to create something really wonderful on his own account, literally on his 'doorstep' as he had just purchased Earlywood Corner, a house set in two-and-a-half acres of garden that had once formed part of the Earlywood Estate. With the purchase of the house he also inherited his nearest neighbour, Alexander Rutland Davey, who lived at Coombe Edge, a few hundred yards down the Sunninghill Road. He was the same 'Mr Davey' as mentioned in item 10 in those all important minutes of the Sunningdale Golf Club.

Although Harry Shapland Colt recorded that he had been 'consulted by Mr Davey with a view to laying out a new course at Earlywood', thereby implying that it was entirely Davey's project, the original notion to build the golf course can only have come from Colt. The idea, however, could well have developed out of a conversation between these two friends and neighbours when Davey mentioned that he was interested in The Upper Cottage that was included in a parcel of 50 acres nearby that was coming onto the market. Both Davey's and Colt's land marched with the Earlywood Estate, then owned by Hugh Pollock, a London solicitor from Lincoln's Inn Fields, and his wife Evelyn. The Pollocks had purchased Earlywood

7   *The young Harry Colt driving off from the 9th tee at Rye, the first course he created, circa 1895. The caddie is collecting a handful of sand from the sandbox to elevate the ball for one of his opponents to drive off.*

House along with the 250-acre Earlywood Farm in 1882 and had leased the house to Colonel Mark Sever Bell, VC.* When Bell died in 1907 the Pollocks decided to rearrange their farm. By that time about a fifth of the land had been hived off by the Ascot to the Camberley branch line of the London & South Western Railway, and was only accessible by a single bridge. Pollock decided to put the outlying land and cottage on the market through Messrs Lofts and Warner of Mayfair. Davey can only have been inspired by a previous description of the land:

> A most attractive property of about 50 acres adjoining Earleywood, beautifully timbered and undulated and forming a choice site for the erection of a mansion. There are excellent views on all sides and on one position of the estate an ornamental cottage residence.[3]

At best, Alexander Davey was an occasional golfer. He lived a mere ten minutes away from Sunningdale and was in an ideal position to become a member, even a founding member or bondholder, through his friendship with several members of the committee, yet he declined to join the fledgling club at any time. He could have been a member of the old Royal Ascot Golf Club, whose early membership records have been lost, but then he would surely have joined Sunningdale as well like so many of their number. Nor were there any other golf courses in the vicinity at that time. But this grave 'omission' did not preclude Davey from working with Colt, as he was able in many other ways.

Alexander Rutland Davey was born in 1872, the eldest of three sons and a daughter of Alexander George Davey, FRCS, of Melrose Hall, Ryde, on the Isle of Wight. Through his mother, Penelope Susan, they were scions of the Lowthers of Cumberland. His father was a prosperous surgeon, a Justice of the Peace, and well connected on the island—as chairman of the appeals committee he endowed a cot for £1,000 and was presented to Queen Victoria when she opened the children's hospital in Ryde in 1899. He was also on the board of the Earlswood Asylum for Idiots. The young Alexander did not follow his father into medicine but instead read for the bar, joining Lincoln's Inn. By the time he was 25 he was a partner of Roberts & Co., a firm of Parliamentary Agents in the City. It was a time of plenty. Their clients were diverse, Davey acting for such companies as the Charing Cross, Hammersmith and District Electric Railway Company (now the District Line), the Victoria City and Southern Railway, the Weston-Super-Mare Grand Pier, and a host of utility companies. He also acted for several public companies, including the Berkshire brewery Gillman and Spencer that had won prizes for the excellence of their beers in the past. When the shareholders lost confidence in the chairman and directors, Davey was voted onto the board. Alexander's siblings

---

* Lieutenant Sever Bell of the Corps of Royal Engineers won the VC during the First Ashanti Expedition. On 4 February 1874 at the Battle of Ordashu, he exhorted an unarmed working party of Fantee labourers to work while surrounded and under heavy fire, thereby saving the day.

followed other occupations open to the professional classes. One brother, George Davey, entered the church. After Oriel College, Oxford, he served as a temporary chaplain throughout the First World War, and after being the incumbent of several parishes became an assistant priest at St Martin-in-the-Fields, Trafalgar Square. The other brother, Cecil, went into the Army, ending up as a Brevet Major in the Isle of Wight Princess Beatrice Volunteer Battalion of the Hampshire Regiment. His sister Elizabeth married Lionel Hordern, a lieutenant in the Royal Navy and one-time ADC to Prince Alfred, Duke of Edinburgh.

With a reasonable private income (his capital was enlarged by nearly £6,000 after the death of his father in 1900) as well as agent's and director's fees, Alexander Davey was considered well-off and lived in some style. He had built Coombe Edge in 1898. It was a typical red-brick, gabled Home Counties Edwardian house with a coach house, set in over eight acres. There he lived with his wife Winifred, attended by three female indoor servants, Ellen Berry, Mary Kempson and Fanny Shoesmith. There were no children.

Although Davey most likely did play golf, his real passions were for croquet and tennis. A member of the Lawn Tennis Association, he had his own grass court at Coombe Edge along with an immaculate croquet lawn. For 20 years he and his wife entered the major croquet tournaments in the Home Counties, the likes of Hurlingham, Ranelagh, Stoke Poges, Horsham and Folkestone. Competing either singly or as a pair with his wife, they had a moderate degree of success—on the few occasions they made the finals they invariably lost. It was, however, on the circuit that the Daveys came into contact with their neighbour and fellow croquet-aficionado, Sir Hubert Longman. Together they were responsible for founding the Windlesham Croquet Tournament, jointly staging it every other year, mostly using their own lawns. In fact Sir Hubert went on to become the President of the

8 *Sir Hubert Longman (front row, left) with his fellow directors of Longman, Green and Co. He was on the founding committee and the first Captain of Sunningdale, and thus invaluable when setting up Swinley just nine years later.*

Croquet Association, where he was highly regarded, not least for his high moral sense of fair play. At one tournament a hunchback was barred from playing, as it was thought that his appearance would put the other players off their game. Longman intervened and the unfortunate fellow was instantly reinstated. The Longman Cup was named in his memory and it is still the premier nationwide croquet competition today. Having been involved with Sunningdale since its inception, Sir Hubert Longman (the first and last baronet) had had a wealth of experience in establishing a golf club from scratch, and as such there was no better person for Davey and Colt to invite to help set up and front their new club.

And so, with the approval of the Sunningdale committee and the admirable Longman in place, Colt and Davey began their project. Alexander Davey started by making an offer of £1,000 for the Pollocks' 50 acres including The Upper Cottage, which, after close negotiations, was finally accepted. Davey then went to Barclay's Bank in Bagshot and secured a loan for £1,100 to cover the initial purchase and expenses including tenant right of up to £20, compensation for J. Osborne, the Pollocks' tenant, for crops and cultivations on leaving the land his family had farmed for generations. With the approval of the loan Alexander Davey was one step nearer to fulfilling his own scheme, the purchase of The Upper Cottage set in some seven acres of garden, a spinney and a paddock that was to be hived off from the parcel of land. For this he agreed to pay the sum of £150 to the newly formed club. In time he was to sell Coombe Edge and build a house on his new acquisition. He called it Boden's Ride, after the track of that name that led into the old forest. It stands adjacent to the 18th fairway.

While Davey was pursuing the farmland, Colt, dressed in his characteristic light tweed coat, plus-two breeches, heavy hob-nailed boots and canvas leggings, began a survey of all the woods and wasteland bounded by the railway line and bordering those 50 acres. Over several weeks, he paced north, south and west through scrub and dense woods, heath and bog. Mostly of Bagshot sand, it was largely covered with purple moor grass (*Molinia caerulea*) and heather (*Calluna vulgularis*) associated with poorly-drained, acid soil. There were clusters of old, gnarled Caledonian pine scattered over the whole area, along with acres of densely grown, naturally regenerated Scots pine; clumps of silver birch, alder and other scrubby trees were dotted over the dryer patches. He made a special note of the Fernhill Allotment, recently burned, marked out by ridges and stone, which had once been for the poor of Winkfield parish to collect firewood and to graze the odd, hardy sheep. At first sight it was an unprepossessing place. He walked every inch of the land, noting each natural feature. He could see a really good course emerging in his mind's eye from the combination of the farmland they would own and the heathland and woods that would have to be cleared. Finally he came up with a design for an 18-hole course in his head, then transferred the boundaries to the 25-inch Ordnance Survey map of the area. He had at last identified the extra land he wanted. It was just 179 acres.

With the map in his hand Alexander Davey went to see the head forester of the Department of Woods and Forests to negotiate the lease, as the land they wanted then formed part of Windsor Great Park under the aegis of the Ranger. Being considered wasteland of little or no commercial value, the parcel that was to become part of Swinley Forest Golf Club had vacillated between an endless succession of notional owners (see Appendix II) and common land. Swinley Wake and Bagshot Heath had been a part of the Royal hunting preserve for centuries, and as such had subsequently become part of the Crown Estates. With the arrival of the Duke and Duchess of Gloucester at Bagshot Park in the early 1800s, followed by Prince Arthur, Duke of Connaught (Queen Victoria's third son) in 1875, the surrounding Crown lands were consolidated into a large estate of over 6,500 acres with the purchase of various parcels of charity land and the residue of an estate owned by the Marquess of Downshire. With all his skills as a barrister Davey negotiated very favorable terms for a Crown lease for the 179 acres for an initial 31 years. While the course was being built and the Club established, the first three years' rent was a mere £25 per annum. For the next seven years it was £1 an acre, rising to £1 5s. 0d. for the next seven years and £1 10s. 0d. for the seven years after that, ending up at £2 an acre for the remaining term. The decent standing timber was also included in the agreement, 'The Crown to be paid 2/- per tree for those of more than 6″ quarter girth'[4]—large pit-prop size, roughly 20cm or a little over 7½″ in diameter.[*] A local firm of solicitors, Bailey, Shaw and Gillet in Ascot, were left to deal with drawing up the actual lease with the Crown. With the money in place from Barclay's Bank they also drew up the contract for the purchase of Pollock's land in the name of Alexander Davey, 'to be held in trust by him for the Club'.[5]

Although Davey was successfully handling the negotiations and finance for the land, and Colt was formulating his plans for the actual course, the great breakthrough for the whole project came when they were joined by the Earl of Derby. His interest in Swinley was first aroused at the Sunningdale committee meeting, when he could well see the advantages of such a club to him. Possibly the gruff tones of Edward VII exhorting him to have his own course were still ringing in his ears? Maybe being so close to Coworth, his Berkshire home, meant that geographically it would be virtually on his own land, but with the advantage of not having the trouble and expense of maintaining it? Whatever his reasons, he took up the challenge with enthusiasm and from there on adopted the project as his own. He made it quite clear at the outset that if he was going to be involved in the new club it should develop in the way he, and he alone, would wish. And so it was *his* letter that was circulated to *his* friends inviting them to join in the new venture. The letter proposed that the new club would have:

---

[*]   Up until 1972, the volume of timber was measured in hoppus feet—1 H.ft = 1.273 cu.ft. 1″ quarter girth equalled 4″ imperial.

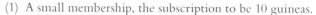

9   Harry Shapland Colt, secretary of Sunningdale and golf course architect, was the inspiration behind Swinley Forest Golf Club.

(1) A small membership, the subscription to be 10 guineas.
(2) Ladies to have the right of playing on all days in the week, subject to such restrictions as might be thought advisable.
(3) Membership to be subject to the unanimous vote on the part of the committee.
(4) Rules of the Club not to be altered except by a majority of two thirds of the bondholders.[6]

These proposals were later adopted at that first committee meeting.

A draft Form of Bond, based on the one used at Sunningdale, had also been prepared by the Club's solicitors. In the end Lord Derby decided that no more than 100 bonds at £100 each should be issued, and that he alone should approve all applicants. He also insisted that he must endorse any new member of the committee and greatly approved of the addition of Evelyn Lucas, who like Longman was a founder member of Sunningdale and had at one time been their honorary secretary. But Lucas was brought in to serve as a committee member, not as secretary, for that position was reserved for Harry Colt, along with the other most important assignment—the design and construction of the whole course. He was to be paid £200 per annum 'until it was a going concern'.

Despite the meticulous planning, the committee made one, none too serious, error and that was the choice of date for their first meeting. Lord Derby had failed to tell his fellow members that on the chosen day, 15 October 1909, he was Senior Steward at the Second October Meeting at Newmarket. He also had a runner, a bay filly called Queen's Journal, in the Southfield Plate for three-year-olds that was run on the Caesarewitch Course. The horse was ridden by the gifted apprentice Frank Wooton and started at 15/8 on favourite. Queen's Journal ran a very good race, but the legendary black colours and white cap were beaten by a short head into second place by Sir Ernest Cassel's 100/8 against colt Wiseacre. Lord Derby received £30 prize money, with £200 to the winner. He may not have had a winner on the racecourse that day, but by the end of that day's racing at Newmarket he was certainly an integral part of another course that was to become famous throughout the world—Swinley Forest Golf Club.

CHAPTER 2

November 1909 had exceptional weather, with less than half an inch of rain falling in the whole month. One day of blue, cloudless sky followed another. Each weekday morning the tall, lank figure of Harry Colt was seen to be leaving his house, carrying a meagre lunch in his piece-bag as he set off across the fields to the land he was to transform into Swinley Forest Golf Club. He was invariably in great good humour, as all his projects were going well. His latest, Stoke Poges, had opened in July to great acclaim:

> If there were no palatial clubhouse and no beautiful gardens and grounds, the course itself would take a great deal of beating anywhere within thirty miles of London. Mr. H. S. Colt, to whom belongs the credit of designing it, has scored a great success and his reputation as a green architect, already high, will be greatly enhanced by this the latest of his works.[1]

But Swinley was a very different venture from Stoke, where his job had been relatively straightforward. There he had begun with a blank canvas of some woodland and beautiful parkland that 'Capability' Brown had sculpted out of an original deer park in 1750 and Humphry Repton altered 40 years later. The soil was good and free-draining, and the turf, grazed by deer for centuries, was immaculate. The house, the first country club in England, had been designed by James Wyatt. The land at Swinley—arable, pasture, thick woodland and heath with its bogs and stream—could not have been more different. With the cottage going to Alexander Davey there was no house of any description. Yet Colt greatly relished the challenge, and set about his new project with enthusiasm.

Swinley Forest was one of the first of many forest and heath courses to be designed by Colt in a long and successful career. He had cut his teeth laying out the links course of Rye Golf Club in 1894 when working as a partner of Sayer and Colt, a firm of solicitors in Hastings. But it was only when he went to Sunningdale as secretary that he saw first-hand the many advantages of converting heathland, with its well-drained, rock-free, sandy soil and gently undulating terrain, for golf. Bernard Darwin, the grandson of Charles Darwin and prolific writer on golf, agreed: 'By

10 *Notwithstanding the heavy tweeds, waistcoat, stiff collar and tie of the day, Harry Colt was a remarkably fine scratch golfer. He divided his time between competing in major competitions around the country, designing golf courses at home and abroad and his duties as secretary of Sunningdale and Swinley.*

a merciful dispensation of Providence, fir trees, sand and heather, which are beautiful things in themselves, are the ingredients from which inland golf courses should be made. The prettiest courses are also the best.'[2] Heathland was the closest land type to a links course, and there was a seemingly endless supply of this virtually unusable wasteland surrounding London, along with most other major towns and cities in the country, where the foresighted golf course architect could practise his art. Contrary to popular belief, inland courses developed at exactly the same rate as links courses. At that time Colt was not alone in recognising that this unlikely heathland or forest terrain could be shaped into splendid golf holes, and there was more than enough work at home and abroad to keep him and the other three legendary designers of the time, Willie Park Jnr of Sunningdale and Huntercombe fame, J.F. Abercromby and W. Herbert Fowler as busy as any of them wanted. In fact Park literally worked himself to death. Of the quartet to embrace golf course architecture as a profession, Colt and Fowler were both amateur players, the other two former professionals.

Although Colt was greatly impressed with Willie Park's design and execution at Sunningdale, and learned much from it and in the 12 years he was there as secretary, he made some significant changes to the Old Course. He moved some of the greens (the 6th, 7th, 8th, 11th, and 12th) on the Old Course, setting them on plateaux in his inimitable style of 'developing natural features'. He also enlarged and extended the fairways to compensate for the 'Haskell',* the new rubber-cored ball that had come into fashion around that time.

---

* The new ball was known as a 'Haskell' after Coburn Haskell, an American dentist, who invented it in 1898. It consisted of a solid rubber core wrapped in rubber thread and encased in a gutta-percha (later Belata) sphere. It replaced the old 'guttie' made from the latex of the Malaysian Gutta-percha tree (*Palaquium*) that had been used since the 1850s, the invention of the Reverend Dr Robert Adams Paterson, a Presbyterian minister from St Andrews. When it was found that the 'guttie' played better with nicks and scratches, the entire surface of the ball was dimpled with a saddler's hammer that gave it the appearance of the modern golf ball. Colt was on the committee of the Royal and Ancient when the new Haskell ball was found acceptable for play in 1901. It gained popularity when Alex Herd used a 'Haskell' when he won The Open in 1902. The new ball not only flew nearly twenty per cent further than the old guttie, but rolled further as well.

Harry Colt began his construction at Swinley by engaging G.A. Franks, a local agricultural contractor, to fell and grub up the superfluous trees, then to plough and seed down the whole area. Franks agreed to pay 2s. 6d. a tree over six-inch quartergirth (smaller trees were thrown in free) with £300 to be paid in advance. In the end he was committed elsewhere, and so the contract went to Edward Berry, a local timber merchant from Sunningdale. Harry Colt was a good judge of character and drove a hard bargain. He limited Berry to just 30 per cent of the profit, and allowed him £1 per week for expenses, with a small advance to set up a sawmill in the woods. By the end of November Colt had a clearer idea of what he wanted to do. He had made a detailed plan of the property, or as much as the dense woodland would allow, and produced copious rough drawings of each proposed green and tee. It is unlikely that he made a scale model of Swinley in Plasticine, as he was to do on some of his later commissions: they were expensive to make and in this instance unnecessary, as only his fellow committee members and trustees were involved. Also, as he virtually lived on the site, he knew that there could be much fine-tuning as the work progressed. One of many features of a Colt-designed course is that it was not only as attractive as possible in its own right, but he also allowed for panoramas and views over the surrounding countryside—known as his 'landscape aspect'. When he was planning the Toronto course, for instance, he actually camped on the site for a week to better understand the terrain and to take in what he called the 'vistas', all of which were incorporated into his overall plan. At Swinley there was a great deal more felling than was purely necessary 'from a golfing point of view'.[3] But the greatest single feature that is so instantly recognisable of a Colt course is the bogey (par) three holes and, to a lesser extent, the short bogey fours.

Colt had an instinctive feel for the fundamentals of strategic design. At Swinley he had to operate within a framework of three defining features—the position of the clubhouse, the railway line, and the wetlands at the centre of the far end of the proposed course. Obviously the clubhouse had to be built on the land actually owned by the trustees, and with the single bridge over the railway line it made sense to site it as close to the road as possible. The railway line formed the eastern boundary. While it would have been possible, but expensive, to drain the marshy area, Colt found that he did not need the land in his final plan and deliberately left it untouched as a natural feature—90 years later, an artificial pond on the 5th was made at the edge of the wetlands. Colt then set about placing five bogey threes, their positions dictated as far as possible by the terrain and his favoured natural plateau. Each one was unique for its distance, difficulty and beauty. He then worked all the other holes into the framework, in the same perfect rhythm and harmony, around those five bogey threes and the wetlands towards the far end of the course. In designing a course from scratch Harry Colt strove for variety, often providing four or five good short holes, such as the 4th, 8th, 10th, 13th and 17th at Swinley,

11 *Looking back over the 15th hole. One of the rides cut through Swinley Forest so that Queen Anne could hunt in a chaise runs across the fairway just below the hill.*

several good length two-shot holes, varying from an extra-long brassie shot for the second to a firm half-iron shot for the 6th, 15th and 16th, one or two three-shot holes, the 5th and 12th, and two or three difficult drive and pitch holes, the 3rd and the 11th. He also tried to alternate the par 3s between the odd and even numbers so as to give partners of a foursome a share of each, as at Swinley with the 4th, 8th and 10th, also with the 13th and 17th. To him, the lengths of 'the various holes should be such as to incite the player to attempt strokes with every club in the bag of fair capacity'.[4] Another mark of Colt at Swinley is his usual 'long plain-sailing hole for the first one, followed by another to send on the players from the first tee … [which] was desirable from a secretary's point of view as if his members cannot start, they always become critical and impatient'.[5]

It has often been suggested that Swinley was designed to accommodate Lord Derby's game, as he had a tendency to slice the ball. Colt was such a perfectionist that he would never have compromised his design for anyone, and Lord Derby would certainly not have even thought of suggesting it, let alone demanded it. That said, Colt's fairways were wide enough to accommodate the most moderate shots. What is remarkable about the whole scheme, however, is that Colt put it together virtually before a single tree had been felled. It was 'a mystifying experience, and nothing is quite so mysterious as the way in which the architect [Colt] can map out his whole course in considerable detail when in many places he can only see a few yards in front of him … the man must surely have a sixth sense.'[6]

Sometime later, Bernard Darwin recalled meeting him on site:

> We wandered one fine winter's day in what seemed [like] a huge primeval forest. Mr Colt showed me as we fought our way through the undergrowth where the holes were to be, as I gazed and wondered at the gift of this golfing architect which seems as mysterious as the water diviner. I carried away memories of lovely bits of woodland and glassy glades through the forest, and I have been trying quite vainly ever since to identify them. When I came next, there was a golf course in being and my glades had vanished into fairyland.[7]

Colt began by making a careful selection of the trees at Swinley he wanted to fell, both for the construction of the course and for his famous vistas, which Bernard Darwin called 'a ruthless attack on nature'.[8] He also selected whole areas of woodland and some specimen trees, including a few large horse chestnuts and clumps of Scots pine, which were left for amenity and natural hazards as was typical of a Colt course. He began by marking over 2,300 trees of timber quality, which were then translated onto a felling plan. This was then sent to the estate office in Windsor Great Park. The head forester came out personally to approve his selection on behalf of the Crown. At the same time Colt arranged to buy portable tramlines and trucks from the Department of Woods and Forests, as he knew well the damage done to the ground through timber hauling.

It was Boxing Day 1909 when the same committee met again at Lavershott Hall, except that the triumvirate of Sir Hubert Longman, Alexander Davey and Harry Colt had been joined by Major Evelyn Lucas,

12 One of the greatest writers on golf, Bernard Darwin was a friend and admirer of Harry Colt. He was the grandson of the naturalist Charles Darwin, author of the Origin of the Species.

late of the Duke of York's Own Loyal Suffolk Hussars. Again, the Earl of Derby was absent. He always spent Christmas at Knowsley and, although he did not care much for shooting, the Boxing Day shoot was a long-standing tradition. Henry Alexander Trotter, an early bondholder and committee member of Sunningdale, was also voted onto the committee, but living near Salisbury he was not present at that second meeting either. Both Lucas and Trotter were golfing friends of Lord Derby, and took their place on the committee with his blessing.

It was at this meeting that the name was officially changed from the Fernhill Golf Club to the Swinley Forest Golf Club. It is likely that the change was made at Lord Derby's suggestion, as Swinley Forest, the Royal hunting preserve, was thought a more appropriate nomenclature for a club he was associated with than that of a mere fuel allotment for the poor of the parish. At the same meeting Longman proposed that Colt should be given £100 for his 'services up to date'.[9] Clearly Colt had not submitted a design fee or put in an estimate of what the whole scheme was to cost. In the end he was paid an honorarium of £200 a year to cover the design and to oversee the building of the course, in addition to running the fledgling Club.

The meeting progressed well in Sir Hubert's library. The Crown lease had been approved by their solicitors and put into the names of the trustees—the Earl of Derby, Sir Hubert Longman and Henry Trotter. When Colt voiced his suspicions of Berry the timber merchant, they decided to employ a bookkeeper and general manager, H.W. Munday, at £2 5s. 0d. a week, to safeguard their interests.

Alexander Davey's turn to speak came next, and he confirmed that arrangements were being made for the transfer of all the land (except for his six acres and cottage) from his name to that of the trustees. It was then agreed that he should have access to his land and cottage from a new road behind the proposed clubhouse and through the middle of the adjoining field. In the end, the road to Boden's Ride went in front of the clubhouse, where it has remained, there being no other way onto the property. Davey also brought up the question of further rights of way over the proposed course.

Known as The Devil's Highway, the Roman road from London to Silchester (that marches with the 6th, 7th and 8th holes) had long been a right of way. The railways had made the country more accessible to townsfolk, who came out for the day in their droves. National newspapers published weekend walks, including the delights of 'a walk through Swinley Forest at midsummer [that] leads us deep into the woods of fresh bracken and splashes of vivid masses of rhododendron blossoms'.[10] Fearing a rush of walkers inspired by such purple prose, Davey offered to see Pollock and ask him to have notices erected on his land to avoid the possibility of further rights of way being created over the course. The same went for the Crown lands.

As with everything in his life, be it a long and distinguished political career, as Mayor of Liverpool, a stint as Ambassador or on the Turf, once Lord Derby was committed to a project he gave it his full attention and backing. At Swinley he began by indenting for 25 of the original 100 bonds, for which he advanced £1,000. With this handsome sum, he could ensure that his personal friends, rather than those of whom he merely approved, would form the nucleus of what he increasingly saw as *his* club. It was that £1,000, held in the name of the trustees, that financed the initial works—the original loan had been used up in the purchase of the land and the tenant right. Lord Derby's cheque was deposited in Barclay's Bank, Sunningdale, and the funds were there for Colt to draw on as and when needed. Although Lord Derby was not present at the meeting, it is clear that his wishes (and most likely those of his wife) were well represented when the draft agreement for 'taking up bonds' (and the Form of Bond itself) were discussed. The first idea, to allow bondholders to 'nominate Ladies as members for fixed periods',[11] was deleted and Rule 14 (1) concerning visitors and guests was amended to:

> A bondholder may introduce in respect of each Bond held by him one guest on
> every day of the week to the Clubhouse or Green, either a Lady or Gentleman,
> without payment of any Greenfee, but Saturdays and Sundays such guest, if a
> Lady, shall either play with the Bondholder, or be staying in his house.
> 14 (2)
> All members may introduce Ladies to play with them on payment of 2/6d.

If the Earl and Countess of Derby's strongly-held views on women on the links and in the clubhouse were disregarded at Sunningdale, at least they could be indulged at Swinley.

Soon after beginning the work at Swinley, Harry Colt realised that he could not cope on his own. He was overseeing the building of the course whilst still carrying on his duties as secretary at Sunningdale, as well as devoting time to all his other far-flung projects around the country. He decided to take on an assistant with more experience than his pupil, Mr Aylmer, and after much searching and many interviews finally engaged Auguste Legouix, a farmer from Jersey. They were to remain friends and colleagues to the end of their days. Colt began by putting Legouix, his wife and young son Joe in Earlywood Cottage, a small three-bedroom house in the grounds of Earlywood Corner, and they were fully installed by the time work started at Swinley on the 3 January 1910.

14 *Nearly 14,000 trees were felled to create Swinley. The temporary sawmill was sited halfway up what became the first tee.*

Although Harry Colt had initially agreed with the head forester at Windsor Great Park to fell just 2,300 trees, in the end nearly 14,000 were cut down, a large percentage of which was of timber size, the remainder being either smaller, burned, or stunted. Of those felled, over 5,000 trees had to be removed completely. Colt and Legouix tried every method of grubbing out known at that time. They began by hiring a powerful steam engine which was very successful with the smaller trees. To remove them, a long steel hawser was attached to the tree about ten feet from the ground, and the engine engaged. When the 'engine gave a grunt'[12] the tree was out, roots and all. The larger Scots pines were more difficult. The hawser was attached higher up the trunk and the engine was put in the lowest gear, then

> a regular battle would ensue; the engine grunts became loud snorts, and although the betting was at least 100 to 1 on the engine, the tree would make a fine show of resistance. When it gave way all the roots were by no means out of the ground, but only those on the far side of the engine, as when the tree fell the large side branches would get fixed in the earth, and act as effectual brakes to all the efforts of the engine.[13]

These roots were subsequently disposed of at great expense. Colt had estimated that each tree cost one shilling to remove with the steam engine, taking into account the hire of the machine, coal and labour, a fraction of the cost of extracting the remaining roots. He and Legouix tried everything. They hired patent root extractors that did not work, nor did the 'scientific levers'. They tried shire horses, with partial success. They even drilled the stumps and filled the deep holes with dynamite, then blew them up. That was not a success either. In the end, they resorted to the muscle of the labourers with their mattocks. As it was not so important for the trees at the side of the course to be grubbed up entirely, Colt used a cunning ploy recommended by his friend Edward Hudson, the founder of *Country Life*. At his suggestion, the trees were cut down at ground level with a cross-cut saw. The stumps were then drilled with a series of two-inch holes, filled with a little saltpetre and topped up with water. The holes were then plugged. After about twelve weeks, the plugs were removed and the empty holes filled with paraffin. The stumps were then set on fire and left to gradually smoulder away to little or nothing. The patches of heather were also dug up, gathered and burned with the brushwood and branches, the ash being kept for use later.

15   *It is hard to believe that Swinley was playable within 18 months of this photograph being taken.*

Just as Colt had suspected, halfway through the contract Edward Berry, the timber merchant, was caught embezzling the funds. Not only had he not paid his advance on future sales, he had also kept all the monies from the sale of the timber. Colt wrote to Berry's customers, informing them that in future they were to pay the trustees direct for timber. Berry was furious, saying that the letters had seriously damaged his credit rating. Later, Alexander Davey employed W.P. Richardson, a private detective, to find out what Berry had embezzled, then sued him in the name of the trustees in the County Court for the return of the outstanding £394. Berry counterclaimed. In the end Berry was declared bankrupt, and the trustees received nothing except a large bill from the solicitor. From then on the majority of the timber went for pit props, being sold direct to a Mr Wentham for 5s. 6d. a ton.

With the capable Auguste Legouix in place, they decided in the end that it would be easier to pay for everything piece-rate. Collins, who had been Berry's foreman, took over the felling and extraction on his own account. He received 2s. 3d. a tree to fell and grub up the roots, and a further 1s. 6d. to drag it to the sawmill and cut it into timber. A final payment of £100 was paid to clear up the whole site. A larger sawmill was also hired to cope with the vast quantities of timber being extracted. But it was not all slash and burn. A belt of Scots pine and chestnut was planted alongside the railway line at a cost of £120.

As the trees were removed Harry Colt's inspired design began to take shape. Once an area was cleared completely all the land destined to become the fairway, tees and greens (including the trustees' land) was deep-ploughed using teams of horses. It was then cross-ploughed and left for the weather to break down the soil. The land was then worked over again with a sub-soil plough down to a minimum of 12 inches. Colt and Legouix kept a close watch on the preparations and, when they were satisfied with the ploughing, the whole area was disced, then harrowed. A small army of men followed the teams of horses picking up every last scrap, heather roots, splinters from the clear fell and the cultivations. It was all burned in slow fires, and the ash kept for 'use presently for the grass'. Some of the areas were re-ploughed until they were both satisfied that the tilth was fine enough. To the unpractised eye the whole of the proposed course looked a sorry sight, as if nothing could possibly grow in this desert. But they were wrong. Legouix, with his experience in creating rich pastures in Jersey, ordered up massive quantities of lime (around 98 per cent carbonate of lime), which was applied at around one ton to the acre, more where needed in some places, less in others, and none where he wanted heather to grow. The arable and pasture land was also liberally limed, the lime coming by train on a branch line to the Swinley brickworks nearby and then being transported by horse and cart along the forest tracks to Swinley. It was an unpleasant and somewhat dangerous task for the labourers shovelling the lime off the back of the carts into large piles and then raking it over the land by hand for an even application.

16 *John Macdonald standing by the 4th green. He came from North Berwick as first green-keeper and was to stay for 30 years.*

Slowly the lime leached into the sandy, acid soil and, when it was totally slaked and had lost its burning properties, the land was then well manured. Massive amounts of best-quality horse manure, 'short and free from straw' (well-rotted), were brought from London (where there was still an inexhaustible supply), again by railway, and applied at a rate of around twenty tons to the acre. As with the lime, more went on the poorer areas and less on the better. The horse manure was then worked into the soil with spike harrows and left to settle. After that, Cambridge rollers were drawn over and over the land to consolidate the seed bed, which was then left for at least six weeks after the final rolling. Colt was a great believer in compacting the soil as much as possible for a firm seed bed, having seen how the seed germinated better in the wheel-tracks of a cart that had passed over a newly sown pasture, where 'the marks of the wheels could be seen quite plainly by the dense growth of grass'.

Apart from the advantages of letting the land settle and consolidate after such heavy cultivations and manuring, the 'rest' allowed the weeds to germinate and to be removed before sowing. This was particularly relevant for the trustees' land. Having been farmed for decades, there was a vast residue of weed and cereal seeds (some of which had lain dormant for centuries) that suddenly germinated. Colt could see the advantages of having a really good green-keeper on site as early as possible, and to this end he engaged John Macdonald from the North Berwick Golf Club (founded in 1832, the 13th oldest golf club in the world). He was given a cottage and £1 15s. 0d. a week. Macdonald, a master gardener, came with his wife and five sons—the sixth, Angus, was born in the cottage a few months after their arrival, with two more daughters born later. As was so typical at Swinley, he was to involve his whole family and stay for over 30 years.

Another assertion of Colt's was that it was 'difficult to over-drain a golf course',[14] and at Swinley, with its generally free-draining Bagshot sand, he was able to keep the new drainage to a minimum. He had managed to avoid the expense of draining the wetlands in his overall design, but with all the extractions and cultivations some wet areas did form, which Colt dealt with when he was certain that no more would appear. Some were just 'damp patches', and it was enough to dig out the soil, fill the hole with coke breeze, tamp it down and then replace the topsoil. In the few wetter areas, he laid a series of land drains, building up a drainage system of six-inch main drains with three-inch spurs running off them. These emptied into either the one existing ditch, a deep open trench (past the 6th tee) that had been dug long in the past, most likely to improve the hunting, or into newly constructed ones. The clay pipes were laid in trenches between 30 inches and three feet deep (thus below the level of cultivation) and covered with a six-inch layer of gravel. It is a measure of the skill of Legouix, who set the levels to the open ditches, that, with regular maintenance, they are still running today 100 years later. Colt worked out that the cost was around 1s. a yard for the main drains and 9d. a yard run for

17   *The 5th hole under construction. Colt, in keeping with the current fashion, made very small tees, the ladies' being just below the men's.*

18 *The 5th hole 100 years on from Colt's original tees.*

the three-inch drains. When the pond was made on the 5th it was discovered that Colt had most likely thought of putting one there himself, as the drains all run in that direction but stop someway short of the area.

With the whole course fallow, Colt then put his design from paper into reality. He began by placing the 18th green close to the site of proposed clubhouse, then the 1st tee. A stream ran across the proposed 1st and 18th fairways, forming an attractive natural hazard as well as a useful drainage outlet. From its course Colt then worked out the position of his first tee—not too far from the proposed clubhouse, nor too far from the stream for the reasonably proficient golfer to carry over it. It was to cause him a problem later. Being virtually a private golf course there was no need for two starting points, as with other courses that had to accommodate a larger membership mostly playing at weekends. As at Stoke Poges he constructed two teeing grounds throughout the course (today there are four—blue, white, yellow and red, giving an even greater variety of distance). These were very small, little more than flattened mounds, as can be seen today on the pair of Colt's original tees below the 5th tee. With his uncanny knack of being able to read the ground perfectly most of Colt's work was done by eye. It is likely that he altered the position of one or two of the holes from his original plan, as well as the position of some of the tees, to take in some natural feature not noticed in dense forest or under thick scrub before the clear fell, as 'he was always ready to take advantage of any possibility which might present itself, or to make improvements and modifications as work progressed'.[15] Typical of his plan was the marriage of the green and the foreground over which the approach shot is played. To Colt, natural features like a hollow or a ravine, a bank or a collection of banks, all added interest to the play, as any error in the approach shot is accentuated by the nature of the ground. It is further punished by the next shot being made that much more difficult, as at the 9th at Swinley where there is a series of man-made ridges that were divisions of the original Fernhill Allotment. That said, Colt strove for great variety in every aspect of his courses, and if the approach was flat, as at the 1st, then he left it that way. He was also a promoter of 'the blind approach of the Punch Bowl variety',[16] which he used to great effect, like his 11th at Hoylake and (formerly) the Maiden at Sandwich. He did not, however, manage to fit one in at Swinley. Another advantage in positioning the green beyond rising ground is that bunkers are easier and cheaper to cut out of a slope than on the flat. While it was desirable to leave the placing and construction of some of the bunkers until the course was in playing order, it was obviously easier to create them at the same time as forming the greens. Colt was always conscious of saving money, but would never compromise for the sake of cost.

Under Colt's exacting eye Legouix, Macdonald and Aylmer marked out the position of each tee and green with stakes, then paced out the distances between each—had it been done by a surveyor's chain, the distances would have been to

19 *One of the many features of a Colt-designed course is his use of natural features. Here on the 9th he has utilised the banks (formerly the divisions of the Fernhill fuel allotment) as a hazard.*

Length of Holes.

	Yards.			Yards.
1st	380	10th	230
2nd	370	11th	275
3rd	325	12th	490
4th	160	13th	160
5th	490	14th	360
6th	460	15th	480
7th	400	16th	430
8th	160	17th	195
9th	445	18th	375
Total outward round ...	3,190	Total inward round ...	2,995

Total for the 18 Holes   6,185

20 *Colt's original 'Length of Holes' chart. Note that the distances are all to the nearest five yards, having been paced out rather than measured accurately with a chain, hence the optimistic distance of 6,185 yards.*

the nearest yard rather than the nearest five yards as recorded in the table for the length of holes. 'Anything round about 6,000 yards', maintained Colt, 'seems to be long enough [for a course], even with the new-fashioned [Haskell] ball,'[17] and consequently Swinley was always believed to be a little over his ideal. So good is Colt's design that it is impossible to state for certain which greens are entirely natural (land 'which Providence has intended mortals to putt on'[18]) and which had to be made, either partially or in their entirety. When designing and positioning the greens he began by paying attention to the 'entrance', that is, the portion of the fairway onto which the approach shot is pitched. He took great care in the preparation of the ground, making sure that the turf was of the best quality and free from any obstruction, so that there was no danger of the ball being kicked to one side, pulled up, or shot forward. Colt also maintained that the shape and size of the green was determined by the nature and direction of the stroke played onto it, with the widest part being towards the back. Keeping the entrance to the green fairly narrow, and making the green broaden gradually further back, made for an interesting approach shot while at the same time provided a sufficiently large surface for putting. Again he took into account the natural terrain when setting out the green itself, making use of any slope or undulation to create added interest

21 The Times *golf correspondent praised 'the infinitely resourceful' Harry Colt when describing his 4th hole where he used an Arrison bunker here to great effect. It was said to be named after Colt's partner, C.H. Alison, who used it extensively in Japan where they so pronounced his name.*

and difficulty. His talent for making 'interesting' greens was widely recognised. The golfing correspondent of *The Times* praised 'the infinitely resourceful' Colt and in particular his 4th green at Swinley where

> there is a most ingenious preventive of the back-wall policy. The green can be reached with a good iron shot from the tee, and since there is a wall of turf behind the green, it would seem that the player might play too strong a stroke in the certain belief that the ball would rebound into the middle of the green. But at the foot of the wall, there is a moderately deep trough or dip in the green and it is there that the ball will lie, so that the player will have a difficult put [*sic*] out of a valley and over the crest of a ridge—a just and moderate penalty for the exuberance of his tee shot.[19]

That said, Colt was always at pains not to make the green itself too difficult with too many 'abrupt undulations' and steep gradients. With the proposed number of members of Swinley, Colt knew that he did not have to overly worry about excessive use, nor wear and tear. Also, the type of member that would be approved of by Lord Derby considered that both tennis and golf were games to be played only in the summer and early autumn, leaving the winter free to hunt and shoot and the spring for the early salmon runs.

To construct the new greens at Swinley was a very slow and laborious process in 1910-11. Colt had heard of the 'horse scoops' used in America, and adopted them for all his early work. This invaluable piece of equipment was shaped like a huge shovel with two handles and was worked by a pair of heavy horses. After the ground had been deep-ploughed, the labourer then manoeuvred his horses into position and lifted the handles so that the scoop was angled into the soil. As the horses moved forward, so the scoop filled with soil. When it was full, the handles were depressed and the soil dragged to the top of the mound. The system worked well and to great advantage—with horses the soil did not pan and so the drainage problems associated with heavy machinery were avoided. The rest of the mound was created by hand with shovels, wheelbarrows and rakes. With such a slow method of construction it was also easy for Colt to fine-tune his ideas as the work progressed, so that Swinley was as perfect as he could possibly make it.

Once the green had been built and consolidated with rollers, the surface was prepared for sowing. Colt always preferred to sow his greens rather than turf them, and at Swinley he had Legouix and Macdonald, both grass experts, to oversee the work. As with the fairways, the surface of the green was limed and manured. Colt prided himself in producing greens that were firm and well drained, and to this end a quantity of charcoal and coke breeze was mixed with the subsoil. Again the greens were left after consolidating until the weeds germinated, when they were removed by hand. Also the prodigious worm population, largely imported in

22 *The original Collcutt and Hamp Golf Club. Thomas Colcutt was the architect of the Savoy Hotel, Wigmore Hall and the Imperial Institute in South Kensington in London.*

the horse manure, had to be eradicated. A proprietary worm-killer from Suttons was used and applied on 'a warm, muggy day with plenty of water'. The worms appeared on the surface in vast numbers, and 'were brushed into heaps and carried off in a wheelbarrow'.[20] An ounce of sulphate of potash per square yard was applied at the same time, as it was found to be the most effective against eel worms and 'other noxious grubs'.[21]

At the beginning of the year (1910), it was decided that the committee should not delay in building a clubhouse, a pair of cottages and some stables, and a firm of architects, Collcutt and Hamp, was given the brief to come up with something suitable. Thomas Collcutt was a gifted architect. He had won the prestigious King's Medal for Architecture in 1902 and was President of the Royal Institute of British Architects, 1904-6. Collcutt and Hamp could have been chosen by Lord Derby, who would have known of them as the architects of the Savoy (as well as of the Wigmore Hall, not far from Derby House in Stratford Place, the Palace Theatre and their finest work, the Imperial Institute in South Kensington). It is more likely, however, that Colcutt came to Sir Hubert Longman's attention as the architect who 'removed the top storey recessed from the main building in which was placed a large smoking and card room'[22] in his London club, the Athenaeum in Pall Mall. Collcutt and Hamp had produced some preliminary drawings by April, but it was generally agreed that they were too grandiose and that they should come up with something on 'a smaller scale'.[23] In the meantime the committee accepted the estimate of Howard Brothers of Sunninghill to build the pair of cottages for £775. Three months later the architects came up with another set of plans that, with minor alterations, was accepted. The clubhouse, yard and outbuildings were then put out to tender to three local builders, Watson, Norris and Hughest, who all came up with sums of around £4,700. This was thought to be excessive, and the architects were called in yet again to modify the plans to reduce the price. Finally, Watson & Co. were given the contract on their price of £3,879, plus another £120 for a servants' hall and extra lavatory on the ground floor. Another addition was made before the building was finished, when the garage was extended to house a manservant; a boot room and knife room were also added. Barclay's Bank, Sunninghill came up with a loan of £5,000 for the clubhouse and a further £2,000 to finish the course, both at 4½ per cent with no personal guarantee from the trustees. Later, the bank limited the loan to £7,000 and demanded all the timber receipts and bond money as and when it came in.

By late September 1910 the fairways were ready for sowing—the trustees' land had been grassed down in the previous March. In April 1909 Harry Colt had been approached by Suttons Seeds to represent them and to advise their customers 'on turf etc.' in return for 'a reasonable retainer' (he had a similar arrangement with Shanks Mowers). It was a shrewd move on behalf of Suttons to secure Colt as they were then well behind their rivals, James Carter & Sons (Carter's Tested Seeds), in the new and lucrative golf course seed market. By the time he came to sow Swinley he had already tried and tested Suttons' grass seed mixtures and found them excellent. For the fairways he used what was then called Dutch fescue at 8 bushels (200lbs) per acre. The same mixture was used for the tees. Although most of the construction work was done by hand, Colt always had an eye for any labour-saving device. He had bought

> a very useful machine … at quite a moderate price called the Little Wonder Sowing Machine … An even distribution of seed can be depended upon by using it and by employing an intelligent man, who walks at an even pace up and down the quarter to be sown, pegs being used at the ends of the portion dealt with.[24]

In fact, 'the intelligent man' Auguste Legouix sowed the fairways twice, two-thirds of the mixture one way and the remaining third across the land. The seed was then raked in carefully, the labourers being instructed to make 'sure that there were no little furrows in the land from the prongs of the rakes; otherwise the grass [would] come up in long lines and not indiscriminately on the surface'.[25] It was then heavily rolled. For the greens Colt used a mixture of poas (meadow grass), fescues and agrostis (bentgrass) at the rate of one pound of seed for 16 square yards. Later he experimented with a recently discovered agrostis found only on the west coast of the United States and in Kamkatcha, on the eastern seaboard of Russia. The greens were wired off against rabbits until the grass was well established—in fact all the early golf courses relied heavily on rabbits to do much of the 'mowing' of the fairways. Colt was indeed fortunate at Swinley as the late autumn of 1910 was warm and damp, which made for an even, swift germination over the whole course. Nor was the winter that harsh either, when a bore hole was sunk and water laid on around the whole course for the sum of £400. It was money well-spent, as 'the summer of 1911 brought the necessity of irrigating greens to the notice of every green-keeper, and for some weeks, whenever available, it was probably in use day and night'.[26] Had the sowing been left until the following March it would have been disastrous, as the summer of 1911 was the hottest on record and equal to that of 2006. There was also a small forest fire by the 7th.

With the grass on the greens established and the fairways growing well (both in the care of the green-keeper John Macdonald), Colt set about placing his bunkers and hazards that were not constructed at the same time as the greens. For this he played each hole, acutely observing the run of the ball on landing in each place. From this he worked out the optimum place for each new carry and bunker, with the good, the average and the less good player in mind—as he wrote, 'the hazards applicable for the tee shot will be suitable for the full shot played in approaching the green, and one or two cross-hazards giving a long carry will be acceptable to most people'.[27] Colt favoured the diagonal bunker, and used it to great effect at Swinley. He was, for instance, so pleased with the layout of his 4th (par 3) that he used it again immediately for the 8th at Denham, followed later by others, like the 15th at Southerndown, Bridgend in South Wales, and the 6th at Calcot Park, near Reading. In the design and placing of the remaining bunkers Colt believed that they should be difficult but not impossible to play out of, and that the stroke made should depend on skill and not brute force alone.

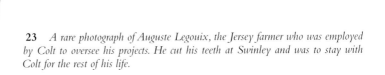

23 *A rare photograph of Auguste Legouix, the Jersey farmer who was employed by Colt to oversee his projects. He cut his teeth at Swinley and was to stay with Colt for the rest of his life.*

24 *Swinley 12 months after sowing. Colt was fortunate that the grass was well established by the time of the long hot summer of 1911.*

To Colt, the appearance of an artificial hazard was just as important as its function. The rugged look of many of the bunkers at Swinley, and much of the subtle mounding around the greens, were clearly inspired by the natural bunkers of a links course. Besides heather, Swinley has all the natural hazards—sand, long grass, gorse and water—which Colt used in making it one of the most attractive courses in the country. He was a great believer in creating an irregular course, 'with a bay of turf here and there and a promontory of heather to slightly turn the line of play to right or left as the case may be'.[28] He allowed the heather to spill out over the fairway, as if growing naturally, so that the 'artificiality be further reduced'. Most of the heather was sown at Colt's direction from seed gathered by a gang of women during the initial cultivations and broadcast at the side of the fairways, in front of some of the tees for carries and, typically of Colt, around the top of the man-made bunkers to further soften their line against the sward.

Another feature of Swinley is the banks of rhododendrons and azaleas that do particularly well in acid soil. They are all around the course and make a spectacular backdrop to greens, most notably the 12th. The rhododendrons were carefully sited at the outset, each of the many species being chosen with care. They were mostly of the Sikkim-Himalaya varieties brought back to England by

Sir Joseph Dalton Hooker (1817–1911). Hooker lived in the house he built called The Camp in Windlesham, named after 'the camp set up after the Battle of Culloden' to house the troops who 'were such scoundrels that they could not be kept in town'.[29] These 'scoundrels' were put to work creating Virginia Water by the Duke of Cumberland, then Ranger of Windsor Great Park. Joseph Hooker and his father, Sir William Hooker, were the greatest British botanists of their time, which spanned three centuries from the end of the 18th to the beginning of the 20th centuries. A traveller and plant-collector, Joseph Hooker was one of Charles Darwin's closest friends, and like his father Sir William, was director of the Royal Botanic Gardens, Kew.

One of the most important of all Hooker's travels was to the central and eastern Himalaya (1847–9). As a former naval surgeon, the Admiralty allowed him to sail to Calcutta with Lord Dalhousie, the newly-appointed Governor General of India. In 1848 he set off for Sikkim, a small and impoverished state bordered by Tibet, Nepal, Bhutan, and British India to the south. Altogether Hooker collected some 7,000 species in India and Nepal (he was briefly imprisoned for crossing the northern border), and on his return to England classified and named them all. The first publication of the expedition, *The Rhododendrons of the Sikkim-Himalaya*, was edited by his father. Joseph Hooker's travels added 25 new rhododendron species to the 50 already known, and these spectacular new varieties introduced into Britain sparked off the rhododendron craze among Victorian gardeners. Hooker created a woodland garden at The Camp 'richly planted with his own Sikkin rhododendrons'[30] and occasionally advised friends on the planting of their gardens. Sir Joseph Hooker and Sir Hubert Longman were not only near neighbours and friends, but had an author/publisher relationship as well. Longman, Green and Longman had published two of Sir Joseph's early works, but they were better known as the publisher of his father, Sir William Hooker, and many of his friends and fellow scientists, most notably Charles Darwin.

25 *Silvered copper medal of Sir Joseph Dalton Hooker by Frank Bowcher, 1897. Sir Joseph, one of the greatest botanists of his day, lived close to Swinley at The Camp, Windlesham and it was his varieties of Sikkim-Himalaya rhododendrons that were in Colt's original planting plan.*

26 *Colt was always concerned to make his courses as attractive as possible. Here at the 9th green, as elsewhere, he removed many more trees than he originally intended to create what he called his 'vistas'.*

It would only be natural for Harry Colt, at the suggestion of Sir Hubert Longman, to consult Sir Joseph on what and where to plant at Swinley. The rhododendrons that were originally planted were all the Sikkim-Himalaya varieties. The plants would have certainly come from the Sunningdale Nursery (now the Wyvale Garden Centre) that marched with Longman's Lavershot Hall. The nursery had been founded by Charles Noble, who concentrated on Hooker's new Sikkim Himalaya rhododendrons (as well those from Western China) and was taken over by Harry White (1857-1938). It would have been he who supplied Swinley. Although they were of course 'pure' when planted, rhododendrons are notoriously promiscuous and these have long become hybridised. Today, the *Rhododendron ponticum* has taken over virtually everywhere.

Colt was fortunate to have Auguste Legouix overseeing the whole project, as he was not only a good manager but also a noted horticulturalist. It was he who planted all the amenity shrubs. Apart from the specimen rhododendrons he also established banks of whins or gorse (*Ulex europaeus, U. gallii* and the rarer *U. minor*) and the common broom (*Cytisus scopariu*). Some of the dreaded purple *R. ponticum*, so beloved by the land-owner for pheasant cover since the middle of the 18th century, was growing wild, while other swathes were planted by Legouix.

27 *One of the great par 3s at Swinley, the 4th is invariably included in golf writers' fantasy courses as their favourite hole. Of all the holes on the course it has been remodelled the most.*

By the end of July, Harry Colt reported to the committee that Swinley Forest Golf Club would be playable on 30 September 1911, a month short of two years from the inaugural meeting to the official opening. Colt and his team had done a very fine job, for which he received no fee other than his remuneration of £200 per annum to design the course, supervise its construction, and to see the Club up and running—later he was to receive just £100 per annum as 'advisory member to the committee'.

Harry Colt, too, was delighted with his design and execution. In his modest way, he always described Swinley Forest Golf Club as 'his least bad course'.

CHAPTER 3

Edward Villiers Stanley, 17th Earl of Derby, was bitterly disappointed. Lloyd George, Chancellor of the Exchequer, had introduced a tax on unearned increments] on land in his 'People's Budget' of 1909—as Sir Edward Marsh, sometime secretary to Churchill observed: 'Earned increments are sweet, but those unearned are sweeter!'[1] The clause was a deliberate and artful ploy to antagonise the Tory-dominated House of Lords (and the property-owning classes), who promptly defied tradition and threw out the Finance Bill. The constitutional crisis that followed led to the General Election of mid-January 1910, with Herbert Asquith's Liberal Party being returned by just two seats. Although it was a hung parliament, the Liberals clung to power and formed the next government. As a result the right of the Lords to veto a bill was promptly reduced to one of mere delay and Lord Derby remained on the Opposition benches. Without a Tory government there was no prospect of his return to mainstream politics. There was, however, much else to occupy him. He was already Chancellor of Liverpool University and was soon to achieve the first of his three lifetime ambitions, to become Lord Mayor of Liverpool, win the Derby, and become Prime Minister like his grandfather, the 14th Earl, who twice held the office. He succeeded on the first two counts. The General Election lasted two weeks, and as the results were being declared on 31 January 1910 Lord Derby chaired the third meeting of the fledgling Swinley Forest Golf Club, the first of many over the next 25 years.

28 *The Conservative majority in the House of Lords rejected Lloyd George's 'People's Budget' that set out to tax unearned income from land. The Chancellor of the Exchequer was a passionate golfer, playing occasionally at Swinley as a guest of Sir Rufus Isaacs.*

For this, and the lunch that followed, the key players of the Club formed up at noon at Derby House in Stratford Place in London. There were Sir Hubert Longman and Evelyn Lucas, who also had houses in London, and Harry Colt, who had come up by train especially for the meeting. As they were to discuss the bonds and the execution of the Crown lease, Derby had also asked the Club's solicitors, Bailey, Shaw and Gillett, to be present. It is significant that Alexander Davey was not there then, nor did he attend any of the committee meetings hosted by Lord Derby. After the Crown lease had been executed in the names of Lord Derby and Sir Hubert, a list of the first prospective bondholders was circulated among the committee members.

The first tranche of names (and those that followed throughout 1910 and '11) was made up largely of Lord Derby's closest friends, with just a few added on to subsequent lists by the other members of the committee. The lists are truly remarkable in their diversity, Derby's being made up of socialites (including the *Hautes Juifs*) and fellow leading owners on the Turf, members of the House of Lords, distinguished ex-servicemen including two holders of the Victoria Cross, politicians from both sides of the House, ambassadors, courtiers, financiers, philanthropists, two Royal Dukes, a herald and some very senior golfers nominated by the other members of the committee. There were three former Viceroys of India. Once again, the hand of Lady Derby can be seen in the composition of the list.

Lord Derby was on the fringe of what was known as 'the Marlborough House set', which was made up of the friends of the Prince and Princess of Wales, later Edward VII and Queen Alexandra—Lady Derby was, after all, an Extra Lady of the Bedchamber. They were frequent guests of Edward Derby's father, the 16th Earl, who invited them and their friends to Knowsley, as with the famous house party of 1900 (see page 4). Two of the guests then were the first two names on Derby's list: Leopold de Rothschild (always known as Leo) and Arthur Sassoon (great-uncle of the poet Siegfried Sassoon). Although both were of his father's generation, all three were leading owners for decades and the greatest of friends—up until the Second World War the generation gap was far less marked than today. Sassoon and de Rothschild were also brothers-in-law, Leopold marrying Marie, the daughter of

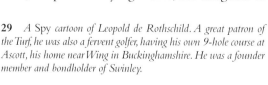

29 *A* Spy *cartoon of Leopold de Rothschild. A great patron of the Turf, he was also a fervent golfer, having his own 9-hole course at Ascott, his home near Wing in Buckinghamshire. He was a founder member and bondholder of Swinley.*

30 *Louisa Sassoon by Frederick Watts. A great beauty of her day, she was admired by the Prince of Wales. She and her sister Marie de Rothschild were great friends of Lady Derby and played regularly at Swinley.*

Achille Perugia, a merchant from Trieste in 1881, while Arthur married her sister, Louisa. They were two striking women, particularly Louisa, who was painted by Frederick Watts in 1882 and 'whose beauty the Prince [of Wales] admired'.[2] 'Mrs Leo', as she was invariably known, was painted by Sir Alfred Munnings late in life on her favourite grey out hunting with the Whaddon Chase. The two sisters and Alice Derby were enthusiastic and reasonably proficient golfers, and it can only have been agony for them to play with the Queen and her daughters, who

> never grasped the rules of the game, and regard it as a kind of hockey allowing much light-hearted scrimmaging, the winner being the player first succeeding in propelling his or her ball into the hole, regardless of the number of strokes played.[3]

For the three friends, the lessons later given to Queen Alexandra by Ben Sayers, the legendary professional from North Berwick and the greatest player never to have won The Open, came not a moment too soon.

As a family the Rothschilds were fervent golfers. Leo built a nine-hole course at Ascott, his house at Wing in Buckinghamshire. The course was an extension of the magnificent gardens and was kept in pristine condition by some of the 70 gardeners under the watchful eye of the resident agent, Jock Tarver, who lived at Lower Ascott. Leo and Marie de Rothschild played regularly on their own course, often after lunch parties when guests would 'proceed to the first tee with a few clubs carried in a "Sunday" bag'.[4] They had three sons, Lionel, Evelyn and Anthony, who were also brought up on a diet of golf. While Lionel took to gardening, Evelyn and Anthony continued with their passion for golf and were two of the original bondholders of Swinley. The two brothers served in the Buckinghamshire Yeomanry in the First World War and both were wounded, Evelyn on the Western Front and Anthony at Gallipoli. Evelyn later served in Palestine where he was seriously wounded at the critical Battle of Mughar Ridge against the Turkish Seventh Army. He died four days later on 17 November 1917. His brother Anthony survived the war to become one of the managing partners of the family's banking house, N M Rothschild in London. He was still a member of Swinley when he died in 1961.

The Leo de Rothschilds also played at the nearby Waddesdon Manor, where his cousin Alice Rothschild had built a nine-hole course on inheriting from her brother, Ferdinand. The course was later extended to 18 holes by her heir and great-nephew James and designed by Harry Colt (again he used Auguste Legouix to oversee the project). It was always said (but never recorded) that Jimmy de Rothschild was so keen on his golf that he went to the secretary of his local club and asked him to suggest a bride. He came up with Dorothy Pinto, always known as Dolly. According to her nephew, George Pinto, who played with her at Waddesdon: 'She was a good, competent golfer. In her prime her handicap was in the high single figures.'[5]

Jock Tarver was not only their agent at Ascott but also a close friend of the Leo de Rothschilds, and it was they who first introduced him to Lord Derby. He was a fine and steady player, winning the first Swiss Golfing Association's Engadine Cup played at Samedan, St Moritz, along with many other tournaments. Tarver competed regularly for the Queen Victoria Vase at the Royal and Ancient, St Andrews, once, in 1920, providing

> the thrill of the day … [when he] was 6 down and 8 to play against Mr Key, but so sternly did he set about his task that he won every remaining hole, with the exception of the 13th which he leveled. This gave him a sensational win on the home green where he holed a good putt.[6]

Tarver remained a member of Swinley all his life, becoming an honorary member in 1938. A close friend and contemporary of Lord Derby was the 26th Lord Willoughby de Eresby, who, shortly after his election to Swinley, succeeded his father as 2nd Earl of Ancaster and Hereditary Great Chamberlain. They entered Parliament almost together in the early 1890s, where they had much in common in that their fathers practically owned the whole of their constituencies—Lord Stanley (as Derby then was) was returned unopposed as Conservative MP for West Houghton, Lancashire and Willoughby de Eresby for Horncastle Division, the centre of their Lincolnshire estates. Willoughby de Eresby was a keen sportsman, playing polo and golf for the House of Commons. Swinley obviously appealed to him as he left Walton Heath, where he had been a member since the inaugural match in 1905. Today he is best remembered for the Willoughby, a cold-fawn-coloured pug that was bred by him and Lady Willoughby de Eresby from new blood-lines introduced from Russia and Hungary. Another close family member was Lord Charles Montague, younger son of the 7th Duke of Manchester and Alice Derby's brother.

Charles Montague, close in age to his sister, shared her love of golf. At his peak he was a scratch player, and once partnered the Frenchman Arnaud Massey (winner of the 1911 Open) in a foursome against the Hon. Howard Stonor and Ben Sayers at the North Berwick Golf Club. The match went to the last hole with Montague winning on the last putt, having been three down at the 15th. It is possible that it was he who suggested that their green-keeper, John Macdonald, should come to Swinley.

Another golfing friend and neighbour of Edward Derby was Captain Christian Combe, a member of the brewing family, who lived at Cranbourne Court near Winkfield, not far from Coworth and Swinley. He had inherited Strathconan in Ross-shire, an estate his father had bought from Arthur J. Balfour, the former Conservative Prime Minister. Lord Savile was another typical early bondholder. After Eton he entered the Diplomatic Service and served under his uncle, then Ambassador to Belgium. He soon retired to Rufford, his uncle's estate and magnificent stud in Nottinghamshire, which he eventually inherited. He spent the rest of his life racing and shooting with the occasional foray onto the golf course.

31 *Lord Derby and his brother-in-law Lord Charles Montague, son of the 7th Duke of Manchester. Montague, a scratch player, was one of the original bondholders of Swinley.*

THE *ILLUSTRATED SPORTING AND DRAMATIC NEWS*

ROYAL·ASCOT·SUPPLEMENT

Troops.
1937

THE MAN BEHIND THE SCENE
Lt.-Col. Sir Gordon Carter, Clerk of the Course

32   *Lt Colonel Gordon Carter, always known as 'Troops' Carter after his telegraphic address, was commissioned after 16 years as a trooper in the 1st Life Guards and ended his military career as Silver Stick. He went on to become Clerk of the Course at Ascot and was befriended by three Sovereigns.*

As the course was being prepared, so Lord Derby added more and more names to his list of bondholders. So closely guarded was the list that when a Mr S. Aiser applied for a bond Harry Colt was told to write saying that 'Lord Derby had decided that all remaining bonds were for his personal friends only'.[7]

It was inevitable that there would be a close and lasting association between Swinley and the Royal Family along with the Household at Windsor. In the April 1910 'entry', the first of many courtiers to be offered a bond was Lt Colonel Gordon Carter. Carter was born in 1854 and joined the Army as a trooper in the 1st Life Guards, gaining his commission after 16 years' active service in the ranks. He fought with distinction in South Africa and was present at the Relief of Kimberley. When he returned to London he commanded the Sovereign's Escort. 'Troops' Carter (as he was known after his telegraphic address) led a colourful life, once joining Earl Fitzwilliam in an expedition to the Cocos Islands to recover Henry Morgan's pirate treasure. They were not successful. On leaving the Army he was appointed Clerk of the Course at Ascot where he was thought indispensable, being the 'main spring of the Meeting'.[8] He remained there for decades, and was met and befriended by Edward VII, George V, George VI (and Lord Derby), ending up as secretary to the King's Ascot Representative and a knight.

Another noteworthy member was Sir Rufus Isaacs, later to become Viceroy of India and the Marquis of Reading. As Lord Chief Justice he was tipped 'to greatly strengthen the judicial team, one single fact speaks eloquently of Lord Reading's golf; he plays most of it at Swinley Forest, and if a golfer can play at Swinley he can play anywhere, for there is hardly a more difficult course either inland or by the sea'.[9]

Sir Rufus Isaacs was elected a member in 1911, the same intake as Major Martin Archer-Shee MP who had served with Lord Derby in South Africa. The family lived nearby at Ashurst Lodge, Sunninghill. Family legend has it that he used to take three quick strides across the tee to drive off, as if playing hockey. Later, Martin Archer-Shee, a 36-year-old Member of Parliament, was to be miscast as the failed undergraduate Dickie Winslow in *The Winslow Boy*, Terence Rattigan's play based on his half-brother George Archer-Shee. The play and the case are well known. George was accused of stealing a 5s. postal order from a fellow cadet at the Royal Naval College, Osborne, and consequently expelled. It was Major Martin Archer-Shee who secured the services of one of England's greatest barristers, Sir Edward Carson (who had famously prosecuted his old university friend, Oscar Wilde). Carson invoked the Petition of Right to bring the case to Court, but the Admiralty challenged the petition and won. The ruling was subsequently overturned on appeal by Carson. The trial began on 26 July 1910, with Sir Rufus Isaacs acting for the Admiralty. Four days into the trial, George Archer-Shee's claim of innocence was finally accepted. After a heated political furore, damages of £7,021 and costs were finally award to the family, largely through the intervention of Major Martin Archer-Shee, the new Conservative and Unionist Member of Parliament for Finsbury. There was no apology. George Archer-Shee later joined up in the South Staffordshire Regiment, and was killed in action in 1914 in the first battle of Ypres when an order to withdraw did not reach his platoon in time.

There is, of course, no record of Rufus Isaacs and Archer-Shee ever playing together at Swinley, but Simon, the present Marquis of Reading and Isaacs' great-grandson, often plays there as the guest of Robert Abel-Smith, Major Martin Archer-Shee's grandson.

Another great golfing politician and member of Swinley was the former Prime Minister, A.J. Balfour. Arthur James Balfour was infatuated by golf. He spoke and wrote wittily on the subject, even contributing the section on humour in *The Badminton Library's Golf* published by Longman, Green and Longman. Balfour's

8.—A. J. BALFOUR.
" Putting the most trying to the Nerves."

33 *A Cope's cigarette card of A. J. Balfour, a prolific writer on golf and golfing humour.*

'Septembers were spent at North Berwick every year from the middle 'eighties until the [First World] War',[10] staying at the Bass Rock Hotel at North Berwick, and venturing out, first in a brougham and a pair of horses, then a 'modern motor car' to play the great courses of the area. He was born and lived in Whittingehame in East Lothian, which he described as 'the paradise of golfers', but did not 'feel the full fascination of the game' until he was 'past his teens'. By his own admission he started too late to excel. On several occasions he won the House of Commons handicap although he 'could not remember what the handicap was'.[11] A frequent guest at Knowsley, Balfour had long been a friend of both the 16th and 17th Earls. He and Edward Derby also met frequently in the House of Commons. In 1903 Balfour, then Prime Minister, showed his high regard for Derby by promoting him to Postmaster General in place of Austen Chamberlain, who went to the Exchequer. Balfour was not a member of Swinley for long, as for some unknown reason he resigned in 1921 and passed his bond to Fitzroy K. Chapman.

Edward Derby's friends had great faith in the future of Swinley, as they took up his offer of a bond long before the course had opened for play. There were some rather surprising early entrants, such as the Reverend G.F. Wills, the incumbent of the Priory Church of St Thomas the Martyr on the edge of one of the Derby Lancashire estates, and Colonel Charles Macauley of the 51st Bengal Native Infantry, sometime Assistant Commissioner of the Dera Ismail Khan district of the Punjab. Hardly fitting into the Derby mould was the great genealogist Henry Farnham Burke, later knighted and variously Somerset Herald and Norroy King of Arms, and finally Garter King of Arms. He was the son of Sir Bernard Burke, founder of *Burke's Peerage* and *Burke's Landed Gentry*. A definite luminary was the Earl of Dunmore who, as Viscount Fincastle, had won the Victoria Cross during the

Tirah Campaign in India in 1897. A Lieutenant in the 16th Lancers, Fincastle and two officers from the Guides Cavalry rescued Captain Greaves of the Lancashire Fusiliers. The badly wounded Greaves, surrounded by Ghazi swordsmen, was shot dead in Fincastle's arms, while another bullet smashed his scabbard. All three rescuers were awarded the Victoria Cross, one posthumously. Fincastle later went to South Africa and served on the staff of Major General Wavell, where he was befriended by Lieutenant Colonel the Lord Stanley, Grenadier Guards. The other holder of the Victoria Cross, who joined Swinley later as an ordinary member, was Field Marshal Lord Roberts.

Another colourful character invited by Lord Derby to become a bondholder was Major Herbert Langton Sapte, the last officer in the British Army to receive his commission by purchase. Major Sapte chose the 35th Regiment of Foot, later the Royal Sussex Regiment. After serving in Egypt and Cyprus he went to South Africa as Military Secretary to the High Commissioner. Sapte came to the attention of Cecil Rhodes after he prevented the Charter Company troops from engaging a unit of the Portuguese army in their push to create a corridor from the land that was to become Rhodesia to the port of Beira on the East Coast of Africa. Notwithstanding this major setback in Rhodes' territorial plan, Sapte was still employed by him later as manager of Consolidated Goldfields in South Africa when he left the Army. On his return to England he joined their London board.

An army friend not forgotten was Viscount Acheson, heir to the 4th Earl of Gosford. He was Lady Derby's nephew and as a lieutenant in the Coldstream Guards had served on Lord Roberts' staff with Lord Stanley. Acheson went on to join the committee of Swinley. A man of a similar mould to his friend Edward Derby was Sir Edgar Vincent, later Lord d'Aberon. Slightly older, Sir Edgar was a keen sportsman, politician and diplomat. After Eton, where he rowed for the eight, he joined the Coldstream

34 *The Earl of Dunmore (right) who, as Lieutenant Viscount Fincastle of the 16th Lancers, was awarded the Victoria Cross for attempting to save an officer during the Tirah Campaign, India in 1897. He is talking to J. Hay Beith, better-known as the author Ian Hay.*

35 *Sir Edgar Vincent, later Lord d'Aberon, was one of Lord Derby's closest friends. They were both successful owners on the Turf and when appointed British Ambassadors, d'Aberon to Berlin and Derby to Paris, their friendship forged on the links served them well in the peace negotiations after the First World War.*

Guards (with the soubriquet Σοφός—wise), leaving to become financial advisor to the Government of Egypt. He then went to live in Constantinople, where he became Governor of the Imperial Ottoman Bank. In the same year (1899) he 'registered his colours on the Turf and entered politics as Conservative member for Exeter'.[12] He lost his seat in 1906, the same year as his best horse Donetta, winner of the Duke of York Stakes, won the Kempton Jubilee stakes. In 1920 the two friends were appointed Ambassadors, Derby to Paris, Viscount d'Aberon, as Vincent became in 1914, to Berlin. It was a hugely important time, and much of the success of the treaties after the First World War can be attributed to their long and close friendship. As a subaltern d'Aberon published a grammar of Modern Greek; in later life, three volumes of autobiography and a learned treatise entitled *Alcohol—its action on the human organism*. He was a passionate golfer, with his own 9-hole golf course at his house, Esher Place in Surrey.

When the Earl of Derby stepped down as Ambassador to France in 1922 he was succeeded by his friend Charles, 1st Baron Hardinge of Penhurst. He was a distinguished diplomat, having been Ambassador to Russia in 1904 before returning to England to take up the position of Permanent Under Secretary in the Foreign Office. By the time Lord Derby had offered him a bond at Swinley in 1910 Hardinge had been appointed Viceroy of India, and it was to be another six years before he could make use of it. Lord Curzon, a full member of Swinley, was Viceroy of India between 1899 and 1905. Another Vice-regal connection with Swinley was Hersey, Marchioness of Linlithgow. She was the mother of the second Marquess and Viceroy of India in 1936-43, and the first female bondholder.

Other bondholders drawn from Derby's close friends followed. At the age of nine Edward Stanley entered Wellington College, the school his grandfather, the 14th Earl, and the Prince Consort had founded. In later life he looked back on his school days with mixed feelings: 'he detested the bullying but recalled some of his school friends with affection'.[13] One such friend was W.G. Raphael, an exact contemporary who followed him to Sandhurst, and was for many years a fellow owner on the Turf. Raphael never made use of his bond, as he died of a heart attack the following year aged forty-seven.

Another early member and bondholder was the 5th Earl of Kenmare, sometime Master of the Horse and a close friend of Lord Derby, whose estates in Killarney contained many of the famous lakes. Although a somewhat pedestrian golfer himself, he was the father of Valentine, Viscount Castlerosse, a fine scratch

36 *Although never a member, Viscount Castlerosse often played at Swinley on his father's (the Earl of Kenmare) bond. A colourful character, he would have his servant follow him around the course with a jug of whisky and water.*

player and subsequent 6th Earl of Kenmare. Castlerosse was the renowned gossip columnist on the *Sunday Express* and the model for the 'eighth Earl of Balcairn, Viscount Erdinge, Baron Cairn of Balcairn, Red Knight of Lancaster, Count of the Holy Roman Empire and Chenonceaux Herald of the Duchy of Aquitaine' in Evelyn Waugh's novel *Scoop* (the other on the rival newspaper being 'the fifteenth Marquess of Vanburgh, Earl Vanburgh de Brendon, Baron Brendon, Lord of the Five Isles and Hereditary Grand Falconer to the Kingdom of Connaught').[14] It is certain that Castlerosse, who used his father's bond, was the most colourful character to play at Swinley. He maintained that 'if you are descended from a famous scoundrel you probably belong to a good family' and was especially proud of one of his forebears, an 18th-century Irish bishop, who, having lost heavily gambling with his dinner guests, would don a black mask and rob them on their way home. In his heyday Kenmare would have his 'servant accompany him on the golf course with a jug of whisky'.[15]

Not all the early bondholders were Lord Derby's personal friends as under the rules of Swinley, other members of the committee could introduce prospective candidates so long as they were approved by him. One such was the great amateur player Norman F. Hunter (known as Norrie), who was introduced by Sir Hubert Longman and Harry Colt. He and Colt often played together with great success, both at Sunningdale, where they won such trophies as the Founders' Cup in 1913, and elsewhere. Like Colt, Hunter was Captain of the Cambridge University Golf Team and played regularly for the Oxford and Cambridge Golfing Society, including on their tour of America in 1903, the first ever by a British team. He was an exceptional golfer—he and Colt even beat James Braid and James Sherlock in a match against the Professionals at Stoke Poges in 1909. From 1886 onwards Hunter competed annually in the Calcutta Cup and the Queen Victoria Jubilee Vase at St Andrews, and, partnered by his brother Mansfield, played for Scotland against England. Hunter was killed at Ypres in 1915.

The brothers Francis Algernon and Leonard Govett were sponsored by their double brother-in-law, Sir Hubert Longman, he being married to their sister Laura, while his sister Sybil Augusta was married to Leonard. Both Leonard and Algernon were fine sportsmen. They had been playing continually on the British amateur golf circuit and in France since their time at Harrow and later at Oxford, where both were awarded golf half-Blues. They were also fine tennis players, Francis playing for many years at Wimbledon. But it was as toxophilists that they really excelled, dominating the sport throughout the 1890s. The sons of Adolphus Frederick, the founder of the stockbroking firm of Govett Sons & Co., they were no less successful in the City. Francis specialised in mining stocks and, with Herbert Hoover, was founder and chairman of Consolidated Zinc (the Z of RTZ). The vast profits from this alone enabled Hoover to finance his Presidential campaign.

37 *Norman F. Hunter, always known as 'Norrie', was one of the great amateurs on the circuit and a member of Swinley. He was considered such a technician that he was chosen to illustrate the 'top of swing with driver', the 'finish with driver' and 'top of stroke, lofting approach' in* Great Golfers, Their Methods at a Glance *by George Bedlam.*

The City was well represented in the original make-up of Swinley, as indeed it has been ever since. Henry Alexander Trotter had served with Derby on the committee of Sunningdale. Leaving Trinity College Cambridge with a First in Law and a golf half-Blue, Trotter joined a firm trading in the West Indies, principally in spirits from Jamaica. Well-respected in the City, he was a director, then deputy chairman of the Alliance Assurance Company for 40 years and a director and later Deputy Governor of the Bank of England. He took up four bonds. His kinsman, Noel Trotter, was no less remarkable. For 30 years he was Postmaster General of the Straits Settlements. He returned to Frognal in Sunninghill, a house near Swinley and to commerce, making his fortune as chairman of several Malay rubber companies. A near neighbour at Rose Mount in Ascot was Peter G.B. Westmacott, a former 3rd Northumberland Fusilier and President of the Institute of Mechanical Engineers. He had met Lord Derby previously when both served on the board of the Lancashire Derbyshire & East Coast Railway Company. His son, J. Westmacott, was also allowed a bond.

At Henry Trotter's invitation came Frederick Williams Taylor, manager of the Bank of Montreal, and H.A. Richardson of the Anglo-Egyptian Bank, along with S.W. Luard, Clerk of the Worshipful Company of Salters. All were proficient golfers who played regularly on the amateur circuit around the country. One who was seemingly never off the circuit was Captain Angus Hambro, Conservative Member for South Dorset, whom Bernard Darwin described as 'the most delightful and graceful of golfers'.[16] Hambro reached the semi-final of the Amateur Championship in 1912 and ten years later he was chosen to captain the British team in the first Walker Cup match, but was unable to make the crossing to the United States. In his time he was Captain of the Royal and Ancient, Chairman of the Rules of Golf Committee and, in 1946, President of the English Golf Union.

At the fourth meeting of Swinley Forest Golf Club, it was decided to call up £75 on each bond and a further £25 on those already allotted. The privileges that went with a bond were discussed at length, and it was decided that for each bond held it would 'enable their nominees to exercise their privileges conferred by the bonds',[17] that is, each male guest could play without the bondholder being present. As the list of bondholders was filling up quickly, it was decided to admit ordinary members with an entrance fee of 10 guineas as well.

Heading the list of ordinary members was Freddy Glynn, 4th Lord Wolverton. He and Edward Derby were exact contemporaries and close friends, leading similar lives. Wolverton was the grandson of the founder of the family bank, Glynn Mills Currie & Co., of which he eventually became senior partner. He served in South Africa with the North Somerset Yeomanry, and on his return in 1902 was appointed Vice-Chamberlain of the Household by the Prime Minister, Arthur Balfour. He became a steward of the Jockey Club, and in 1908 took his horses to Derby's Stanley House stables at Newmarket, where Sir Edgar Vincent also had

38 *Captain Angus Hambro, described as the most delightful and graceful of golfers, divided his time between the House of Commons and the links.*

his in training. 'He never had the luck to own a really good horse'[18]—although one horse called Ugly came close by winning 21 races over six seasons. He was a keen yachtsman and big game hunter—once, on safari in Somaliland, he slew 17 lions. Lady Wolverton and Alice Derby were also great friends, golfing partners and confidantes, Edith Wolverton once writing to her from Cannes: 'We have quite settled down into our life out here; gambling, golf and grand dukes.'[19]

But the Derby's had their own, rather grander Royal Dukes at home and Lord Derby invited the Duke of Connaught and his son, Prince Arthur of Connaught, to be honorary members. The Duke of Connaught was the third and favourite son of Queen Victoria. From early childhood he was passionate about the Army and in due course made it his career, rising to Field Marshal in 1902. He had married Princess Louise, daughter of the 'Red' Prince of Prussia, and in 1879 they moved into Bagshot Park. It was to be some time before the Duke could take up his membership, as he was appointed Governor General of Canada before the course was playable and returned four years later. The Prince was an enthusiastic golfer, and at one time considered buying a villa in the South of France where 'there was golf to play and tennis to watch'.[20]

His son, also Prince Arthur of Connaught, was brought up at Bagshot. He, too, was a keen golfer, and a member of Walton Heath—he even went to Sandwich for

39 *Lord Derby leading in Sansovino, his first Epsom Derby winner, in 1924. Tommy Weston, the jockey, was so nervous before the race that he accidentally caught his white silk stock in a button of his all-black jacket, giving the impression that the button was white. After that, the white button was added to the Derby colours of black jacket and white cap.*

his honeymoon. He brought up all his children to play, his daughter Lady Patricia Ramsay being elected an honorary member in 1922. Her husband, Admiral the Hon. Sir Alexander Ramsay, often played at Swinley. When he thought that he perhaps should be paying a green fee, he sent a cheque for £10, which was returned with a note saying that 'as he was a member of HRH the Duke of Connaught's family, he would not be asked to pay a green fee'.[21]

Another ducal member of Swinley was the 6th Duke of Portland. In 1879, he inherited Welbeck Abbey, Nottinghamshire, from a distant cousin, an eccentric recluse who shunned visitors. The 5th Duke had had 15 miles of tunnels dug under the house and gardens which housed libraries, a billiard room large enough for 12 full-size tables and an enormous subterranean ballroom to take at least two thousand people—all of which remained unused. William Portland is remembered for many things, not least his philanthropy. Along with Edward Derby and his friend Sir Edgar Vincent, he was a leading owner on the Turf. His horse St Simon won the Ascot Gold Cup and the Goodwood Cup in 1884. St Simon went on to sire three of the best horses of the age, Florizel II, Persimon and Diamond Jubilee, the last two winning the Derby for the Prince of Wales. Portland won the Derby twice, once with Ayrshire in 1888 and the next year with Donovan. To date, the original owner-members of Swinley have had six Epsom Derby winners and 10 Oaks Stakes between them, with Lord Derby accounting for two Oaks, three Derbys—Sansovino in 1924, Hyperion in 1933 and Watling Street in 1942—along with the winners of six St Legers, two 2,000 Guineas and seven 1,000 Guineas.

At the end of July 1911 Swinley had a membership of 84—38 bondholders, 44 ordinary and two honorary members. It was a truly remarkable collection of people made up of some not-too-close neighbours, the cream of the amateur golf circuit, and the core of the City. The rest were chosen by Lord Derby himself. He monopolised the choice and put his stamp on the Club—he was, after all, underwriting all the expenditure by personally guaranteeing the overdraft of £5,000.

But Lord Derby was no autocratic despot. His large frame and imposing presence belied an inner warmth, while his easy manner and contagious geniality won him many friends from all walks of life from both political parties, while Chips Channon, that acute social observer, found him 'fat, smiling and amiable'.[22] Derby was amusing and a good conversationalist at every level. He loved gossip. Lady Wolverton once wrote that he had 'the greatest genius for collecting it [gossip] of any human I know'.[23] The Swinley committee was certainly in awe of him: the bird-like publisher Sir Hubert Longman, the deferential Harry Colt and Alexander Davey, who did not fit into any camp, and the new members, Henry Trotter and Evelyn Lucas. Acting singly or together, they were no match for Lord Derby, who had the knack of putting his expressed wishes across in the nicest possible way, but would brook no argument. In political life he was less sure of his ground, Earl Haig going so far as to write in 1918: 'D[erby] is a very weak-mind fellow I am afraid and, like the feather pillow, bears the marks of the last person who has sat on him.'[24]

There is no evidence that any of the committee really minded Swinley being taken over by Lord Derby as his private fiefdom. What is more, he set the mould for many a subsequent chairman. What is certain is that Colt and Davey were upset that Lord Derby, with his aversion to close neighbours, would not allow any form of development on the periphery of the course, as was the case at Sunningdale and at St George's Hill.

> The first person to theorise about the connection between golf and surrounding land values was Harry Colt who as secretary of Sunningdale between 1901 and 1913 would have witnessed the developments taking place around the golf course. He wrote 'if a good margin of the course can also be obtained, so much the better, as this land will be almost certain to possess good building value in the future'.[25]

Davey would have wanted to develop his six acres at Boden's Ride—he had, after all, a perfectly good house at Combe Edge, with its fine croquet lawn, close by, and was not that interested in golf. When the Crown Estate began selling off building plots on the west side of the railway line, Derby made it very clear that none of the new purchasers within a radius of three miles should be even considered for membership of Swinley. His animosity against Alexander Davey went further. Although he was not present at the meeting, Lord Derby's wishes were made clear when the resolution was passed that 'Mr Davey be restricted to a single dwelling for a term of 7 years or for the lifetime of Lord Derby'[26] on his plot of land. This somewhat vindictive restriction was a measure of what Derby thought of Davey. The control could not have been enforced anyway as the land was already firmly in Davey's name, although access past the clubhouse to his land would have been difficult. In the end Davey did build his 'single dwelling', Boden's Ride.

With the clubhouse nearing completion there were many last-minute decisions that were handled by Colt. It was decided that the gas from the Ascot Gas Company was too expensive and it would be cheaper to install a private plant supplied by the Acrogen Gas Company. He interviewed a couple from the West Surrey to manage the clubhouse, but found them wanting. Eventually Mr and Mrs David Martin were engaged at £7 a month.

After much searching Colt came up with a professional. Earlier in the year he had played for the Oxford and Cambridge Golf Society in a match against the Professionals at Stoke Poges (where presumably he had an advantage). Playing for the Professionals was Lawrence Ayton, a member of the famous Ayton family of St Andrews. His grandfather was the first Captain and one of the 16 founders of the Mechanics Club for artisans and tradesmen in 1843 (the name changed to St Andrews Golf Club in 1851). His father David 'was well-known in St Andrews as a fine player, with a graceful, easy and very full swing [and] a frequent prizewinner on that green'.[27] One such prize was the professional tournament at the 1881 R & A Autumn Meeting that he won with 94 strokes over 18 holes, notwithstanding 'the strong gale from the south-east which proved very troublesome both in the driving and in the short game'.[28] The 7th, par 4, hole on the Jubilee Course at St Andrews is called the Ayton Hole in honour of the family. Colt canvassed the opposition for a professional for Swinley, and it is likely that it was Lawrence who suggested his older brother, David Ayton Jnr, whom Colt would have known from his frequent visits to St Andrews over the previous 20 years. Obviously David passed muster and he was subsequently employed, aged just 25, at £1 per week with a cottage, starting on 1 September 1911.

With the building work finished by early September and the course in place, all that was needed to complete the whole project was to furnish the new clubhouse. Regrettably, the Stanleys, in all generations, 'had little sense of elegance, style, fashion or taste. It was not that they had bad taste, but that they had no taste at all'. It was said that 'Knowsley was, in fact, nothing but a large, tasteless hotel'.[29] The contents of his houses were taken for granted. When the Earl of Crawford, a Trustee of the National Gallery and close neighbour, lunched at Knowsley, he was appalled at the general ugliness of the furniture, but felt moved to remark to Derby that he had 'a very fine set of Charles II dining-room chairs'. After he had gone the Earl snorted, 'Damn cheek that fellow noticing my chairs'.[30] With Derby's total lack of interest in decor there was little prospect of the Swinley clubhouse being furnished in anything other than 'utilitarian'. A mere £100 was allowed (and fully spent) to furnish the whole house, and the local sale rooms were scoured for 'old oak furniture'.[31] Much of the furniture in the clubhouse today, such as the oak settles, is from the original purchase.

40 *Knowsley, just seven miles from the centre of Liverpool, has been home to the Earls of Derby since 1385. At the time of the 17th Earl, it was said that he had eight houses but lived in none of them.*

It was suggested that there should be a grand opening of Swinley, but Lord Derby, who disliked razzmatazz of any kind, vetoed the idea so it was 'formally opened on Saturday without public ceremony'.[32] Instead Edward and Alice Derby invited the Leo de Rothschilds and Jock Tarver to stay at Coworth. The morning of 3 October 1911 was quite perfect, warm and sunny with a slight breeze. The air was fresh, the stifling heat and parched countryside of the record heatwave of July only a memory after the heavy rains that had followed throughout August and September. And so, after breakfast, the party assembled in the hall, the men dressed as for a cold winter's day's shooting in thick heavy tweed plus–twos, high-buttoned coat and waistcoat with a stiff collar and tie. The two women were only marginally less constricted with their jackets buttoned up to the neck, ankle-length skirts and jaunty hats. The party then went out to the three cars lined up at the front door—the third car was for the golf clubs. At precisely 11 o'clock, the Derbys, the de Rothschilds, Jock Tarver and their clubs headed off through the park and out along the Great West Road to Sunningdale, then over the railway crossing, past a large windmill and a public house, where the line of cars turned right. They passed Combe Edge, Alexander Davey's house, then turned left at Colt's Earlywood Corner, where the young Joe Legouix marvelled at the Rolls Royces as they bumped up the unmade estate road.

At the top of the lane and over the railway bridge, the cars swung into the gravel drive where two small groups were waiting. As the chauffeurs opened the car doors Harry Colt in his position as secretary stepped forward to greet the chairman and his party, while John Macdonald, the green-keeper, David Ayton, the professional, and David Martin, the steward, caps in hand, looked on at a respectful distance. The other members of the committee were all there with their wives, Hubert and Laura Longman, Henry and Dorothy Trotter, Alexander and Winifred Davey and Evelyn Lucas on his own. After a few pleasantries (Colt already knew the de Rothschilds and Jock Tarver well, having played with them all on the course at Ascot) the players moved off to the first tee, followed by the caddies. Colt was delighted with the appearance of his course, with that particular shade of green all over that comes only with freshly sown grass. Macdonald and his assistants too had all done a fine job: the fairways cut by a gang mower drawn by a pony wearing leather boots, the greens cut with the brand-new Shanks' petrol motor-mower.

It was thought appropriate that Lord Derby should take the inaugural stroke and he drove off in fine style. Alice Derby then went up to the forward tee, only a few yards ahead of the back tee. Her caddie took a handful of wet sand out of his pocket and set it onto the tee. He then placed the ball on the little pyramid, firmed it down, then handed Lady Derby a driver. She gazed down the fairway, past the belt of newly-planted trees on the left, over the stream and up to the first green on the top of the slight hill. There was an air of expectancy as she drove off. They watched the ball soar into the air. It was a fine shot, at least 70 yards. Then, down it came and landed right in the stream with an insulting 'plop'. She tried again, with exactly the same result. Try as she might, she could not get over the stream, but would not sacrifice the distance by keeping her drive short. At the fourth, failed attempt, Lord Derby shouted:

'Damn it, Colt. Can't you see? You've put the stream in the wrong bloody place. Get it moved.'

It was an unprepossessing start.

CHAPTER 4

It was a forlorn bunch that gathered around the stream that crossed the first fairway. The grass sown by Auguste Legouix and carefully tended by Macdonald had taken particularly well, and it seemed a terrible waste to disturb it. But it had to be done. Harry Colt paced the fairway, marked out the new course of the stream, and three labourers set about digging out a deep channel. Part of the spoil went into the bed of the old stream, which is clearly visible today where it has sunk a few inches to make another 'natural' hazard. The change may have accommodated Lady Derby's drive, but today 'It's a blasted nuisance', said Ian Pearce, a former secretary. 'It plays havoc with the drainage.'

In fact the Earl was to repeat the process sometime in the 1920s at Gullane Golf Club, where the Derbys took a house every year. In common with many others he found the 2nd, with its twin hills and stream running through the steep fairway, particularly difficult, as Malcolm D. Macdonald described it in his *The Measure of a Golf Hole*:

Now the second hole on Gullane One	It's all uphill from tee to green
Is not so very long,	This God-forsaken place,
But the fool who doubts its manhood	And no matter how the wind blows
Will be proven very wrong …	It's always in your face.

Derby left £400 with the secretary to have the hole altered. When he returned the next year, the whole of the fairway had been remodelled. The stream had been piped and filled in, and 15 horses with scoops had removed the top of one of the hills to make level what was a deep fairway. Derby was delighted and renamed the hole 'Easy Going', which 'it isn't, as it is like a permanent wind tunnel'.[1]

Such was the understated nature of Swinley, no one had thought of working out a stroke index before the Club opened. This is surprising, as Harry Colt was still a member of the Rules of Golf Committee and he had designed and set up at least ten golf courses from scratch, and Sir Hubert Longman was a stickler for detail. After a lengthy discussion, Lord Derby came up with a typical Swinley solution. Knowing that Longman and Colt were both members of the Royal and Ancient, he asked what stroke index was used there. When they explained how the index worked, and that

41   *The view from Colt's first tee up the fairway and across the 18th clearly shows the line of the old stream and the new after it was diverted.*

42   *Like moving the stream at Swinley, Lord Derby paid £400 for the hill (left) to be removed at the 'second hole on Gullane One' so that it was easier for him to play during his occasional visits to the course.*

the St Andrews version would hardly be applicable to Swinley, Lord Derby dismissed their argument by simply declaring, 'if it is good enough for them, then it is good enough for us'. And so Swinley began in its own unique way, not quite conforming with the norm, but not too unconventional to be classed as eccentric.

From the very beginning Swinley was a popular course and was widely used by its members. The generous concession to bondholders which allowed their guests, both male and female, to play at any time without payment of a green fee, the men accompanied or not, swelled their numbers. A new class of weekday or '5-day member' with a subscription of five guineas a year was approved, or three guineas for a Service membership for officers serving within a 20-mile radius of the course. As the surrounding clubs, the likes of Sunningdale and Walton Heath, took on more members and so became crowded, particularly at weekends, so Swinley with its small, exclusive membership became all the more desirable. It was also run efficiently by Harry Colt, who 'was organised to the letter'[2] and remained secretary at a notional salary of £100 a year, although he cannot have been there much, dividing his valuable time between looking after Sunningdale and an ever increasing workload designing new courses. During 1911-12, he was busier than ever, pushing himself to the full. He was working on Betchworth Park and St George's Hill (a similar woodland course to Swinley), both in Surrey, The Eden at St Andrews and Blackmoor in Hampshire. He even travelled to North America three times, where he designed Toronto, one of the best courses of the day, and was a paid advisor to George Crump who was responsible for Pine Valley, New Jersey. Thus, much of the day-to-day running of the Club was left to the green-keeper, John Macdonald, the professional, David Ayton and the steward with his wife. Colt also took on an unpaid pupil green-keeper, a Mr R. Eckersby.

If all of Colt's multifarious jobs were not enough, he had taken on another role of reporting to the Championship Committee on possible courses for all the top competitions. Although not a links course, Swinley might then just have qualified, but he did not mention it to his fellow committee members, as to host even an Amateur Championship would have gone against the very nature of the Club. Swinley was for the enjoyment of the members alone, and, of course, their friends. The committee was, however, open to requests from deserving bodies to use the course and clubhouse. The first such match allowed was between the Royal Artillery, Deepcut and Royal Artillery officers at the Staff College, Camberley, in 1913.

The staff found that Harry Colt, as the Club's secretary, was 'no easy man to serve'[3] and most of his employees were frightened of him. That said, he was scrupulously fair and cared deeply for their welfare, in particular the caddies'. With his 'energy and foresight',[4] he was the first to recognise the problems connected with the employment of boy caddies during his early days at Sunningdale. At that time a girl from the village was appointed caddie-mistress at Swinley with a remuneration of 1d. a round booking fee. Later she left to become a kitchen maid

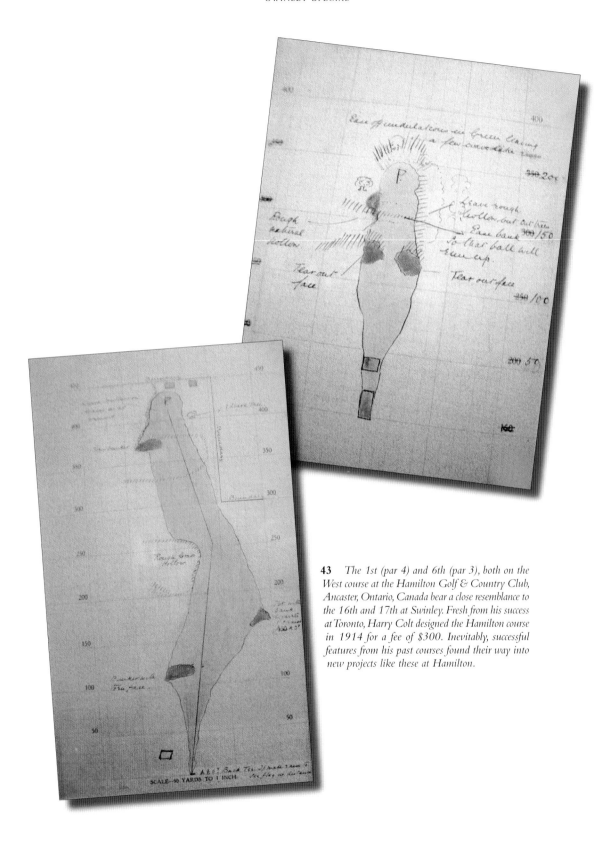

43　The 1st (par 4) and 6th (par 3), both on the West course at the Hamilton Golf & Country Club, Ancaster, Ontario, Canada bear a close resemblance to the 16th and 17th at Swinley. Fresh from his success at Toronto, Harry Colt designed the Hamilton course in 1914 for a fee of $300. Inevitably, successful features from his past courses found their way into new projects like these at Hamilton.

44 *A rare picture of Harry Colt, who positively disliked being photographed.*

but returned when she was guaranteed 15s. a week. She was responsible to the green-keeper, John Macdonald. Each morning he would direct the caddies to rake the bunkers, mow the practice green, and generally tidy up around the clubhouse. These chores done, they were then free to caddie. If he was fortunate, a boy could expect to caddie for an average of nine rounds a week, but was scheduled to be there from nine o'clock in the morning until dusk every day. This left approximately two-thirds of the boy-caddie's day with nothing to do. For a lad aged between 14 and 18 the remuneration was good—in 1912, Swinley was paying 1s. 6d., 1s. 4d. and 1s. 3d a round for a first-, second- and third-class boy respectively, so that with tips and some food he could have earned a massive 15s. a week, considerably more than his contemporaries apprenticed to some trade or working on the land. Colt could see the potential damage to the boy, however, unless he was a good enough player to become a professional, as many did. Often forced leisure, idle time and money led to gambling or worse and the easy lifestyle made him unfit for an apprenticeship once his time as a caddie had come to an end. He would become a 'loafer'.[5] There were few openings for him other than the Services.

With this in mind Colt organised practical classes in carpentry and other trades for the boys during their slack times, and compulsory evening classes in a specially-constructed school room during the winter months. As he was running both clubs in tandem, it is certain that the Swinley boys enjoyed the same benefits and training as their Sunningdale counterparts, most likely attending the same evening classes during the winter as well. It was to be some time, however, before Colt's enlightened treatment of the boy-caddie was to become widespread. It was his idea to encourage the Swinley caddies, both men and boys, to form their own committee, and for it to be affiliated to the newly formed Caddies Aid Association—the committee had already given a 'donation of 5s. towards their funds'.[6] Soon after the caddies' committee was formed they applied to Colt for a regular salary, as opposed to single payments, 'for the uncertainties of the Insurance Act'. The Swinley committee was sympathetic but rejected their request, as 'funds did not allow'.[7]

At that time Swinley mostly employed boy-caddies as they suited the membership better. It was generally felt:

> for a good player, who is well acquainted with the green, it is very questionable whether boys are not preferable to men as caddies, apart from the matter of expense. As Sir Walter Simpson [a prolific writer on golf] whimsically puts it, boys are 'more scoldable' and their criticism is less formidable. A gaunt, disapproving man is a wet blanket to your efforts and spirits, but you go on your way unmindful of the best merited derision of a small boy. To instruct a beginner or to pilot a stranger around the course a grown useful intelligence is a useful quality in the caddie; but for the golfer who knows what he is about, has the pluck to play his own game, and is on his native heath, no species of caddie is so desirable as a bright active lad.[8]

For those members who did not rate the boy-caddie, there was:

> another class of caddie … found in the vicinity of London. They wear the outward signs of loaferdom, the seedy black overcoat or the ancient and dinted hat; some of them are wholly undesirable, but there are to be found in their ranks many excellent caddies, with a shrewd judgement and considerable knowledge of the game.[9]

By the beginning of 1913, Swinley was a victim of its own success. Such was the demand for lunches that it was decided at the next meeting of the committee, held in Derby House, that 'a charge of 1/- per head table money should be levied on all non-playing luncheon guests'.[10] The charge was a mere bagatelle to the guests and did nothing to limit numbers. At the next meeting it was decided that, after only two years, the dining room was too small and had to be enlarged. For this, Colt offered to see Thomas Colcutt, the original architect, to draw up some more plans, and Lord Derby agreed to fund the project himself so long as it did not exceed £200.

Shortly before the opening of Swinley, Fred Rains, an early English cinematographer, made a silent film entitled *The Suffragettes' Downfall; Or, Who Said 'Rats'?* Only two fragments remain, but it is enough to show the story of two women friends, both ardent suffragettes, who go off to play golf while one husband is left behind to care for the baby and do the shopping. On his way home from the shops, he stops at a public house and is sold a rat. On reaching home, he puts it on a dish under a large, domed, silver cover. In the second fragment, the man and his wife are seen arguing, seated at the dining table before a 'Votes for Women' poster on the wall. The maid enters and the rat is soon discovered. She screams, drops the dish, and both she and the wife berate the wretched husband. The maid goes out and the wife hits her husband until her friend arrives on the scene. The film ends with the wife signing a declaration forsaking the suffrage movement and the golf course, and promising to look to her duties in the home.

Although the film bore little resemblance to real-life women golfers, it was banned from cinemas in England, being thought too 'inflammatory'.[11] By 1913 women's golf was firmly established with its own governing body, the Ladies' Golf Union. There were dozens of fixtures around the country, a far cry from the segregated nine-hole golf courses of the previous century. Yet despite these

45 *The golfer's view of the suffrage movement in 1913. The harridan of a suffragette, wearing their colours of purple (dignity), green (hope) and white (purity), is caught in the act of trashing a green. The hideous image and the profile on the medal are typical of the strong anti-suffragist feeling, while the medal is parody of those prison medals the suffragettes awarded themselves, with the tri-coloured ribbon with bars denoting the dates of their imprisonment.*

advances, golf was still considered a bastion of male privilege and 'a pronounced symbol of masculine exclusivity'[12] and, as such, a fair target for suffragette action. The suffragette movement was born out of the WSPU, the Women's Social and Political Union, founded by Emmeline Pankhurst with her two daughters Christobel and Sylvia to forward the emancipation of women. By 1905 the press had lost interest in their campaign, but when Christobel and another heckled Sir Edward Grey at a political meeting with cries of 'Will the Liberal Government give votes to women?' they were arrested. After a scuffle with the police and a fine of 5s. each (which they refused to pay), they were sent to prison. It was the first time that women had resorted to violence in an attempt to win the vote and from then on members of the WSPU carried the soubriquet 'suffragette'. Further demonstrations and violence followed, along with mass imprisonments and hunger strikes that culminated in the concerted campaign in 1913. The 'guerrillists' led by Christobel Pankhurst believed that 'if it was necessary to win the vote, they were going do as much damage to property as they could'.[13]

The year began with attacks on personal and private property across the country. Telephone and telegraph wires were cut, paintings slashed in public galleries, the Orchid House at Kew burned, and windows of London clubs smashed. Then, on the night of 14 February, the suffragettes mounted simultaneous attacks on 17 golf clubs, from Leicester to the Royal St George's, Sandwich, from Pontypool to the Royal West Norfolk at Brancaster, and also Swinley Forest where:

> the greens were torn up with trowels and words burned in with [sulphuric] acid conveying such messages, such as 'Votes or War', 'Justice before Sport', 'No Votes, no Golf', 'Peace with Honour', 'Better be Hostile than Indifferent' and the ever familiar 'Votes for Women' and 'No Surrender'.[14]

There were no arrests after these unprecedented attacks, which was probably just as well as the general mood was ugly. The secretary of the Professional Golfers' Association believed that if any of the perpetrators were caught damaging greens they should not be handed over to the police but left for the members to deal with, adding: 'heaven help them if they are caught'.[15]

Although there were a fair number of active politicians as members of Swinley, it was indeed unfair of the suffragettes to attack the greens, for as a club it was unique in its attitude to women members. Swinley was totally emancipated, with female bondholders (albeit the only one then was a dowager marchioness), members and guests playing on an equal footing with men, unlike at Sunningdale where a woman playing in any match automatically had to let those behind through, whatever their number.

The reaction to the attacks on the greens was totally predictable. Christobel Pankhurst defended the action in *Votes for Women* which she edited:

> Some people say the suffragettes have acted very unwisely in destroying golf greens because this had made golfers very angry. Yet what is there to fear from their anger? What have male golfers ever done for the Suffrage cause, and what will they ever do if they are left to play their game in peace? Some golfers are members of the Liberal Government and they have done the women's cause a very great injury … The editor of *Golfing* says that golfers are not very deep politicians. Perhaps they will be now that the Suffragettes have taught them the very close connection with golf and politics.[16]

The editor of *Golfing Illustrated* naturally deplored the attacks: 'there is something particularly mean and sneaking about the destruction of putting greens … in stabbing golfers in the back, the suffragettes have roused a far wider wave of antagonism than they thought of [*sic*]'.[17] But not all the comment was adverse, as the London correspondent of the *Manchester Guardian* found:

> No golfer is, of course, enthusiastic about the silly mischief which militant suffragettes have done to the greens, but is it possible to find one or two who look on the matter in a characteristic sporting way. One such sportsman was explaining to me to-day that as the business of golf was to get over difficulties, and as many clubs, for instance, were continually spending money in putting up new bunkers, a little bunker or two on the green or a few bald patches only increased the difficulties, and gave new opportunity for your skill. He mentioned, by the way, that the bogey in his club at the injured holes had been increased by two. He touched on the new shots which the new hazards brought into play and seemed rather proud about a little lofting shot with an undercut by which he had carried a nasty little bunker one foot from the hole. He spoke of it, after all, as a new form of stymie. He expected to see golf club makers with a new suffrage lofting putter on the market in a day or two. He was told that a man who talked like that was liable to be expelled from his club.[18]

As a result of these actions, Lloyd's were quick to offer golf clubs insurance against future attack. The rate was £1 a green for a year's cover, the underwriters to pay for damage to each, up to a maximum of £50. The one stipulation was that all 18 greens had to be insured, not just those 'closest to the highway or comparatively accessible to Suffragist raids'. Thus for a premium of £18 the insurers were liable for a maximum of £900 if every green on the course was damaged—'destruction which could scarcely be regarded as a reasonable possibility even in the wildest dreams of the militant women'.[19] The Swinley committee felt, rightly as it turned out, that as they had been attacked once they would not be again and so declined any additional insurance. Sunningdale did take up Lloyd's offer, while Walton Heath, where the house that was to be presented to Lloyd George was fire-bombed by the suffragettes, employed 100 of their beefiest caddies to patrol the course at night.

The greens would have recovered well by the time Sir Rufus Isaacs wrote to David Lloyd George on 12 May 1913:

My Dear LG,

Wednesday morning 11.30 Swinley Forest is our appointment—my wife had not heard from yours about Wednesday but anyway you are returning with me here—we had not heard from [the] Mastermans yet how they propose to come …

Yours ever,

Rufus[20]

Sir Rufus Isaacs was the Attorney General and one of the original bondholders of Swinley, as was the Chief Whip, the Master of Elibank, while David Lloyd George, then Chancellor of the Exchequer, was a member of Walton Heath. Besides their respective positions in Herbert Asquith's Liberal Cabinet and their mutual love of the game, the three men had something rather more sinister in common. They were all implicated in what became known as 'The Marconi Scandal'.

At a Cabinet meeting in 1911 it was decided to set up an 'Imperial Wireless Chain'. Using the new Marconi invention of radio, it would connect Britain with her Empire for better defence against the growing military might of Germany and Japan. The contract was put out to tender, and in March 1912 Marconi's price was accepted, subject to the ratification of the Cabinet. The chairman of the British arm of Marconi was Godfrey Isaacs, brother of Sir Rufus. That same March the American Marconi Company decided to increase its capitalisation, and before the shares were even approved and available to the public Godfrey and Sir Rufus Isaacs each bought a large tranche of the American stock for themselves. Ten days later the shares opened on United States and British exchanges, closing the day roughly four times higher than what the insiders had paid for them. Rumours abounded in the market that 'Lloyd George has been dealing on the Stock Exchange heavily to his advantage with private political information'.[21] Cecil Chesterton, brother of G.K. and co-editor of the political weekly *The Eye-Witness*, claimed that Lloyd George, Sir Rufus Isaacs, and the Master of Elibank had all used their prior knowledge of

46 *Sir Rufus Isaacs, a competent player, was considered the 'backbone' of the Houses of Parliament golf side.*

47   *The golf course has always been an ideal place to discuss matters privately, and so it was when the Chancellor of the Exchequer, David Lloyd George, Sir Rufus Isaacs and Charles Masterman, Financial Secretary to the Treasury, played at Swinley the day before a Select Committee looked into their involvement in what became known as 'The Marconi Scandal'. He always maintained that he 'was never a long hitter but unlike what might be imagined, I was always straight'.*

the contract to profit from share transactions in Marconi and associated companies. A Commons select committee (made up of a Liberal majority) was set up in the New Year (1913), where it was revealed that Sir Rufus had indeed purchased 10,000 £2 shares in the American Marconi, and had immediately resold 1,000 shares to David Lloyd George. It later transpired that the Master of Elibank had also bought 3,000 Marconi shares for himself and another 3,000 on behalf of the Liberal Party. That Swinley game, on a deserted mid-week course, played between David Lloyd George, Sir Rufus Isaacs and Charles Masterman, Financial Secretary to the Treasury, was the day before the opening of the Select Committee. It is not hard to imagine the topic of conversation throughout their game.

In the end it was found that all three had indeed bought shares in the American Marconi Company, but only after the tender had been let, which effectively negated the charge of direct connivance or insider trading. The Tories felt that the ministers had been 'wanting in frankness', while their own Cabinet colleagues considered 'their dealings to have been certainly indiscreet and very nearly improper'.[22] By the end of the year, Isaacs was appointed Lord Chief Justice—'... so reverent to behold, in scarlet and in ermines, and chain of England's gold.'

By March 1913 Harry Colt felt that the time had come to resign as secretary of Sunningdale. He had tried to leave two years before as his workload took him increasingly around the country and abroad to Europe and America, but the committee begged him to stay on. This time there was no argument and Colt had his way. Soon after, David Ayton left Swinley to become the professional at Clacton-on-Sea. He was there for only a few months, being a very early volunteer for the Army. He survived the First World War and later became the first professional at the new Point Grey Golf Club, Vancouver. Ayton had proved to be an admirable choice for the short time he was at Swinley. Well-taught by his father and grandfather, he was a very fine golfer, playing several times for Scotland and in many exhibition matches. At that time the professional's duties were 'to play a round of the links when required, at a fixed fee, whether with skilled players or with trios [novices] who need instruction'.[23] In addition, in keeping with a long family tradition, Ayton was a skilled club-maker, but at that time there was no proper workshop at Swinley so his talents were confined to their repair. After the success of Ayton, members of the Swinley committee decided that his successor should be equally competent and therefore they should take their time in finding the right replacement. In the absence of Colt who was abroad, Sir Hubert Longman had approached Jack White, the professional at Sunningdale, to take over and 'to place someone in charge of the shop and keeping a man in it who could play, teach and do repairs as an interim arrangement'.[24] The arrangement was to last one year and White's appointee was to be housed in the professional's cottage.

To employ Jack White was a bold move. On the one hand it was a great coup to have someone of his undoubted stature (the 1904 Open Champion) as the professional, albeit a notional one; on the other hand it was a risk, as he was a dipsomaniac and over the years had spent many weeks in homes drying out. Time and time again he was threatened by Sunningdale with dismissal, and time and again he was reinstated with a final, final warning. In the end he had to supply a doctor's letter every two weeks, certifying that he was in good health and sober. Whatever his condition at Sunningdale the arrangement worked well for Swinley, as members could book him or his nominee for a round and the professional's shop was suitably manned. It was to be another ten months before a professional of their choosing was engaged.

Although there were many members who lived in the close vicinity of Swinley, there were a fair number who had London addresses, and for them to play at their club would have entailed a whole day's excursion. There were those who would motor down, often driven by their chauffeur who would go to the room beside the kitchens and stay, suitably fed and watered, until it was time for him to drive his master home. Only in December 1913 (an exceptionally cold winter) was a stove, a gift of Lord Derby, put into the room. Their own external 'earth closet and urinal', also a gift of Lord Derby, came six months later. The chauffeur-caddie (like the chauffeur-loader) is a figment of period-film directors' imagination.

There were other members who travelled to Swinley by train. The trains of the London & South West Railway left from Waterloo and went either to Ascot, on the Ascot-Aldershot line, or Sunningdale, on the Staines-Wokingham line. Either way it meant a taxi-ride to Swinley that could not be relied upon. Sunningdale had a proper station, but up until 1902 none of the London trains stopped there on Sundays. And so a delegation from the golf club lobbied the superintendent of the L&SWR for at least one train, preferably the 9.24 from Waterloo, to stop there on a Sunday. The request was denied. When Sir Hubert Longman, then Captain of Sunningdale, heard of their refusal he consulted his father-in-law, Adolphus Frederick Govett, who was a director of the L&SWR Company (as well as the Waterloo and City Line, known today as The Drain). It was through him that the Sunningdale team was introduced to the general manager of the Company, Sir Charles Owens, a lieutenant colonel in the Engineer and Volunteer Staff Corps who had been knighted for the 'satisfactory working of the railway arrangements in connection with the dispatch of troops to and from Southampton during the [South African] War'.[25] Owens was also a keen golfer and, it would appear, open to bribery. With the offer of an honorary membership of Sunningdale he arranged for the 9.24 from Waterloo to stop at Sunningdale. Once Owens was hooked the committee played him for all he was worth—cheap fares for golfers, more Sunday trains stopping and the like. Other golf clubs followed in their wake, with special concessions for golfers—'golfers' tickets' and purpose-built halts for Sunday golfers, like the one set up by the Great Western Railway in 1912 for Denham (another Colt course of a similar date) in Buckinghamshire. In fact it was only in the 1930s that 'the commuters using Denham Golf Club Station outnumbered golfers'.[26]

With the precedent set, Alexander Davey was told to approach the London & South West Railway Company for a similar platform to be set up at Swinley—presumably Sir Hubert was embarrassed this time to ask the favour of his father-in-law. Davey saw Sir Charles Owens, who was still a director of the L&SWR. He no doubt could see himself as an honorary member of Swinley as well as Sunningdale and granted everything Davey asked of him on the most favourable of terms. The L&SWR agreed to put up a wooden platform, with lights, beside the track and below the bridge on the flatland at the end of the embankment—roughly where the water tanks are today. In due course the platform would become classed as a 'halt'; that is, a more permanent fixture and included in the timetable. The Company also agreed to 'stop all Sunday trains and any weekday ones if sufficient passengers required it'.[27] Swinley already had a concession for Sunday golfing tickets from Waterloo to both Sunningdale and Ascot, and this consideration was extended to the Swinley platform as well. Davey had done well with his negotiations as he achieved everything for a modest outlay of £25 a year for ten years. The system worked well, with the golfing passengers merely notifying the station master at Ascot that they wished to alight at the next stop. The station master in turn sent a porter scurrying up the train to inform the engine driver, who duly pulled up at the Swinley platform. On the return journey the passenger literally flagged the train down. It was a boon to the London golfer who could leave London Waterloo at 9.24 and travel direct to the Swinley Forest Golf Club platform, arriving on the course within an hour and a half. The service was initially widely used, but faded out soon after the First World War through lack of support. The 'platform' never did receive its 'halt' status, and when the ten-year option lapsed it was not renewed.

That summer of 1914 which led up to the First World War was the last of its kind. It heralded the end of a gilded, leisured age, and of a society which the aristocracy, the upper- and moneyed-classes would never see again. The testing rounds of golf and days out at Swinley continued against the rumblings of war and general mobilisation. The course was playing well, and two extra green-keepers had been taken on to bring their number up to five and a boy. Another man was engaged whose duties were solely to sign in visitors and collect green fees from a 'sentry box' (paid for by Lord Derby) by the gate. Extra staff were taken on in the clubhouse to help the new stewardess, Miss Waltham, the original couple having left under a cloud. Mrs Bowyer had recently been engaged as cook at an annual salary of £45 to cope with all the lunches. As usual during Ascot Week the course was crowded every day after the racing. Outside matches, nearly all with a military connection (such as the Staff of the Royal Military Academy, Sandhurst, against the cadets) were allowed on weekdays, and with the five-day and Service members the course was used all the more.

For too many of the members and staff that summer was the last time they ever played at Swinley. On 4 August 1914 war was declared on Germany, and life as they all knew it was never to be the same again.

CHAPTER 5

The enthusiastic crowds that converged on Buckingham Palace echoed the general feeling of delight of the whole country on the night war was declared on Germany, a view not shared by Lord Kitchener who believed that it would take far longer than Christmas to defeat the enemy. There was an immediate campaign against all things German, especially that of their philosophers and composers. Anti-German feeling was whipped up to fever pitch; the Hun became a baby-bayoneting hate figure. Dachshunds were kicked to death in the street, while the German shepherd dog, a less easy target, had its name changed to the more Allied-friendly Alsatian, followed as late as 1917 by George V changing his family name from Sachsen-Coburg und Gotha (Saxe-Coburg-Gotha) to the more acceptable Windsor (a move that prompted his cousin the Kaiser to crack a rare joke about going to the theatre to see a performance of 'The Merry Wives of Saxe-Coburg und Gotha'). Various German cousins who lived in Great Britain took on more acceptable British titles or abandoned their German ones altogether. Caught in the middle was Prince Albert, Duke of Schleswig-Holstein-Sonderburg-Augustenburg, second son of Prince Christian and HRH The Princess Helena, the third daughter of Queen Victoria. 'An outstanding golfer playing down to [a handicap of] about 6',[1] the Duke was elected an honorary member of Swinley in June 1914. He was also an enthusiastic member of the Golf Match Club (see page 143), nearly holding the record of those playing more than ten matches when he 'won nine, lost two and halved one'.[2]

But nowhere was this anti-German feeling more keenly felt than on golf courses up and down the country. Emotions ran high in the clubhouse, where it was generally agreed that although 'the fortunes of war will vary, the pendulum will swing, but the final issue can never be in doubt … [for] the Germans have never shown themselves the least inclined for golf'.[3] However, there were those of German (and Austrian) birth who lived in Great Britain who did play golf, and it was against these members that a loose confederation of 50 golf clubs around London passed a resolution that they should 'cease to frequent their respective clubs for the duration of the war and those not naturalized should be immediately expelled'.[4] Swinley was not of their number, although the neighbouring Sunningdale did pass a similar resolution: 'If it is found that any Member of the Club has taken up arms against this country or its Allies,

48 *Prince Albert, Duke of Schleswig-Holstein, a grandson of Queen Victoria, was an enthusiastic golfer. Notwithstanding his service with the German Army, he remained a member of Swinley throughout the First World War.*

his name be at once removed against the List of Members'.[5] There were 19 signatures. This caused a problem with one of their honorary members and former Captain (1910), the afore-mentioned Prince Albert, Duke of Schleswig-Holstein, 'the brightest, kindest and most entertaining of companions'.

Prince Albert, known as Abbie, was born at Frogmore House in

1869 and later brought up at Cumberland Lodge in Windsor Great Park. While his elder brother Christian went from Wellington to Sandhurst and was commissioned into the 60th (the King's Royal Rifle Corps), Albert, though thoroughly English, served in the Prussian Army, reaching the rank of lieutenant colonel in the 3rd Uhlans of the Guard. On the death of his brother in South Africa in 1900 Albert became heir to vast estates in Silesia 'and therefore it was considered necessary for him to make his home in Germany and serve in the Prussian Army'.[6] Albert was close to his first cousin, the Kaiser (he was with him in the Imperial Yacht *Hohenzollern* in the Baltic shortly before war was declared). Although on the retired list, he felt it incumbent upon him to offer his services to his cousin, on condition that 'he would, under no circumstances, serve on the Western front'.[7] He was therefore attached to the staff of General von Loewenfeldt, in charge of the Berlin defences.

Notwithstanding this non-combatant role, various factions at Sunningdale continued to take a dim view of Prince Albert's membership, some suggesting that his name should be 'erased from the list of Captains of the Club'.[8]

49 *Timing and swing are the mark of a good golfer and shot, as with Prince Albert, Duke of Schleswig-Holstein, 'the brightest, kindest and most entertaining of companions'.*

Swinley took a more pragmatic view of His Highness' honorary membership. As he was out of the country there was obviously no possibility of him embarrassing anyone by coming to play until the war was over, so there was absolutely no point in going through the idiotic motion of pretending he did not exist. Anyway, he was a popular member and in the words of an officer of the 11th Hussars at the Charge of the Light Brigade, who recognised a Russian Battery Commander whom he had met at a ball in London six months before: 'The aristocracy knows no bounds'. Towards the end of the 1920s Princess Albert's younger sister, HH The Princess Helena Victoria, was also elected an honorary member of Swinley. Like her brothers she was a keen golfer, but not as proficient. When she was staying at Glenconner House in East Lothian in Scotland, as a guest of the Prime Minister, Herbert Asquith, and his wife Margot, the two women decided to play at the nearby North Berwick Golf Club where the Princess was well known. Before the game, Margot Asquith, President of the Ladies Parliamentary Golf Association, quietly asked the Princess' caddie how good a player she was, to which he replied with typical Scottish caddie cheek: 'A verry puir player—much like yerself!'[9]

As with golf clubs throughout the country, the war had a profound effect on the finances and management of Swinley. It was Brigadier General J. Ponsonby DSO, Coldstream Guards, who suggested that 'all members serving in H.M. Forces be permitted to pay half subsc[t] and that members using the club pay a green fee'.[10] At that time, 1916, Swinley was showing a drop in income of nearly £900 'in comparison with 1914'—contrary to popular legend, there was never a time that the Club's expenses were divided up equally among the members at the end of the year. Harry Colt worked out that a half-subscription for Service members would cost the Club a further £200 that they could ill afford. In the end the committee came up with a typical Swinley compromise—each case would be considered on the merits of the individual and that '6d. extra [be charged] for Fish Course and Sweet course (each)'.[11] In addition, the Department of Woods and Forests was approached for a reduction of rent for the duration of the war.

Apart from the loss of revenue Swinley was also greatly affected by the enlistment of club servants into the Forces from the very outset of the war. Most joined up immediately, some even going to the regiments of Service members. The boy caddies waited until they were old enough, all doubtless inspired by Lord Derby and his sterling recruitment work in his beloved Lancashire. It was Lord Kitchener who realised that men would be more eager to enlist if they could serve alongside their friends, neighbours and work colleagues, rather than be lost among the regular soldiers of the Army. And so, towards the end of August 1914, the first of the 'Pals Battalions' was formed when 1,600 men from the City of London enlisted in the 10th (Service Battalion) Royal Fusiliers. It became known as the 'Stockbrokers' Battalion'. Soon after, the Niblick Brigade was formed, made up of golf professionals and assistants who were drafted into the 60th, the King's Royal Rifle Corps, based at Winchester.

50 *Edward Hoare became honorary secretary in 1915 and kept Swinley and his family bank, C. Hoare and Co., going throughout the First World War and beyond.*

51 *Girl caddies were employed during the First World War at Swinley as well as disabled Servicemen. As their French counterparts tended to grow larger than the boys, the latter were described as being like 'Helots [serfs from Sparta], downtrodden and outcast'.*

Lord Derby himself raised a battalion of 1,500 Liverpudlians, mostly from the docks. 'This should be a battalion of Pals', he told them. 'A battalion in which friends from the same office will fight shoulder to shoulder for the honour of Britain and the credit of Liverpool.' Within the next few days he had raised another three battalions for the King's (Liverpool) Regiment. Lord Derby presented each new recruit personally with a silver badge of his family crest (an eagle perching above a baby in a cradle) as a memento of his enlistment. In recognition of Derby's role in raising the four battalions, a brass version of the 'Eagle and Child' was adopted as their cap badge, much to the fury of the other regular battalions who wore the White Horse of Hanover. It was not long before the 'Pals Battalions' became commonplace throughout the country. On the back of this success Lord Derby was appointed Director-General of Recruiting in October 1915, just before the advent of conscription.

In common with all other golf clubs Swinley turned to female labour for both indoor and outdoor staff. Two women were employed as part-time green-keepers under John Macdonald, who had registered under the Derby Scheme* for call-up. Being in his fifties, and with eight children, there was little chance of his being conscripted.

Edward Henry Hoare, the new honorary secretary, was a key figure in keeping Swinley going through the war years and beyond, just as he did the family bank, C. Hoare & Co. He had become a partner in 1910, having worked for years in the City as a solicitor. At the outbreak of war he stepped in to become managing partner so as to allow his nephews, Harry and Arthur Hoare, 'leave of absence to join the forces'.[12]

Another inevitable change came with the caddies. As the boy caddies (among them Macdonald's sons) grew up and left for the war, or were diverted to the land—it was thought that 'strong boys should not be carrying golf clubs as long as there is useful work for them to do elsewhere'[13]—they were replaced initially by schoolgirls, then joined by disabled servicemen. Girl caddies were 'no novelty … [and had] been tried intermittently and with reasonable success over several courses'. Le Touquet, another Colt course, was 'where plenty of girls have been employed [in the past] and they seem to grow larger than the boys so that the latter have something of the appearance of Helots, downtrodden and outcast'.[14]

Due to its proximity to many military installations, Swinley was approached by the Army Forage Department for permission to 'harvest the grass on their links for hay for Army use'.[15] Permission was readily granted as the alternative was to lose some, if not all, of the course to agriculture, although Harry Colt, as a Deputy Commissioner for the South-West District of the Ministry of Food,

---

* The Derby Scheme, instigated by the Earl of Derby, encouraged men to register their name voluntarily on the principle that, once registered, they would only be called up for service when necessary. As an added incentive, married men were advised that they would be called up once the supply of single men was exhausted. The scheme was not a success and was replaced by conscription with the Military Service Act of January 1916.

would have used his influence to see that his favourite golf course would not have been ploughed up. Near the end of the war a neighbouring farmer, a Mr H.C. Minchin, 'provided labour and appliances for cutting the fairways'.[16] Six years later he was to say that Colt had promised to give him honorary life membership in recognition of his services. The suggestion was refuted. He was, however, allowed to play *gratis* during the week.

From the very beginning of the war, golfers noticed a significant rise in the price of golf balls when all existing supplies of rubber were diverted to the production of military hardware such as tires, hoses, belts, grommets, gaskets and the like. As golf balls became harder to come by, the five-minute rule for finding them in the rough was relaxed. It was not just Swinley that was raided at night by gangs of small boys collecting balls to sell back to members the next day. Caddies were also bribed to filch the odd ball. One anonymous member wrote that he 'had a personal experience of a loafer offering me half a dozen balls … His pockets were full of them and as most golfers are careless about the number they own, the amount that can be stolen is quite staggering.' What made it worse for him was that it happened in St James's, 'outside a first class London club'.[17]

It would appear that there was very little activity at Swinley over the war years, with few meetings of the committee (and none at all in 1919). Lord Derby was too busy to convene a meeting, having succeeded (and been appointed by) Lloyd-George as Secretary of State for War, which he remained until 1918, the year he went to Paris as British Ambassador to France. Colt had sold Earlywood Corner and moved right away to East Hendred in South Oxfordshire. That left Longman, Davey, Lucas and the honorary secretary E.H. Hoare all still living within a few miles' radius of Swinley. Davey was even closer, having completed building his house, Boden's Ride (to the left of the 18th fairway), on his original land in 1916. In fact Davey faded out of the Swinley picture altogether some time after 1921. He sold Boden's Ride to a fellow bondholder, Edward Peacock, and moved south, buying two small farms at Burwash in the Dudwell Valley in East Sussex. It is possible that he intended to create another golf course with Harry Colt, his friend and erstwhile neighbour. It was not to be.

And so, on the afternoon of 20 April 1920, a quartet of the committee met in the imposing board room of C. Hoare & Co.'s Bank in Fleet Street in London. Major Lucas took the chair, flanked by Alexander Davey and Harry Colt, with Edward Hoare, still managing partner, as honorary secretary. It was the first proper meeting since the beginning of the war and much had happened in the meantime. Edward Hoare began by reading a list of 25 members who wished to resign. It was a surprising list, not least as there were six names of members that were not recorded as being members in the first place. There was a Mrs Astor, *née* Ava Willing and noted Philadelphia beauty, who was divorced from her husband, John J. Astor, who was drowned when the *Titanic* sank. She later rejoined as Lady

Ribblesdale, the wife of Lord Ribblesdale, sometime Master of the Queen's Buckhounds (see page 195). Also on the list was the Duke of Palmella, sometime Portuguese Ambassador to the Court of St James's. Others who resigned were two of the first-rate amateur players, A.V. Hambro and Captain A.G. Taylor, which could suggest that the course had deteriorated to a state that they could no longer play it with enjoyment. Arthur Balfour was also on the list of resignations. Whatever the reason, or reasons, for the mass exodus, there were many more, all 48 of them, who wanted to join in their places.

For the first time Lord Derby had little input in selecting any of the new members. He wrote to Colt excusing his absence as 'it was impossible for him to leave the Embassy in Paris to attend this meeting',[18] but added his thanks to Edward Hoare 'for his work during the past year and that he be congratulated upon the large number of nice members who had joined the Club since he had become Honorary Secretary'. At that time there were 159 members, including four on the foreign list. The fortunes of Swinley had improved considerably, and Colt suggested that '6 months interest be paid upon the Bonds'; others thought that a year's interest was appropriate whatever the state of the Club's finances. This was the first (recorded) time that a dividend was proposed to be paid, but the decision was deferred for all members of the committee to vote. In the end, as usual nothing was done and the dividend appears to have been waived for yet another year. At the same April 1920 meeting it was decided to increase the membership to 200, and when that target was reached to start a waiting list. Also decided unanimously was 'The election of H.R.H. The Prince of Wales as an honorary member of the Club'.[19]

Throughout four changes of name—Prince Edward of Wales, The Prince of Wales, Edward VIII and Duke of Windsor—David (as he was invariably known) was always a keen and reasonably proficient golfer with a handicap that hovered around 13. Like many a golfer, he began by caddying for his father, later George V, one Ascot Week in a game at Windsor with the Duke of Roxburghe and the professional Ben Sayers. He was paid 1s. a round, a third-class caddie rate at Swinley. When Sayers suggested that he give him and his brother, Prince Albert, lessons, their father refused, retorting that a 'game that could make a man unaccountably mad at himself ought not to be encouraged'.[20] They were, however, allowed to play at Sandringham, where they were coached by their tutor Henry Hansell, a member of Sunningdale, and by James Braid. Later the Prince's golfing skills were honed by Archie Compston, the professional at Coombe Hill. Like his grandfather Edward VII, he was Captain of the Royal and Ancient at St Andrews, driving himself in wearing 'a multicoloured Fair Isle sweater, with a jigsaw of patterns' which, he admitted later, was 'the only outstanding feature of my appearance at St Andrews on that occasion'.[21] He won or was runner-up in several tournaments, most notably in the Parliamentary Match of 1933 when he played Lady Astor in the semi-final. She 'did not want to beat the heir to the throne' and threw the

52   *The Prince of Wales driving himself in as Captain of the Royal and Ancient at St Andrews. It was a very poor shot and he later admitted that his Fair Isle sweater was the 'only outstanding feature on that occasion'.*

match on the 17th, leaving the Prince to win 'two up and one to play'.[22] Although he had played at Sunningdale (through Hansell's introduction) as a boy, he was delighted with his membership of Swinley as an alternative, particularly when he moved to Fort Belvedere at Virginia Water, his folly on the other side of the Great West Road and adjacent to Coworth, Lord Derby's Berkshire home. At the next meeting of the Swinley committee two more of Hansell's pupils—Prince Henry (later created Duke of Gloucester) and his sister, Princess Mary (afterwards The Princess Royal), were elected honorary members.

Although Lord Derby had been delighted by the way Swinley had been managed during his absence in Paris, he began to feel that he was losing overall control of what he continued to regard as *his* golf club through the transfer of bonds. Also, as the price of the bonds was escalating, the new bondholders were reaping the benefit of the transferees with no financial advantage to Swinley. It was therefore decided, by a two-thirds majority of the bondholders circulated, that the trustees should, out of a special fund, 'pay off and redeem at par any Bond or Bonds' of a deceased holder or of 'a Holder who has been divested of his property in a Bond or Bonds by operation of law'—otherwise a bankrupt or criminal—or by agreement. It was also agreed that any bondholder wishing to dispose of his bond had to offer it back to the committee on 'payment of the original sum of £100 for each such bond, together with any interest due thereon'.[23] There was to be no going back once the sale notice was complete. After serving as honorary secretary for 11 years Edward Hoare decided that he had had enough and resigned his position, but remained a member of the committee. His place was taken by Major Lucas, but as he was to receive a small honorarium for his services he resigned as a member of the committee. Lucas took to his new job with enthusiasm, and according to *Country Life*:

> Mr Lucas is the new hon. secretary of Swinley Forest, and watches over that truly admirable course with the tenderest solicitude. He used also to play at Ascot and Sunningdale, and no doubt does so still, but his heart is probably at Swinley. Certainly it is a course that affords a great excuse for a romantic passion, for not only is the place a most charmingly pretty and peaceful one, but the golf is just as good and exciting as it can be.[24]

At the end of the first meeting Evelyn Lucas brought up various points—forthcoming society matches, the invitation for Swinley to join the Berkshire and Buckinghamshire Golf Union, a new septic tank and the like, all of which were agreed. There was one other item: 'The Secretary reported that he had a demonstration of a Hoover Cleaner and Beater and recommended the purchase of one at a cost of £19-10 if and when he considered it necessary'.[25]

53 *Major Evelyn Lucas replaced Edward Hoare as secretary in 1926 where, according to* Country Life, *he 'watches over that truly admirable course with the tenderest solicitude'. As he received a small honorarium, he resigned from the committee.*

There is an oft-told story of an American visitor to Swinley asking a club servant where he could find the showers, only to be told: 'There are none. Their lordships take their baths at their own homes.'[26] The same story is told of the Royal West Norfolk, Brancaster. Although Swinley did have 'a bathroom and showerbath in the gentlemen's Lavatory',[27] the gift of Lord Derby, who 'very generously offered to defray the cost up to £50', it did not necessarily mean that they were actually used—hence the remark. Old habits die hard. Even today the showers in the members' locker room are not as widely used as those in the visitors' changing room. In the 1980s Sidney Spiro, the Anglo-American Corporation of South Africa's man in London and later a director of Hambro's Bank, was playing one Sunday with Rupert Hambro and some friends. When they were changing for lunch Spiro stripped off, wrapped a towel round his corpulent waist and made for the showers. When he noticed that he was the only one there, the South African turned on his companions and declared in high dudgeon: 'The trouble with you bloody public schoolboys is that you are just so filthy!'[28] In a scene straight out of Greyfriars School, the Bunteresque Spiro once went in to change for lunch, opened the door and a pot of Nivea Cream emptied all over his head. Nor was it one-sided. When it was raining, Spiro would use his caddie's clothes to dry his hands.

Unlike virtually every other golf club in the world Swinley has rarely mounted a team to play against any other club or society. Even today the singles and foursomes competitions are approached with little enthusiasm. It was ever thus. In the 1920s it was proposed that 'matches be arranged between the Club and certain Societies, and it was left to the Secretary to arrange such matches, the number in any one year not to exceed six',[29] but there is no record of any such matches ever being played. Golfing societies were, however, allowed during the week, on the strict understanding that 'in no case would the courtesy of the green be given'.[30] In addition, it would appear that the military could do no wrong. Officers attending the Staff College and the Royal Military Academy, Sandhurst, were allowed to play with their wives, or maybe a friend, from Monday to Friday. The same facility was extended to the officers of the Household Cavalry and the Brigade of Guards then stationed at Windsor.

With the Earl of Derby's almost feudal view of the bond between aristocracy and the working class, it is surprising that he did not come up with the idea of forming an Artisans Club at Swinley. Artisan clubs had worked well elsewhere in rural areas, where wages where generally lower and the 'work-and-play' arrangement provided them with the opportunity to indulge in a sport otherwise prohibited by lack of funds. Equipment, too, was often a problem and members would donate used balls and the odd club—'gifts given and received with no embarrassment on either side'.[31] Equally surprising was the attitude of Harry Colt, who in 1910 had founded the Ridgemount Workman's Golf Club attached to Sunningdale.

There he would certainly have experienced at first hand the mutual benefits of an Artisans Club, yet he did nothing either. So, as late as 1923, it was decided (but not recorded) that there should be an Artisans Club at Swinley, and it is likely that Colt was the instigator. He was certainly the first President, with Edward Hoare, the Hon. Sydney Marsham and Major Lucas appointed as Vice-Presidents. It is also a possibility, however, that it was John MacDonald, the green-keeper and the first Captain, who put the Artisans Club together as a family club. He had six sons, all of whom went on to successful careers as golf professionals, and two daughters. The eldest son Donald was a scratch player and part-time professional at the parent club, and he, John junior and David MacDonald (who also worked under their father as assistant green-keepers) were all founding members. The advantages of an Artisans Club to Macdonald would have been great, with its large unpaid labour force at his disposal and access to the course for his family, provided of course they became members.

The club was formed and named the Fernhill Workmen's Golf Club, Swinley. There were 57 original members, each paying an annual subscription of 2s. 6d. The club was made up of the local tradesmen, servants (often of members) in the neighbouring houses, a postman and artisans, all of whom had to be approved by the committee of the parent club. There were railways workers, too, who were ideal. Each stretch of line was cared for by a 'lengthman', and it was all too easy for those working on the track running past Swinley to play a round before or after a night shift. Unlike Sunningdale, where there was a chauffeurs' course for them to play on while their masters used the Old Course, the Swinley members' chauffeurs were not so fortunate. There was no point in them applying for membership of the Fernhill Club as its members had to play before 9.30 in the morning and after 5 o'clock in the evening. The rules of the club were strict and rigidly enforced. Each player had to wear a badge while playing and stand aside 'if they find themselves being pressed by a Member of Swinley Forest Golf Club'.[32] The worst 'crime' was for a member to play with a non-member. There was a fine of 1s. for the first offence and expulsion for the second, as with a breach of any of the others rules. By 1926 the Fernhill Workmen's Golf Club was well established with 59 members each paying a 5s. subscription. In May each year they played for the Fernhill Cup, presented by Edward Hoare and Sydney Marsham, while in July there was a stroke competition for the Major Lucas Cup, with *The News of the World* (a great sponsor of golf) presenting the gold medals to the winners. It would appear that the annual match between the parent club and the Fernhill Workmen's Golf Club began in 1924, and has been played ever since, save for the years during the Second World War. By 1929 they became known as the 'Fernhill Artisans'.

The original £5 5s. subscription for Swinley remained unchanged until the end of the First World War, but as inflation and the need for repairs and improvements rose it doubled to 10 guineas. By 1926 it was felt necessary to raise it again by

54 *Report of the Artisans' match in* The Times, *Monday 20 May 1929.*

THE PRINCE OF WALES.

Plays Golf for Swinley Forest Team Against Ferndown.

For the past three years the members of the Swinley Golf Club at Ascot, whose ground is the beautiful course on the west of the railway line to Bagshot, have had an annual match with the Fernhill Artisans Golf Club. The Swinley Club was established about 20 years ago by the Earl of Derby, who still takes a great interest in its management. It has the Prince of Wales, Prince Henry and Prince George on its long and distinguished membership list. The Fernhill Club has about sixty members, and by permission of Lord Derby they are allowed the use of the Swinley ground in the early mornings and in the evenings.

When the Prince of Wales learnt recently of the forthcoming match he at once expressed a wish to be one of the Swinley team, and the fact that they each had the same handicap —16—caused the selection of Mr. William Jones as the member of the Artisan's team to play against the Prince. The match took place in beautiful weather on Saturday afternoon, and Mr. Jones was defeated by 2 up and 1 to play.

After the game Mr. Jones had tea with the Prince and the latter signed the autograph books of Miss Irene Jones, Mr. Jones' daughter, and of Mr. Ben Ferns.

Following are the details of the match:

Swinley Forest.		Fernhill Artisans	
H.R.H. Prince of Wales	1	W. E. Jones	0
Major E. P. Lucas	0	J. Fulker	1
Mr. J. Murray	0	P. Huxford	1
Mr. A. C. Wilson	0	J. Macdonald	1
Mr. W. Stonor	0	W. Huxford	1
Mr. A. Watson	½	C. Abbott	½
Mr. C. M. Woodbridge	0	T. Hamlet	1
Mr. E. H. Hoare	1	W. Wedge	0
Hon. S. Marsham	0	H. Longhurst	1
Mr. D. F. N. Fitzgerald	1	R. Bates	0
Mr. A. F. Evans	0	J. Woodley	1
Mr. E. R. Peacock	1	J. Strong	0
Mr. C. H. Poole	1	J. Hammond	0
Sir C. Thompson	1	J. Macdonald, senr.	0
	6½		7½

£1 10s., to be able to guarantee the caddies £1 per week and to repair their shed and improve the chauffeurs' room. That same year the Crown lease on the 179 acres had expired, and it was left to the Club's solicitors, Bailey, Shaw and Gillett, to negotiate a new contract. They were so successful that Lord Derby instructed the secretary to invite the Chief Commissioner of Crown Lands, A.S. Gaye, 'to accept honorary membership of the Club in token of the Committee's appreciation of his courtesy and consideration during the negotiations for a fresh lease of that portion of the course situated on Crown Land'.[33] The commissioner 'gratefully accepted the offer'. The terms can only have been hugely favourable and an honorary membership easy to bestow, for not that long after (in 1931) Edward H. Savill, the founder of the Savill Gardens in Virginia Water, was also invited to become an honorary member for his role as Deputy Ranger of Windsor Great Park.

Swinley has always been very low-key and understated, but 18 May 1929, a Saturday, was special when the Prince of Wales agreed to play for the parent club against the Fernhill Artisans. At that time the Prince of Wales was playing his best golf, and a single match on a Saturday afternoon would not satisfy his needs. That day he began by playing seven holes with his equerry, Lieutenant Colonel the Hon. Piers Legh, to familiarise himself with the conditions, then returned to the clubhouse in time for his illustrious foursome. There, waiting for him, was his partner, Walter Hagen. This beefy American was

55 *Swinley has always had a close relationship with the Royal Household at Windsor, so the Hon. Piers Legh, equerry to the Prince of Wales, was no stranger to the course. When the Prince played for the parent club against the Artisans, Legh played a 'warm-up' seven holes with him.*

56 *Playing golf was not the only passion for the Prince of Wales: he was also a follower of the professional and amateur circuits. When presenting Walter Hagen with the cup for The Open in 1928, he invited him to Swinley. They played a match against Sir Philip Sassoon and Aubrey Boomer, the professional from St Cloud.*

certainly one of the greatest (and most flamboyant) players, who had dominated the professional circuit there and in Great Britain for two decades. He had won The Open four times, the US Open twice, and the US PGA Championship five times. He captained the Ryder Cup team six times and played in five matches. Bernard Darwin admitted that 'there [may] have been more skillful players and certainly more mechanical players and faultless players than Hagen, but none with greater sticking power or a temperament more ideally suited to the game'.[34] He had met the Prince of Wales on several occasions, and it is likely that they had agreed to play together sometime in the future when they last met and the Prince presented him with the cup after winning The Open in 1928.

Their opponents were Sir Philip Sassoon and Aubrey Boomer, the professional from St Cloud, Paris (yet another Colt course, constructed in 1913). Sir Philip Sassoon, third baronet, was one of the gilded men of his age. 'He had a long and hazardous friendship with the Prince of Wales whom he worshipped, though their intermittent quarrels were famous.'[35] Sassoon had been Member of Parliament for Hythe since 1912, and held various offices including that of Parliamentary Private Secretary to Lloyd George. He built Port Lympne in Kent, today perhaps better known for the zoo started by John Aspinall. A talented sportsman on the golf course and particularly on the tennis court, he was also a formidable amateur opponent. Boomer, his partner, was another great professional golfer, but not quite as successful as Walter Hagen.

The foursome lunched in the dining room with Piers Legh. Even at that time there was still a division between amateurs and professionals, when the amateurs were often the better players. In some clubs, though not at Swinley, professional players could not enter the clubhouse by the front door, or sometimes even enter the building at all. At one such club Hagen hired a Rolls Royce and parked it outside the front door as a changing room, having been refused the use of the clubhouse dressing room.

After lunch the glorious weather held while the Prince of Wales headed the Swinley team against the Fernhill Artisans. He was paired up against the local postman, William Jones, both men playing off the same handicap of 16. In the end, 'Jones the Post' 'was beaten 2 up and 1 to play'.[36] The Artisans were just too good for their parent club, beating them 7½ to 6½. A.C. Wilson, Swinley's best player, had the misfortune to be drawn against, and lose to, John MacDonald, while A.F. Evans lost to the new assistant green-keeper, Joe Woodley. After the match, the Prince entertained Jones to tea in the clubhouse.

By the early 1930s Swinley was once again becoming a victim of its own success. Dozens of members and their guests turned up at the weekends to play. Other non-members came using a voucher from a bondholder, some came just for lunch and not to play. Members who had made a day of it began to complain that there were so many in the dining room that their second round was being delayed by the interlopers. Even at Swinley the change in society precipitated by the First World War had become all too evident. Although there were still the rich landed members, the majority now worked for a living, often in the City. Most still worked up to lunchtime on Saturday, leaving Sunday their only day to play. So once there, they liked to fit in two rounds of golf and lunch, hence the congestion. Where once to play two rounds in a day at Swinley was something of an effort, everything had changed through the steel-shafted clubs that became commonplace after they were finally sanctioned by the Rules of Golf Committee in November 1929. These clubs caused as great a change as the introduction of the Haskell ball, as, although it was generally accepted that they made little difference to the big hitter, 'the new clubs helped the weak player to get perceptibly farther'.[37]

In February 1932 Major Evelyn Lucas resigned as secretary. He agreed to stay on in an honorary capacity, and once again Harry Colt stepped into the breach to look after the course for the same salary. Lucas' legacy was a healthy bank balance with income far in excess of expenditure, but it would appear that he had let the maintenance of the course slip. Colt's first actions were to fertilise all the fairways and treat 'for the eradication of weeds and worms'. Two more green-keepers were engaged and a new three-gang mower and another tractor were purchased. Once again Colt used Suttons Seeds products, and once again he declared that 'he had been employed by Messrs Sutton for some years on the scientific side and had received a salary from them'.[38] As Colt was by then living in South Oxfordshire, and still had a busy golf architectural practice, it was decided after only three months to appoint a salaried, full-time, resident secretary. Colt was deputed to find such a man.

And so it was that the old tried and tested triumvirate of Edward Hoare, Harry Colt and Evelyn Lucas met at Hoare's Bank in Fleet Street in London to interview the candidates for the post of secretary. In the end, they chose Colonel N.J. Stone, who had served with distinction during the First World War with the Essex Regiment. On retiring from the army in 1928 he answered an advertisement for the post of secretary of Ganton Golf Club, near Scarborough in Yorkshire. Three hundred hopefuls applied, and Stone was among the initial 36 to be short-listed. The list was further whittled down to 11, and with the help of Henry Gullen, secretary to the Royal and Ancient (and a previous secretary of Ganton), the committee chose Stone despite his having no previous experience of managing a golf club. His salary was £250 a year, free house, lunch and tea. To compensate for his lack of knowledge he was given £25 to see how other golf clubs operated during his holidays, and two guineas expenses. So Colonel Stone left Yorkshire where he had cut his teeth, 'with their regret' and their good wishes, and was taken on by Swinley at £400 per annum, a free house and 'free food in the Clubhouse with the exception of drinks'. He began at the end of September 1932.

In the meantime the Swinley committee had seriously misjudged the situation when they tried to contain the numbers playing, particularly those on bondholders' vouchers. Lord Derby outlined a plan to increase the income to cope with the rising expenses—inflation had risen by 50 per cent over the past decade, largely due to Britain coming off the Gold Standard. In the future, bondholders' second and subsequent guests would have to pay a green fee of 10s.; then, as a departure, holders of vouchers themselves playing without the bondholder could introduce 'three other visitors on the voucher—each of them paying a green fee of 10/- —Visitors introduced on this voucher to be of either sex but must play with the holder of the voucher subject to the byelaw in force with regard to Ladies playing in three-ball matches on Sundays—.'[39] During the week, green fees were a mere 2s. 6d. when accompanied by a member, 5s. when unaccompanied. Societies had a better deal, as their green fee was 10s. 6d. a head including lunch.

For over 20 years Swinley had operated without a whiff of scandal—the odd unpaid subscription, but that was it. In July 1932 the caddie master J. Underwood went missing for four days. Colt then went through his books and found that the Caddie Insurance Account was short of just over £100. On his return, Underwood confessed to having taken the money in order to pay off some heavy debts. The money, however, was soon repaid by Mrs Underwood. Underwood had been at Swinley for years, and the committee decided that no good purpose would be served by prosecuting him, particularly as the money had been repaid by his wife, but decided that he could not be trusted to handle cash in the future. They looked around for a subordinate job for him and eventually came up with a solution. John Macdonald the green-keeper would take over the duties of caddie master at £2 a week, the same as Underwood had been guaranteed, and out of that he would pay Underwood a wage not exceeding £1 10s. to act as his deputy. So that Underwood did not handle any cash, the player would pay the head steward 4d., then take a

57   *There can be few golf course with a finer natural backdrop than the 12th green at Swinley when the rhododendrons are in flower.*

ticket to the caddie master or his assistant, who would allot him or her a caddie. The fee was then paid direct to the caddie.

Macdonald cannot have been too enamoured of his additional responsibilities, even though he received an extra 10s. a week. The son of a Presbyterian Free Church of Scotland Minister, he would have been appalled at the theft, but Underwood was a friend of long standing. The cottages where the senior staff all lived were (and of course still are) very close together, fostering a close community spirit on the compound. Macdonald and Underwood were fellow founder members of the Fernhill Workmen's Club. Underwood's fall from grace would naturally have upset his old friend and colleague, and Macdonald would have been uncomfortable taking over his job. When Macdonald soon 'expressed a wish to relinquish his supervision of the caddies',[40] Swinley's tried and tested team of Colt and Lucas (along with the new secretary) formed a sub-committee to deal with Underwood, who was gently eased back into his old job under careful supervision. It could not really have been otherwise. The four men had all known each other virtually since the inception of Swinley, and had become close friends, Colt going so far as to describe John Macdonald and his wife as 'two of my greatest friends'.[41]

Evelyn Lucas was particularly close to the Fernhill Artisans, and it was he who gave them a garden shed as their first clubhouse so long as 'they removed it forthwith from his garden'. The parent club were only too pleased to provide a site (the same as their pavilion today), but accepted no liability for loss or theft. The hut served them well enough, but when it began to deteriorate a few years later they decided to ask permission to build a new purpose-built clubhouse. The parent club agreed in principle and gave the Fernhill Artisans the land on payment of 'one new golf ball each year'[42] ground rent, and the proviso that if the club should disband then the pavilion would revert to the parent club. The money was raised through the reserves, contributions from their members and a dance. When the pavilion was opened on 11 June 1938 Sir Edward Peacock made the opening speech, Mrs Lucas performed the actual ceremony, and Major Lucas made the speech on her behalf. The Artisans have thrived in their new premises ever since, extending it twice.

By 1935 Swinley had once again outgrown the clubhouse. The secretary, Colonel Stone, and his wife lived upstairs on the first floor, and his office (the former chauffeurs' room behind the present pantry) was too small. Swinley's architects, Collcott and Hamp, were again asked to come up with plans to create a new office (the present inner secretary's office) and these, together with the estimate of £235 to build it, were approved. Not long afterwards, the dining room was extended with two staff bedrooms and a bathroom above at a cost of £856.

One particular feature of Swinley is the loyalty and length of service of its employees and their families. Thus it was inevitable that at least one of John Macdonald's six sons would return. In 1938, at the instigation of Harry Colt, he brought back the youngest, Angus Macdonald, as professional. Colt always had 'a

particular liking' for him, and found him 'a bright and intelligent boy with a considerable amount of character'.[43] Angus was apprenticed to Jack White for three and a half years as a club-maker at Sunningdale, where the clubs were 'renowned for their excellence'. After five years as a professional at Camberley Heath, followed by three at Basingstoke, Macdonald returned to Swinley on Colt's recommendation:

> I cannot imagine anyone whom I would sooner have as professional of a club where I constantly played. He has charming manners, a very pleasant address, bears the most excellent character in every way, and is worthy of every trust. It is impossible to speak too highly of Angus.[44]

Colt, always a good judge of character, proved right. He was popular with the members, his Swinley clubs highly sought after, too.

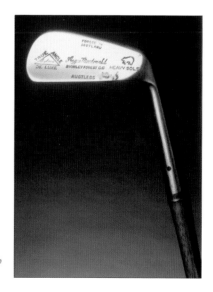

58   *The professional Angus Macdonald, part of the Macdonald golfing dynasty founded by the first green-keeper at Swinley, John Macdonald. He was also an expert club maker.*

Since its inception Swinley had been bumping along, making either making a very small profit, or more usually a slight deficit. As the years went by, the slight deficits mounted up to such an extent that essential works had to be postponed through lack of cash. Eventually the committee addressed the matter of their ailing finances and found that it was largely due to their generous concession allowing bondholders' guests to play at all times of the year for free. The revenue from green fees in 1938 was a mere £508. But in that year, of the 3,700 visitors who made use of the clubhouse and the course only 1,720 actually paid a green fee, leaving the remaining 2,024 to enjoy the 'privileges afforded by the club upon the introduction of bondholders without in any way contributing towards its upkeep'.[45] Lord Derby, with three bonds to his name, always made his guests pay a green fee, unless they were members of his immediate family or were special friends, and proposed that his fellow bondholders should do likewise, at least at the weekends and public holidays. Also 'anybody from any Embassy' was allowed to play on his bonds 'and only pay Green Fees of 2/6 on weekdays and 5/- Sundays'.[46] The Aga Khan played at Swinley on Lord Derby's bond as a diplomat. The motion that bondholders' guests should follow the chairman's lead was put to the vote and duly carried.

A batch of correspondence that has recently come to light at Knowsley shows Lord Derby (at least as far as Swinley is concerned) in the most favourable light. He took immense trouble over the affairs of the Club, keeping up a constant dialogue with Colonel Stone. Small items of expenditure came out of his own pocket; some were larger, like a new tractor in 1936. Friends and acquaintances were continually writing to ask him to propose them for membership, which he invariably did adding that his closer friends could play on his own bonds until elected. Those who were blackballed received a letter of commiseration.

It was a solemn meeting of the Swinley committee in the clubhouse on 10 September 1939, just nine days after the declaration of war on Germany. The policy of appeasement, the 'peace with honour' negotiated by the Prime Minister, Neville Chamberlain (a member since 1921), collapsed with the invasion of Poland, and once again the world was thrown into turmoil and Swinley was placed on a wartime basis. Colonel Stone's salary was reduced by £100, and all the house staff let go except one waitress, Margaret Ellis (who was to serve the club for 25 years), and a couple, Mr and Mrs Folland. Mrs Folland was appointed cook, such as it entailed, as all that was on offer was cold lunch priced at 3s. 6d. The Follands' services were also dispensed with in 1942, and Mrs Stone took over the cooking.

Apart from John Macdonald the green-keeping staff were liable to call-up. All six remained, but it was decided that if any did go they were not to be replaced. By the end of the war there were just two green-keepers left working. The professional, Angus Macdonald, took on the extra role of caddie master, with help at the weekends. In fact he was to remain at Swinley for most of the war, as he signed up as a Special Constable just the day before his call-up papers arrived, which excused him military service.

The committee initially dismissed the idea of an Anderson shelter for the staff, although one was soon installed in the stables between the two Macdonalds' cottages when the full extent of their danger was realised. Swinley was on one of the bombing routes into both London and the Vickers factory at Weybridge, and many German bombs and incendiaries were dropped in the area on their way back, particularly around railway lines. Sheena Macdonald remembers spending practically every night in the shelter with her parents and grandparents, and one night in particular when an incendiary bomb ignited the plantation behind their cottages (where the practice ground is today). 'We stood and watched the forest burn. The flames lit up the sky all night and in the morning there was nothing but a black, charred mess.'[47] Unlike Sunningdale, which was badly damaged by a stick of bombs, Swinley survived unscathed.

In typical fashion, Swinley operated throughout the war and made the best of the limited manpower and resources available. They still managed to run a playable golf course in spite of having only two assistant keepers—John Macdonald, for 30 years the head green-keeper, finally retired in 1940 on a pension of £130 which was paid until his death in 1945. The artisans, all engaged in essential services or retired, also played a vital part in keeping the place going. Money was so tight that they could not afford to reduce the members' subscriptions, even for Service members, but those renting houses in the neighbourhood were allowed in as temporary members for 30s. a month.

Any serving officer could play at Swinley for a fixed green fee of 2s. 6d. a day including Sundays, but the privilege was abused by officers in the Home Guard and the generous concession was immediately denied to them. At least Swinley was spared the fate of many other golf courses in wartime. Some had large concrete blocks placed on the flatter fairways as a deterrent against the enemy landing; others had their clubhouses requisitioned or their perimeters strewn with barbed wire and pillboxes. Golf courses, too, made for excellent rifle ranges, but again, Swinley was spared—in fact Boden's Ride to the north of the course had been a range in the 19th century.

Shortly after war was declared the Ministry of Agriculture wrote to Colonel Stone requesting that between 15 and 20 acres were surrendered for agriculture, the expected contribution for an 18-hole golf course, but on the proviso that it should not 'substantially in any way interfere with the normal use of the course'.[48] Stone relinquished just two acres that were ploughed up for potatoes and barley, with the remainder fenced off for grazing. Sir Edward Peacock also gave up his paddock leased from the Club beside Boden's Ride for the war effort.

Throughout the war there were intermittent meetings of the committee, chaired by Edward Hoare and with Sir Edward Peacock and Sir Thomas Barnes, the King's

Procurator General and Treasury Solicitor. They were an impressive triumvirate, at the very pinnacle of their respective careers. Yet collectively they were responsible for losing the professional and caddie master for what now appears a trivial reason. When Angus Macdonald applied to the committee to sell golf balls, the staple product of any professional shop, he was turned down and in consequence 'he resigned his appointment'.[49] He left to assist his uncle, the professional at another Colt course, Calcot Park, near Reading. J.P. Mears became caddie master at a weekly wage of £3 5s., the caddies themselves receiving 7s. a round, including tips and lunch money.

At last the war was over and Swinley reverted to its pre-war eminence, with few changes: 'The normal scale of green fees and conditions of play [were] to be re-introduced on 1st January 1946'. The war years had taken their toll on Colonel and Mrs Stone and they retired early in the same year, although Mrs Stone continued to cook the Sunday lunches until a replacement was found. They were given honorary membership for their great contribution during the war. After much searching a new secretary, Lieutenant Colonel P.C. Snatt, was appointed at an annual salary of £400. Although Lord Derby had wished to resign his position as President of Swinley and, amazingly, his membership—the committee begged him to reconsider and he died soon after with the matter unresolved—he would certainly have approved of the appointment of Snatt, who had first been commissioned into his beloved 1st Battalion, the King's (Liverpool) Regiment in 1910. Snatt was wounded in the first expeditionary force in the First World War, when he was awarded the Military Cross, and wounded again when acting as a specialised signals officer. He transferred to the Royal Corps of Signals on their formation in 1920, later going on the first expeditionary force to Egypt. By 1937 he was a lieutenant colonel living on half-pay on the Swinley Road in Ascot. A keen golfer, he was a member of The Berkshire and the Army Golf Club. In a sequence straight out of one of P.G. Wodehouse's Oldest Member's tales, at the age of 49 he met and wooed the 31-year-old Miss Myra Manningham-Buller on the golf course. It can be no coincidence that his father-in-law, Sir Mervyn Manningham-Buller Bt, and the new Mrs Percy Snatt became members of Swinley in 1946, the year of his appointment as secretary. Eliza Manningham-Buller, the former Director of MI5, is her niece. The diminutive Snatt, with his neat military moustache and clipped voice, was 'a fearsome fellow' who intimidated the staff, artisans and small boys alike. He even had his own personal putting green that members could use but by invitation only.

Slowly the Club reverted to its normal routine as members drifted back from the war. One committee member, Sir Thomas Barnes, was deputed to look after the new Crown Lease, the rent having been waived during the war years. Then the societies were once again allowed to play during the week, starting with Barclay's Bank (where the Swinley account was kept), the Old Etonians against the Household Brigade, and the Bank of England Golfing Society. The following year, the Ladies Parliamentary Golfing Society and the Junior Carlton Club were allowed to hold their matches there, all at £1 per head including lunch. Notwithstanding the post-war shortages, Swinley was thriving once again, with sufficient funds to allow Service members serving overseas for more than a year to pay a reduced subscription.

The first Walker Cup after the war was played on the Old Course at St Andrews in 1947. The American team, under their non-playing Captain Francis Ouimet, arrived at Southampton and put in some practice at Swinley on their way to London. It was a great occasion, and the conservative committee allowed them to play and lunch without charge, but drinks were extra. The practice stood them in good stead as the United States beat Great Britain and Ireland 8-4.

At that time there were many resignations at Swinley, although, as after the First World War, many more wished to join than wished to resign. Not surprisingly these new members, as well as the original ones, found it increasingly irksome to arrive on a Sunday to find much of the car park occupied by the cars of Artisans already playing on the course. These members took the view that if the Artisans could afford a 'motor car' then they could afford to pay for their golf and not be subsidised by them. While there were many genuine Artisans who were manual workers whose membership was the only way they could play golf, there were those (the car-owners) who joined as the only way they could play on a private course in their area. They were, of course, in breach of the original spirit of the Artisans.

Matters came to a head when Lt Colonel de Chimay and Brigadier R. Senior wrote to the committee to propose that members of the Fernhill Artisans 'should pay some form of subscription and that in future all candidates for election should be approved by the Committee of the Club'.[50] It was left to Sir Edward Peacock to discuss the matter with the Captain of the Fernhill Artisans' Club. He reported back to the next committee meeting, reiterating the origins and main aims of the latter club, namely to provide golf for club servants and those who could not afford 'to enjoy the game on any other course in the neighborhood'. He was also censorious of the way in which the rules and regulations were flaunted, which was 'noticeable in the election of members'.

The negotiations were entirely amicable. The Swinley committee told the Artisans that they wanted a greater say in the running of the latter's club with an active chairman to liaise between the two clubs. They then restricted the number of Artisan members, threw out all honorary members, and reserved the right to interview all candidates and bar any they thought did not qualify for membership. Finally they made all members resign and reapply for a new membership by the end of the year, 1947, when they were thoroughly vetted by the parent committee. Once reset on the right lines the Fernhill Artisans continued in perfect harmony with the parent club, then as today.

59 *The Fernhill Artisans first purpose-built clubhouse that replaced a garden shed donated by Major Evelyn Lucas. It was later extended with a legacy from Sir Edward Peacock.*

By the beginning of 1948 most of the key players in the founding of Swinley Forest Golf Club had either died or long since gone away. Alexander Rutland Davey had faded out of the picture some time before: Sir Hubert Longman, the lynchpin of Swinley since its inception in 1909, had died in 1940. Edward Henry Hoare, a stalwart of Swinley for over 40 years, and Major Evelyn Lucas, the loyal secretary and committee member, were soon to die within a year of each other. The creator of Swinley, Harry Shapland Colt, had bowed out completely. His legacy to Swinley was great, and by the time he, too, died in 1951 the course he created had survived drought, fires and two World Wars intact, virtually the same as it was the day he finished building it. But it was the death of the Earl of Derby on 4 February 1948 at Knowsley that was mourned throughout the country. Memorial services were held in Liverpool Cathedral, at Newmarket, the home of the famous Stanley House Stud, and at Westminster Abbey, where the Lord Chamberlain, the Earl of Clarendon, represented the King and Queen. Another mourner was Sir Edward Peacock, representing King George's Jubilee Fund and the Swinley Forest Golf Club. Although Lord Derby was not the actual founder of Swinley he had embraced it from the very start, putting his own inimitable stamp on the Club to give it the air of a private golf course that it enjoys today. For Swinley, his death was the end of an era.

CHAPTER 6

Shortly after 10 o'clock on Sunday 10 April 1949, the 'tall and robust figure'[1] of Sir Edward Peacock left his home, Boden's Ride, and strolled towards Swinley Forest Golf Club, where he was the senior member of the committee. It was a glorious spring morning, warm and sunny—in fact, just five days later the highest ever April temperature of 77°F was recorded. The night before, Peacock had called a supplementary meeting of the committee to discuss a memorial to the late Lord Derby, but only two of its members, Sir Thomas Barnes and Frank W.R. Douglas, both near neighbours, could turn up at such short notice. The three friends then set off to play, followed by their caddies, whose rate had recently risen to 7s. a round with a 6d. booking fee to J.P. Mears, the caddie master.

These three members of the Swinley committee had much to talk about during that Sunday's golf, including no doubt the final outcome of the Lynskey Tribunal, where John Belcher, the Labour Member for Sowerby in North Yorkshire, had taken the Chiltern Hundreds and resigned his seat two days before. Sir Thomas Barnes, the King's Proctor and Solicitor to the Treasury, had been responsible for putting together the case against Belcher, then Parliamentary Secretary to the Board of Trade, for bribery, or as he put it, 'injudicious actions'. He had denied corruption, but did admit to accepting gifts including a gold cigarette case, wine, spirits and 'entertainment at dog race meetings and boxing matches', along with 'a paid holiday at Margate'[2] for himself and his wife.

Over the years Sir Edward Peacock and Sir Thomas Barnes had regularly played together at Swinley—Peacock (a bondholder since 1913) had been responsible for introducing him in the first place in 1926, the year Barnes married and inherited his father's house in Sunningdale. Peacock also co-opted him onto the committee. Swinley, so close to London, has always been the ideal neutral place for members to meet to discuss important matters, and, as with so many of its members both before and since, friendships forged on the links have proved invaluable in other spheres. For Peacock and Barnes, Swinley had been the backdrop for what was arguably one of the greatest dramatic crises of the 20th century—the abdication of Edward VIII.

Sir Edward Peacock was appointed Receiver General of the Duchy of Cornwall through his friendship with the Prince of Wales and great business acumen. In

60   *Sir Edward Peacock, by James Gunn. Sir Edward 'ruled' Swinley as member of the committee and chairman for 26 years. He lived next door at Boden's Ride. As Receiver General of the Duchy of Cornwall and friend of Edward VIII, Peacock was one of the key figures in the Abdication Crisis.*

1921, 'deeply impressed by his ability',[3] Sir Montague Norman, Governor of the Bank of England, brought Peacock onto the Court, and shortly afterwards he was made a director of 'the eminent banking firm of Baring Brothers'.[4] For years Peacock and Sir Montague worked closely together—during the war they were asked by the Director of Naval Intelligence, Admiral John Godfrey, to find him a personal assistant. They came up with Ian Fleming, then a young RNVR Lieutenant, who was to work in the famous Room 39 as a conduit between the Admiralty, the Secret Service and S.O.E., all of whom were experts in sabotage and resistance. Years later Fleming had his fictional hero James Bond with a nine handicap 'playing a good deal of weekend golf when he was at headquarters. But always on the courses around London—Huntercombe, Swinley, Sunningdale, The Berkshire'.[5] But possibly Peacock's most important role in a long and distinguished career was that of adviser to Edward VIII in the last traumatic weeks of his reign. Like the other three key players, Walter Monckton, Sir Ulick Alexander and George Allen, 'none of them approved of his decision, all believed that he had failed in his duty … [but all] served him faithfully and willingly and felt affection and concern for him'.[6] Living so close, Peacock invited any of the constant stream of visitors to Fort Belvedere, including the Prime Minister, Stanley Baldwin, and Winston Churchill, to dine and sleep at Boden's Ride.

The turmoil of those last days at the Fort was further aggravated by the Simpsons' divorce case, where there was real concern in the King's camp and in the Government that the King's Proctor, Sir Thomas Barnes, would be forced to intervene if he felt that there had been collusion by the respondent, Ernest Simpson, or misconduct by the petitioner, Wallis Simpson. If either was proven there could be no decree absolute, and the King 'might give up his throne and yet be deprived of the chance to marry Mrs Simpson'.[7] Barnes dismissed the suggestion of collusion where 'the co-respondent was a woman whom [Ernest] Simpson (whose married life had ceased to have much attraction for him owing to the King) was anxious to marry and had been "caught" '.[8] He was far more worried dealing with the likely 'misconduct' of the petitioner, where 'it was suggested that the King had probably lived with Mrs Simpson in circumstances of which evidence would be available'. Barnes was in a difficult position. Constitutionally he could not command the Courts to investigate allegations against the King, as the sovereign could not be 'indicted for a crime, sued for a civil wrong or cited as a co-respondent'.[9] In the end a solution of a kind was found, whereby Barnes was ordered to draft two Bills to be laid before Parliament, one 'giving effect for the King to renounce the Throne and the other making Mrs Simpson's *decree nisi* absolute immediately'.[10] As Baldwin suspected, there was intense opposition to the latter from his own Cabinet and Parliament. After the abdication Barnes was 'bombarded with abusive letters urging him to intervene and stop the divorce … and that he should follow up inquiries on adultery as well as collusion'.[11] And who better to turn to for advice than the very man at the centre of the abdication, one who had kept meticulous notes through-out the whole sorry affair? It was none other than his Swinley golfing partner, Sir Edward Peacock. In the end, Barnes did follow up the more 'responsible of his

correspondents', but found that they were merely repeating the gossip of 'the Clubs or the [Law] Temples'. He then interviewed countless people, including the crew of the *Nahlin*, the yacht the King chartered in the Adriatic, servants, hall porters and the like, which convinced him that he would never unearth any credible evidence, and so the decree absolute was duly granted. It was the Attorney General, Sir Donald Somervell, who had the last words: 'Whether or not they ever committed adultery is a question on which I believe those who know him well will differ.'[12]

And so, on that gloriously sunny day, the three members of the committee, Sir Edward Peacock, Sir Thomas Barnes and Frank Douglas, played their round off the back tees. At that time there were still only two, the forward tees being for the ladies, who would not have been playing at the weekend unless

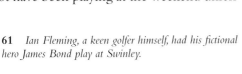

61   *Ian Fleming, a keen golfer himself, had his fictional hero James Bond play at Swinley.*

married to or staying in the house of a bondholder. For the first time Peacock and his friends were using the new score cards, with the amended 'table of strokes',[13] more in keeping with the course and times, that had been devised by the new secretary, Lieutenant Colonel Percy C. Snatt, to replace the one set for the Old Course by the R and A (see page 61).

On that April day the course was particularly full. As a three-ball (then admissible at any time at a weekend), they continually let singles through. There were a couple of Eton masters playing on the Dowager Lady Derby's bond, although all beaks (later extended to the whole staff when the bursar complained) had the facility to play during the week for a reduced green fee by courtesy of the committee. At that time, and under a similar arrangement, Major Chiesman and the officers' mess of the Life Guards, then stationed at Windsor, were given honorary membership of Swinley and were also entitled to play during the week at the same green fee of 15s. One new member who was definitely not out that day was Father Hubert O.F.M., the Roman Catholic priest of St Francis, South Ascot. Sundays were his busy day. Consequently, he had joined without an entrance fee as a five-day member.

The course was in remarkably good condition considering the post-war shortages, although the ravages of the recent forest fire around the 5th were still evident. It was 'far less manicured than today', Lord Alvingham recalled.

> There were no paths, no trolleys, and of course no buggies. It was much more natural then, with these great tree roots spreading all over the place. Divots too wherever you looked although the caddies should have replaced them. The greens weren't much better—you just dropped your clubs next to where you played your ball. The whole place was splendid, the nearest thing to playing on your own private golf course. It all improved when they manured the whole course.

The head green-keeper, Joe Woodley, had remained at Swinley throughout the war. Woodley had been brought in by Colt in 1924, and was to remain at Swinley, boy and man, for the rest of his working life. He was originally from East Hendred in South Oxfordshire, where Colt lived when he left Earlywood Corner and where he employed the local schoolboys to make the scale models of his golf courses. From there it was a well-tried progression to send these boys all over the country for a year when they left school to work with his contractors. If they turned out well Colt would then recommend that they be taken on as an assistant green-keeper when a staff vacancy appeared at one of the courses he had designed, more often than not the very one where they served their apprenticeship. By 1938 Swinley's very first head green-keeper John Macdonald had retired, and Joe Woodley, then senior green-keeper, took over at £3 a week, a little over the minimum agricultural wage. The promotion was further rewarded by 'a water closet in the existing coal store', a new range, and a copper for boiling water in the kitchen. Electricity and gas were only installed in the early 1950s. By 1974 Woodley had clocked up 52 years of continuous service to Swinley, and to mark the great feat a collection of a maximum of £5 per member was made. The committee raised £892.25, enough to buy a new Mini with £5.08 left over to fill the tank with petrol. Woodley was rather disappointed with his gift as he discovered that green-keepers on other courses had received larger cars on their retirement after fewer years. His place was filled by W.L. Barrie, a gardener from the Crown Estates with no green-keeping experience. Nor was he a golfer.

To return to the game on that April morning in 1949, the three committee members, Peacock, Barnes and Douglas, went into the clubhouse, their studded golf shoes going click-clack, clackety-clack on the brand-new parquet floor. They did not even bother to change their shoes in the locker room, with its 'air of a gun room',[14] and were soon outside sitting in the sun where they were joined by Bruce Todd, a neighbour and fellow committee member. Peacock had pressed the wooden bell in the hall, and Alfred Coxall, the head steward, dressed in a smart black coat, materialised to take their order, soon returning with their drinks on a silver salver. Coxall's father, Leonard, was a fine golfer and the first to win the Artisans' [Frank] Douglas Cup in 1935.

After their drinks they wandered into the dining room (now the bar) for lunch. If the feel was that 'of an officers' mess of a decent regiment',[15] the food was 'straight out of the nursery', or as much as rationing would allow—there were still cards on the table reminding members that the rationing was in force, and not to forget 'to hand over their coupons'. The dishes were laid out on a long sideboard—the breaded plaice at one end with a pot of egg sauce, the treacle tart, rice and other puddings at the far end, and the leg of mutton which the members carved themselves in the centre alongside some over-cooked vegetables. As at most weekends the dining room was crowded with members, their visitors and children. At first the committee put 1s. on the cost of lunch to any visitor who had not paid a green fee to deter the hordes, but when this did not work children under the age of 17 were not allowed into the Club and the table money was raised to 2s. a head. In true Swinley fashion no one took much notice of the rule or the extra price, and lunches continued as crowded as before.

It was exactly 2 o'clock when the five men sat down for the specially convened supplementary meeting of the committee. It had been called by Sir Edward Peacock to commission a memorial portrait of Lord Derby. The matter was first raised by Edward Hoare shortly after the Earl's death, and he had asked Lady Derby for a photograph to copy. Bruce Todd, who had been to Wellington in the 1920s, remembered a portrait of the Earl by James Gunn and was deputed to ask the headmaster if it 'might be copied for the Club'.[16] Sir James Gunn was one of the

62 *Members of Swinley generally dislike change. Much of the original furniture is in the clubhouse to this day, although a new parquet floor was laid in 1948, the first one having disintegrated from 40 years of members' spiked shoes.*

63 *The sitting room today, indistinguishable from before the renovations, save that there is no draught howling through the windows.*

64 *The 17th Earl of Derby, oil on canvas, after the portrait by James Gunn that hangs in Wellington College, his Alma Mater.*

leading portrait painters of his day—the Queen so admired his famous conversation piece of the Royal Family (herself with George VI, The Queen and Princess Margaret) at Royal Lodge that she personally commissioned a portrait of herself in her Coronation robes. Todd reported back that the headmaster was delighted for the portrait to be copied, but only in the school holidays, and mentioned another portrait of the Earl by Souter that hung at Windsor Castle. The committee preferred the Gunn portrait, and it was left to Sir Edward Peacock to see him to ask his permission for it to be copied by their chosen portraitist, a Mr Kendrick. Later, Sir Edward chose Gunn for his own portrait for Barings. In the meantime Brigadier Ronnie Senior proposed that a golf 'competition should be inaugurated as a memorial to the late Lord Derby', but it was decided that the portrait would be a more 'fitting memorial and would meet the wishes of the majority of the members'.[17] The horror of anything competitive at Swinley was still very much alive. In the end Kendrick worked throughout the summer holidays of 1949, and the portrait with its erroneous title of:

17th Earl of Derby   Founder of the Club

1865-1948   15.10.1909

now hangs in the alcove of the sitting room. The copy was paid for by donations from the membership and five guineas from the Fernhill Artisans. The Junior Carlton Club offered to contribute, as their members had played on Lord Derby's bond for years, but the committee felt that it should be financed in-house.

The committee also decided that the Dowager Lady Derby, who took up permanent residence at Coworth on the death of her husband, should be made an honorary member of Swinley. Frank Douglas then brought up the question of extending the same honour to her grandson, the 18th Earl of Derby. 'Cement' Douglas, chairman of the Chinnor Cement and Lime Company and formerly a full Colonel in the Royal Army Service Corps, was an all-round sportsman—he turned out regularly for the Richmond (rugby) Football Club, once appearing for England in the 1933 Calcutta Cup. He knew John Derby well as both were officers of the United Grand Lodge of Freemasons, Derby the Deputy Grand Master and Douglas for years the Grand Director of Ceremonies. Douglas was to serve for 24 years on the committee, six of them as senior member.

Derby's honorary membership and subsequent presidency of the Club were well founded. He succeeded Lord Brabazon of Tara as President of the Professional Golfers' Association in 1964, but it was in the 1950s 'when he returned from

65   *The present Lord Derby (left), with Ouija Board, one of the most successful mares in racing history. In her career spanning four seasons she won 10 of her 22 races, seven of them Group 1s including the Epsom Oaks in 2004 and the Hong Kong Vase the next year. Incredibly, she won the Breeders' Cup Filly & Mare Turf in the United States in 2004 and again two years later. The Earl is an honorary member of Swinley and occasionally uses one of his three bonds.*

the United States, where his interest in the game had been further increased by Pro-Am competition [that he] decided he would inaugurate a Pro-Am at Formby'.[18] In consultation with his good friend Henry Cotton the first two successful Pro-Ams were organised, where such luminaries as Peter Alliss, Neil Coles, Christie O'Connor, Dai Rees and Harry Weetman have all played. To honour the 500 years of his family's earldom Derby inaugurated the Assistants Championship (re-launched as the Knowsley Safari Park Tournament) that has been variously won by Guy Hunt, Peter Oosterhuis and Sam Torrance. As a golfer John Derby was an above-average player, but his contribution to the game itself was recognised when the PGA gave him the rather strange title of 'President in Memoriam'. His nephew Edward Derby, the present Earl, is an honorary member and has the three original Swinley Forest Golf Club bonds, numbers 1, 2 and 3.

Throughout the 1950s and into the 1960s Sir Edward Peacock continued to hold sway as chairman of Swinley, although he preferred to call himself the 'senior member of the committee'. At that time the committee was virtually self-perpetuating (which in general suited the members well) through the original Rule 4:

> The Committee shall consist of six Members, three to be a Quorum. The Committee for the time being shall have power to fill up vacancies on the Committee as they occur by resignation or otherwise except as hereinafter particularly provided.

As early as 1954 Lieutenant Colonel A. de Chimay proposed, and Lieutenant Colonel W.L. Abel-Smith seconded, a motion that there should be seven members on the committee, with two members (apart from the chairman) resigning each year. Although they could be re-elected onto the committee by their fellow members, 'two years must elapse before a retiring member can be re-elected to serve again'.[19] The idea was to bring in fresh blood. When it was put to the vote the resolution was won by just three votes: 19 for, 16 against, but under Rule 18 a two-thirds majority was required so the motion was not carried and the committee went on exactly as before. Little has really changed today, when each member of the committee is officially supposed to stand down after five years, with a full year before he can be re-elected. In true Swinley fashion the rules here are somewhat fluid, and a useful committee member can stay on 'if the Chairman in his discretion considers it to be in the best interest of the Club'.[20] Unlike at most other golf clubs, members are discreetly invited to serve on the committee rather than being elected.

At that time the annual general meetings were generally poorly attended—at one such meeting only two members appeared at the appointed hour. Eventually, Sir Edward turned up to address the duo and asked, 'Are you unhappy?' When they answered 'no', Peacock concluded 'so there's nothing to talk about!'[21] and with

66 *Jimmy Harrison never finished a round when playing with Sir Edward Peacock as they would always peel off from the 18th to Boden's Ride for a drink. He and Lord Alvingham were always popular in the match against the Artisans as they constantly supplied their opponents with 'some noxious alcohol'. Appropriately, the Artisans now play for the Harrison Flask.*

that turned on his heel and repaired to Boden's Ride. Peacock was actually not, as this might suggest, an autocratic man. In later life he was mild and gentle, and much loved by all. After he was widowed he continued to live at Boden's Ride, where he was looked after by three old women. He was profoundly deaf. At his dinner parties his housekeeper Cecelia would answer for him as she served at the table: 'We don't think this' or 'We don't think that at all,'[22] as she spoke for her master who had not even heard the question. One evening when Jimmy and Hazel Harrison were dining at Boden's Ride there was a knock at the front door. Cecelia came into the dining room to tell Sir Edward that there were some young men to see him. There on the doorstep were half a dozen of the younger members of Swinley, who had come to complain about the state of the Club. Sir Edward listened to them patiently and when finished he asked:

'Do you enjoy playing at Swinley?'

'Oh yes, sir,' they replied in unison.

'Do you like the food and the service?'

'Oh yes, sir,' they repeated.

'Then goodnight gentlemen!'

Jimmy Harrison was his constant golfing companion from the time in 1952 when Sir Edward made him a member as a young man. The chairman was deeply competitive, so when he was being beaten by his younger partner he would offer him a vitamin pill on the 9th or 10th to put him off. They never finished a round as they always peeled off just after the 18th tee to Boden's Ride for a drink, usually a very strong gin and tonic, then a new-fangled drink that Sir Edward had brought back from the United States. From time to time Mrs Joan Lemieux, Sir Edward's older daughter, lived there with her many children, one of whom, Tessa, became one of the first full lady members.

Sir Edward was passionate about Swinley. It was he who arranged for his former bank, Baring Brothers, to act as trustees. He was also a great supporter of artisan golf in general, and for many years was chairman of the Fernhill Artisans. Once, driving back from Ascot station, he passed a recreation ground where some boys were hitting a golf ball. Peacock stopped the car and sent the chauffeur to call them over. He offered to take all six of them to Swinley, where he arranged for Mears, the caddie master and professional, to give them a lesson and then played three holes with the boys himself. Two became regular caddies and joined the Fernhill Artisans in a record entry of just four months' wait.

Sir Edward Peacock was a fixture at the Fernhill Artisans' annual dinner-dance in the Royal Ascot Hotel. It was a black tie affair and well-attended by all the Vice-Presidents, one of whom was Bernard Rickatson-Hatt, a former adviser at the Bank of England and the committee member responsible for the Artisans. Rickatson-Hatt always went to the dinner on his own, presumably as his wife baulked at the idea of travelling from London by Green Line bus.

Sir Edward continued at Boden's Ride until his faithful retainers died, one by one, and then moved into the thatched cottage next door. Only when he felt he could not go on did he finally resign as chairman in 1961, after 26 years on the committee. He died aged 91 ten months later. He left £500 to the Fernhill Artisans and £1,000 to his beloved Swinley. The Artisans' money went towards the extension of their hut and after much discussion the Swinley committee decided to use their inheritance to make the flowering shrub border in front of the clubhouse and create the putting green that is there today. It was also decided to buy a silver cup for the annual match against the Fernhill Artisans, to be named the 'Peacock Cup' in his honour. In the end a cup that had belonged to 'a member of Lord Derby's family [was] thought most suitable', and is the one that is played for today.

The match against the Fernhill Artisans, one of three annual fixtures in the Swinley calendar, takes place after the annual general meeting, formerly in July but now in September. It is keenly fought by both sides, and since its inception in 1963 the Peacock Cup is usually taken by the Artisans—to date they have won it 29 times as against nine by the parent club, with four ties. Often it was not for want of trying on the part of Swinley Forest Golf Club to win by fair means or sometimes by foul. For years there was great competition

67 *Although it has the arms and crest of the Derby family, the annual match against the Fernhill Artisans is competed for the Peacock Cup, played after the annual general meeting of the Club. It is keenly fought on both sides.*

among the Artisans to play Lord Alvingham and Jimmy Harrison, but only those who were known to hold their drink were selected. Invariably around the 9th or 10th green a flask with 'some noxious alcohol' was produced, which usually assured victory. One year their two Artisan opponents were seen rolling about in a bunker, roaring with laughter and singing 'we're losing, and we're enjoying it!'[23] Another time, the Swinley duo placed a bottle of port into one of their golf bags, but the Artisans, led by the current Fernhill chairman Jim Harris, went into 'port training' all year to beat them at their own game. Appropriately, the Artisans now play for the 'Harrison Flask' donated by his widow, Hazel.

Soon after Sir Edward Peacock moved out of Boden's Ride, the house was sold to a Grenadier—General Sir Rodney Moore, KCVO, KCB, CBE, DSO. He had recently been appointed the first Defence Services Secretary, a senior position in the Royal Household responsible for the liaison between the Queen and her Armed Forces. Later he was made Chief Steward at Hampton Court Palace, his last appointment in a long and distinguished military career that had culminated in 1959 as Chief of the Armed Forces Staff in the Federation of Malaya soon after the end of the State of Emergency. At the end of his posting the Sultan of Pahang presented him with three baby siamangs (*Symphalangus syndactylus*). These apes, the largest of the black-furred gibbons from Malaysia, Thailand and Sumatra, can weigh as much as 50lb with an arm span of nearly five feet, longer than their legs.

The Moores felt that three baby apes would perhaps be too much to cope with on their return to England, so they left two with his Chief of Staff, Brigadier Tony Heywood, who soon had them in a zoo in Kuala Lumpur. The General's ape, called Pandai after the Malay word for clever, travelled back to England in a shoebox dressed in a baby's chill-proof vest—siamangs are born hairless, apart from a tuft on the top of their heads. In his early years Pandai lived in the house and gambolled about free in the garden. He was looked after by Aswan, the General's Malay manservant. As Pandai grew up he became more and more dangerous, so an enormous cage was built off the kitchen at the back of Boden's Ride. When fully grown Pandai was very frightening. Occasionally he escaped, once landing on the handlebars of the bicycle of a butcher's boy delivering meat, who was given £5 for the experience. Another time the ape dropped on the milkman, biting his ear. He was deeply traumatised and off work for three months. Pandai loved jewellery, and visitors were warned to keep a wary distance from his cage as his long black arm would flash out and grab whatever was to hand.

Pandai was a true legend at Swinley. 'The bloody ape', recalls Robert Abel-Smith 'would let out this terrifying holler right in the middle of your back swing on the far end of the course.' Sir Rodney, himself a Swinley member since 1959, never contradicted the story that his 'ferocious' ape roamed free around the garden, even though it was not true—in fact when he was not in his cage he was secured by a long rope. In those days, as Roderick Bullough recalls,

68   *A siamang ape in the wild.*

69   *General Sir Rodney Moore was passionate about all species of ape. His many pets roamed free around Flagstaff House, Kuala Lumpur, when he was Chief of Armed Forces, Malaya, 1959.*

70 *General Sir Rodney Moore and his dreaded pet, a siamang ape, called Pandai after the Malay word for clever. Pandai's fearful holler could be heard all over the course. So frightening was his reputation that balls landing in the garden were never retrieved.*

there was no rough to the left of the 18th fairway. We used to tell our guests that the way to the flag was over the trees, close on the garden fence of Boden's Ride. When their balls inevitably went into the garden, we told them that General Moore was a member and he did not mind anyone retrieving their ball. We would then wait and sure enough, more often than not, they would come out running having met the ape!

The General also had an old English sheepdog that used to get desperately car-sick. His silver Bentley was a familiar sight as it glided past the members on the terrace, with the dog sitting on the front seat with its head out of the fully open window and Lady Moore shivering in the back seat.

When Sir Rodney finally left Boden's Ride for Hampton Court in 1975, two bucketfuls of Pandai-memorial golf balls were divided between his fellow courtiers, Sir Johnnie Johnston and Lord Charteris of Amisfield. Pandai was given to an ape sanctuary, where he was marooned on an island with other apes. Having lived with humans it did not take him long to work out his escape, and he taught the others to swim across the moat. After that they were all fenced in.

There were few at Swinley who were sorry to see Pandai go, but with his passing they lost one of their more bizarre neighbours.

CHAPTER 7

One of the great features of Swinley Forest Golf Club is that it has always employed either the very best, most dedicated and loyal staff, or, really quite often, perfectly *dreadful* people, both of whom tended to stay for decades. But in the 1960s there was a particularly fine group that created a marvellous atmosphere, one that was in tune with the membership.

There were some, like Mrs Norris who was a cleaner for 24 years, who were never seen; others, such as Mrs Knotts, the secretary's typist for 25 years, who worked in the background until she was nearly 80 years of age. Married to a man who worked in the Royal Enclosure Office, Ascot Racecourse, 'she was awfully good, but you never knew what coloured hair she was going to turn up with in the morning—it could be yellow, mauve, red, blue!'[1] Then in the kitchen was Midge Gazzard, 'a dear little heart. She was only a half-pint-sized person. She was wonderful, and would do anything.'[2] She retired at 75 after 20 years' service as assistant to her elder sister, Mrs Kirk who, with her husband, Les, are the real success story of the club. They arrived on 1 April 1960 and, with their bulldog Brutus (followed by Great Britain), became a Swinley institution.

Both Mr and Mrs Kirk had been serving in the Army in Germany and were about to retire at the same time when they saw an advertisement for a couple for Swinley. Kirk bore a striking resemblance to the 17th Earl of Derby and there were some who (ridiculously) attributed his employment to him being his illegitimate son. Some would even have it that he 'certainly behaved like the 17th Earl's son'.[3]

> What with his perfect manners and their great charm, they naturally got the job. Mrs Kirk had only ever cooked for the two of them all their married life, and she was literally thrown in at the deep end. It was just amazing how she coped.[4]

Indeed, nothing seemed to faze her. At that time there was no booking for lunch and members and their guests just turned up. 'Whether there were 5, 25, or 50 she always catered exactly.' Mrs Kirk's fare was plain and simple nursery food, much to the delight of the members. She was also noted for her 'Swinley cheese', an amalgam of what was left on the cheeseboard that resembled a Christmas pudding, to be eaten with fruit cake and port. The present committee have vetoed its return.

The Kirks created a splendid atmosphere among their fellow members of staff—the green-staff and professional's wives all helped out in the kitchen and dining room. Swinley was the Kirks' life, and while they were there they were 'both as happy as can be'. They were devoted to the club and the members. Mrs Kirk knew everybody, and they in turn respected her, although she did have her favourites, most notably Henrietta Tiarks, who became the Duchess of Bedford.

Likewise they were adored by the members. 'The Kirks were quite splendid, just like family retainers', recalled Lord Alvingham. 'They both had a wonderful memory for faces and names. Not only were they club servants, they were friends as well. Mrs Kirk was a marvellous cook, producing good plain food. It was all very simple fare.'[5]

At that time the dining room was popular at the weekends, especially with parents taking their children out from the many neighbouring schools like Heathfield, St Mary's Ascot, Sunningdale and particularly Eton, when Etonians were restricted to a five-mile radius of College for an *exeat*. The Hon. Anthony Warrender, a member since 1979, remembers his parents endlessly taking him and his sister Victoria, who was at Heathfield, to Swinley for lunch:

> We went there every bloody Sunday. It was shepherd's pie or lamb, then treacle tart or rice pudding. We might just as well have stayed at school! Sometimes we went to the Hind's Head where we got prawn cocktail. *That* was great. My father [Lord Bruntisfield] was by then a lunchtime member.[6]

Henrietta, Duchess of Bedford, still remembers 'lunch as being the best shepherd's pie and treacle tart, and cabbage that has never tasted so good since'.[7]

Tea was hugely popular, too, especially among boys on their way back to prep schools such as Sunningdale, with 'buttered toast, two boiled eggs, strawberry jam and cakes'. The dining room at Swinley was 'crammed full of local members and their house parties at weekends when it was their cook's day off'.[8]

The Kirks took the keenest interest in the members and nothing was too much trouble for either of them. In 1984 Andrew Martin Smith was playing a fourball, having left his wife Jenny, who was pregnant with their first child, in London. When he reached the 14th tee he was amazed to see Kirk, in black coat and striped trousers, striding towards him, as 'he was never seen on the course during opening hours'. As he approached, Kirk announced: 'I have a message from your wife, Sir. She's just gone into labour. She says to tell you not to hurry—you just finish your game!'[9] He then trudged all the way back to the clubhouse to his *Times* crossword and serving members their drinks. Kirk was an inveterate *Times* reader and every day combed its pages for news of 'his' members. On one occasion he asked Clive Beck if he had enjoyed the dinner the night before. Much surprised, Beck asked him how he knew where he had dined. 'Your name's in the Court Circular, Sir!', replied Kirk.

Mrs Kirk took particular interest in the younger members, insisting that their children be introduced to her on their first visit to the Club. Once presented, she never forgot them or their names, nor did she fail to ask their parents for news of them. She was kindness itself with the bachelor members, always giving them a treacle tart or some other pudding to take back to London. One such was Robert Buxton, who became a member with some contemporaries in 1964. Once, after an exceedingly good party in London, they decided to continue it at Swinley, taking their girlfriends and hangovers with them. They all needed a sharpener to get on the course, so put in their orders for stiff measures of Bloody Mary, gin and tonics, and glasses of Pimms to Mrs Kirk in the absence of her husband. Buxton's girlfriend at the time was the daughter of the chairman of an international fertiliser company and looked 15, but was in fact 21. Having served all the others, Mrs Kirk turned to her and beamed sweetly: 'And would you like a nice glass of lemonade, dearie?'

Finally, in April 1987, after 26 years' devoted service, the Kirks decided to retire, partially due to his deafness. A subscription list produced over £16,000 from the members, and this was presented to the Kirks with an engraved carriage clock at the Annual General Meeting. Mrs Kirk also presented the Peacock Cup to the winning team—the members, who won 7½ to 6½. When Kirk, 'a much loved and revered fellow' died, 'you would not believe how many members turned up for his memorial service'.[10]

After the Kirks retired, the question of nomenclature among the staff was discussed by the committee. Up to the mid-1980s, all the male staff were called by their surnames—nobody even knew what Kirk's Christian name was. The then chairman, the Hon. Roger Frankland, thought that this practice might be somewhat outdated, even for Swinley. After a short discussion it was generally agreed that it would probably be better if Christian names were employed throughout from then on, 'except for Parker' came the swift rejoinder from Andrew Martin Smith, the youngest member of the committee.

Parker (rarely called Bob) had been a Warrant Officer II in the Royal Army Pay Corps and, as a keen golfer, applied to Swinley as a steward when he needed a job with accommodation for himself and his wife Avis. He failed his interview for steward, but his 2-handicap secured him the job of caddie master and professional where he stayed, incredibly, for 12 whole years. Parker became an institution of gloom at Swinley. By his own admission he did not care much for the members or their guests, and very few of the visiting societies. Members of the committee came in for special censure. In the end Parker found it hard to be polite to his customers, once writing: 'Sometimes I remind myself [that I am] a cross between Victor Meldrew and Basil Fawlty.'[11] He despaired that, if he was found dead in his shop, members would declare: 'I say, Parker's dead. Who's looking after the caddies?'[12] As a consequence the feeling was entirely mutual, and he was not considered popular, as one member recalled:

> … once making the huge mistake of believing he [Parker] could teach me
> something about my game when first a member, I offered him a game/lesson
> on the short loop. He was grumpy about everyone and everything in life …
> When I asked him why he didn't leave (his golf was actually terrible and he gave
> me neither help nor tips) he said he had been given a rolling contract and was
> looking forward to a happy retirement in five years time. He actually said 'You
> see, Sir. I'm jolly happy with life.'[13]

Among the staff Parker was known as 'Arkwright', after the grasping shopkeeper
played by Ronnie Barker in the television situation comedy *Open All Hours*—others,
less benign, referred to him as 'Arsey', a corruption of his initials R.C. It was held
by some that the only reason Parker was tolerated for so long was because his
wife Avis was such a splendid cook, her fruit cake being 'legendary—they made
the best shooting presents to take for a weekend'. Others had it that he was kept
there through a strong Masonic link, ever present at Swinley, he being master of
the local Lodge.

Parker had many detractors among the members and societies. One society
regularly spent around £2,000 on prizes from his shop where, irritatingly, Parker
would not take credit cards. When they asked him to put out the signs for a
'nearest to the pin' and the 'longest drive' competition Parker demanded £30 for
the service. The society bought their prizes elsewhere after that. When Colin
Frizzell was waiting for a knee operation he was unable to play without a buggy.
The winter and spring of 2003 were incredibly wet, and buggies were banned for
three months. Finally, when the course had dried out, Frizzell excitedly telephoned
Parker to book a buggy. The professional replied that the buggy was in his name
but there was no petrol. Determined to play, Frizzell arrived at dawn armed with
his own can and funnel only to find WO II Parker, late of the Pay Corps, standing
to attention beside the buggy, filled with petrol and ready to go.

But not all members were scorned by Parker—in his eyes Algy Cluff (who
bought all his clubs and kit from him) came a close second to the Duke of Beaufort
as his favourite member. When Parker left, Swinley gave him a farewell party
that was attended by the chairman, Sir John Milne, and the staff. No members
turned up, but in the middle of the event Parker received a call from the United
States from Richard Walker, his favourite of all.

Parker had taken over from William Murrant, always known as Bill, a venerable
figure at Swinley who had served the Club for 52 years. Murrant, a quietly spoken
Scot, began at Swinley as a 15-year-old boy caddie in 1926, transferring the next
year to the green-keeping staff. Sometimes on important occasions he was expected
to combine the two roles, as when caddying for the Prince of Wales. One day the
Prince came to play on his own but was accompanied by Mrs Ernest Simpson.
She turned up on the course wearing a very heavy, floor-length, black sable fur

coat. It was a warm afternoon and the Prince told her to change into something lighter, or abandon it altogether. But no, Wallis Simpson knew better. By the time they reached the second green she was sweltering. She removed her coat and handed it to Murrant to carry along with the Prince's clubs. The wretched Murrant returned to the clubhouse a near republican and totally exhausted.

When the caddie master Mears retired in 1950 Murrant was offered the job on a month's trial. He remained on the same wage, but still had to help out Joe Woodley as a green-keeper as and when time allowed. His wife was also expected to work under the club steward. When his review came up a month later it was unanimously decided that Murrant be offered the permanent job as caddie master, at a 'wage of £3 5s. a week and a free cottage'.[14] Mindful of the resignation of Alasdair Macdonald over the sale of golf balls, the committee decided that Murrant could sell them in the shop, but his wage was docked 10s. for the privilege. It was a hugely popular appointment. He was 'the most charming fellow, everybody liked him'.[15] He was also a very good teacher, to which countless generations of members, their sons and daughters will testify. When Murrant decided to retire aged 65 a total of £1,138 was collected from the members, which was invested through some tax loophole for when he finally retired. A further £3,300 was raised through the membership when he finally did step down two years later. He died not long after.

Some members, in particular overseas members, do not visit Swinley for years at a time. One such, a South African, came after an absence of a couple of years, put his head round the door of the professional's shop and asked where Murrant was, only to be told that he was on the course.

'Oh good. In that case I expect I'll see him,' said the member.

'Doubt it,' replied Parker gloomily. 'It's 'is ashes what's on the course!'[16]

At his own request Murrant's ashes were scattered among the azaleas in the 'V' between the 1st and the 18th—the shrubs being a gift of Gerard Pinkney. When Pinkney's name first came up for membership, the committee, 'who were half asleep after a good lunch, asked if anyone knew him'.[17] One of them thought that he was 'that gardener fellow down the road,' so he was duly elected in exchange for supplying azaleas and other shrubs to the club. In fact, the 'gardener fellow' owned Waterers, then one of the largest and most successful nursery gardens in the country. He had a Labrador called Jock, who was so adept at finding balls that his master had four large cardboard boxes in his gun room marked 'bloody awful and cut' (for the children), 'reasonable', 'good' and 'brand-new' (for himself).

As a part of Murrant's original contract in 1950 he was allowed to hire out trolleys after the committee had finally sanctioned their use. Trolleys originally came from the United States (where they were called caddie-carts), and were a boon to those who did not want to carry their own clubs or pay for a caddie. Unlike a caddie, the trolley could not offer advice, clean clubs, replace divots or give the line for putting. But it is never late on parade, requires neither lunch money nor tip, and can be depended upon not to cough or 'sniff on the stroke' or make cynical comments on one's style to other caddies.[18]

The first person to use a trolley in Great Britain was Lieutenant Colonel John T.C. Moore-Brabazon, the first Lord Brabazon of Tara. A pioneer motorist and aviator, he held the very first pilot's licence issued by the Royal Aero Club, and in 1909 was the winner of the *Daily Mail*'s £1,000-challenge to fly a circular mile. A great sportsman, he was still riding the Cresta in his seventies. But it was at golf that he really excelled, going from a complete novice to a scratch player in a few months. He won the White's golf handicap twice. His wit was legendary. Playing on a very wet day at Royal St George's, he made the immortal comment in the suggestion book that 'the water in the bunker by the 12th needs changing!'[19] 'Brab's' original remark has since been attributed to others at many different venues. He was Captain of the Royal and Ancient in 1952-3, and it was there, playing in the Autumn Medal, that he first used his imported American trolley and causing much 'consternation among the caddies'.[20] Although he often played with friends at Swinley, he was not elected a member there until the end of 1969, but died the following May.

Buggies were resisted by the Swinley committee for decades, but by 1994 they finally caved in and Andrew Martin Smith offered to donate one in memory of his father, Julian. It proved a great success, but others were a long time coming.

71   *Pigs will fly. John Moore-Brabazon (later Lord Brabazon of Tara) at the controls of his Shorts' Biplane No 2 in 1909. Brabazon, the first person to hold a pilots' licence, became a scratch golfer within a few months of taking up the game. He won the White's golf handicap twice and introduced the golf trolley into Britain.*

The new buggy was not to the liking of the more traditional members, two of whom were contemporaneously described by an American visitor:

> Both men with persimmon woods and canvas bags were walking the fairways with pullcarts as they had done together for forty years. Bismark, a perfectly behaved little 'English' terrier (so named as he was born in Germany) would wait obediently for each player to hit, and would stop on the fringe of the green watching them both putt out.[21]

At the 17th hole, 'an elegant little par 3', the buggy was spied by Bismark and the two members. As it crossed their path, Bismark, who had been silent since the 10th tee, 'took off after it like a shot, growling and snarling until the offending intruder was safely chased away'. When asked what the matter was with Bismark, his master replied: 'He does not approve of buggies, and for that matter, nor do we. It's the most unsociable thing imaginable.' He continued: 'I've been told that there are courses in your country [the United States] that actually do not allow walking on a golf course! What's the point of playing, then?'

Bismark, with the match well in hand and the area secured of buggies, tottered down the hill and waited quietly on the next tee.

Compared with most other clubs throughout the land, Swinley has always held a liberal attitude towards its female members. This legacy began at the outset through the influence of Lady Derby, when women were treated very much as if they were part of a house party playing on a private course, as opposed to the stereotypical golf club where women were barely tolerated by those who believed that GOLF was an acronym for 'Gentlemen Only, Ladies Forbidden' (or when pronounced 'GOFF' 'Gentlemen Only, Females Forbidden') in their male preserve. Since there was no bar serving drinks at Swinley, they obviously could not be relegated to some back room, as was their fate elsewhere. When a bar area was created in 1950, by rearranging the men's locker room to form the alcove in the sitting room, women were naturally included. But their changing room, accessed only through the bar—some of the younger members used to take bets on how long they would 'take' in the lavatory—was totally Spartan, with only a cold water tap over a sink until an Ascot water heater was installed as late as 1948. Slowly their lot improved. By 1982 it was proposed that they should have 'a new carpet [as opposed to the existing linoleum] similar to the men's changing room; improved lighting, and the provision of a shower and vanity units',[22] but it was to be many years before work was carried out.

On the course the Swinley women were accommodated largely through the initial influence of Lady Derby and, unlike other neighbouring golf clubs, women could play at weekends and public holidays providing she 'shall be staying in the House of the introducing Bondholder'. As the wording stood, it appeared that the bondholder could play with his mistress but not his wife. Before the rule was finally rescinded, Peter Wilmot-Sitwell invited some South African friends, the Ogilvy Thompsons, to play one weekend. To circumvent the rules so that they could all play together, he arranged for his guests to say that they were was staying with Rupert Hambro, a bondholder. Ogilvy Thompson was slightly confused by the arrangement and telephoned Wilmot-Sitwell to say the way he saw it, for his wife Tessa to sleep with Hambro in order for them to play was 'a price rather too high to have to pay' for a round of golf .

By 1933 women were allowed to join as five-day members at a subscription of four guineas in a new Ladies' Section, so long as they were 'relatives of the proposer or seconder'. There was an upper limit of 50 women members, but the quota was never filled, 25 being the maximum at any one time. At that time the all-male Swinley committee under the chairmanship of Lord Derby surprisingly voted that the Ladies' Section should subscribe to the Ladies' Golf Union. Although the resolution was passed, it was never enacted. When Mrs Ritchie suggested it again in 1938, the committee unanimously threw out the proposal as being 'not Swinley'.

By 1952 Rule 15 was altered so that 'a Member, other than a Bondholder, may introduce his wife or daughter to play with him on Saturdays, Sundays and public holidays upon payment of the usual green fees', but when, in 1974, it was suggested that members (as opposed to bondholders) could introduce ladies, *other* than a wife or a daughter, the committee put the motion to the bondholders 'asking them for their views'.[23] They promptly rejected it. Tom Ruck Keene,[*] always known as 'The Admiral' after his famous father who was a real admiral, proposed that the rules 'affecting the introduction of ladies at the week-end'[24] be relaxed, but again the suggestion was brushed under the carpet, as it was when N. Hely-Hutchinson brought the matter up again in 1992. Finally, the rules changed 13 years later in 2005 so that women were allowed to play at weekends with the member, regardless of their relationship to him, on payment of a green fee. The rules changed again in 2006 when women were allowed to join as full members, although they paid the price for their emancipation—a full joining fee and subscription.

Another legacy from Lord Derby was the grant of instant membership to Ambassadors and High Commissioners and the waiving of their entrance fee whilst at the Court of St James's. Some, like the popular United States Ambassador 'Jock' Hay Whitney, were invited to remain members after their term of office came to an end. Others included Henry Catto and the great Walter Annenberg, publisher and diplomat. Annenberg is possibly best remembered in England not as one of

---

[*]   Tom Ruck Keene was an enthusiastic member of the Golf Match Club. He is remembered with affection and the tribute 'Very many of our members are worthy of comment, but perhaps our true heroes are those like Sir Herbert Ingram and Tom Ruck-Keene [*sic*], who went on giving pleasure to their friends in more ways than one, while their balance of losses over wins continued to incline upwards' (*Golf Match Club 1896-1996*, p. xxxiv). He was President of the Askernish Golf Club, on South Uist in the Western Isles, originally laid out in 1892 by Old Tom Morris, 'the father of golf' and winner, like his son Tom Morris Junior, of four Open Championships. There are plans to restore the original 18-hole course that, when completed, will make it 'a links course second to none', the land and position being 'Heaven sent for golf'.

the world's greatest philanthropists that he surely was, but for the classic remark at Buckingham Palace on his appointment. Famously, as he presented his credentials, the Queen enquired on how things were going at the residence then being renovated. Annenberg, somewhat prone to circumlocution, replied nervously, 'Very well, Ma'am, subject to certain elements of restoration and rehabilitation.'

It was Prince Werner de Mésode, the Belgian Ambassador and honorary member of Swinley, who introduced his ex-king, Leopold III, to Swinley in the early 1960s. Leopold was a proficient and avid golfer—even when King he competed in the Belgian Amateur Championships. In 1938, as a widower of just three years, he met his future wife Liliane Baels, twice Club de Genève women's champion, on the golf course at Knokke-le-Zoute. Leopold was greatly taken by her, as much for her game as her looks, for she was reputedly 'as beautiful as a Greek night'.[25] The daughter of a fish merchant in London, she became the Princess de Rethy on her morganatic marriage. After his abdication they spent much of their time in the South of France, where in 1949 he reached the quarter-finals of the French Amateur Championship. Leopold and his wife played with another royal exile, the Duke of Windsor, 'though she always remained critical of his game'. Soon after his introduction he was a regular visitor to Swinley, playing as a guest of the then current Belgian Ambassador.

Most of the Ambassadors who were granted honorary membership of Swinley came from Europe—France, Austria, Germany and Italy—but some from further afield like those of Japan, Chile (including the ever-popular Victor Santa Cruz) and the Korean Republic who, over several incumbents, built up a serious reputation for slowness of play and clogging up the course with a large entourage. Late lunches when the Koreans were playing became the norm. Matters finally came to a head when Robert Harman wrote his first letter of complaint to the chairman after 41 years of membership. He was playing a singles two behind the Koreans one Sunday, and became exasperated at their speed of play—it took them two hours to reach the turn, 'having held up everybody at each hole'. He pointed out that he and Sir Robin Dent had three artificial hips between them and were 'never likely to be the quickest match on the course'[26] He felt 'that this is not what Swinley is about' and that the committee should really look carefully at electing people with 'Ambassadorial status, particularly if they come from a part of the world where golf is played at a different pace … Swinley is of course a unique institution' he concluded, 'and the week-ends are greatly valued by the membership who in the past have easily understood one another'. Thereafter it was felt necessary that future Korean Ambassadors 'should meet the chairman informally to have the procedures and etiquette of the club explained in detail'.[27] Today it is only the United States Ambassador who is invited to become a member for his or her term of office.

Sometimes ambassadors came as guests. Marcus Agius, the current chairman of Barclays, was once asked by his father-in-law, Eddy de Rothschild—the grandson of Leo and Marie de Rothschild, he a founding member of Swinley—to play with

72 *The Princess de Rethy, morganatic wife of King Leopold III of the Belgians. The daughter of a London fish merchant and a fine golfer, she was reputed to be 'as beautiful as a Greek night'.*

La princesse de Rethy (admirée par le duc de Windsor) est une championne (8 de handicap). Elle a un très bon swing.

L'ex-roi des Belges (4 de handicap) est bon joueur. Bon travail des bras et des mains. Mauvais mouvement du corps.

73 *King Leopold III of the Belgians was a proficient and avid golfer. After his abdication, he went to live in the south of France, where he reached the quarter finals of the French Open.*

74 *The Duke of Windsor spent much time on the golf course in his 35 years in exile. The Princess de Rethy, wife of ex-King Leopold III of the Belgians, was critical of his game.*

75 *A royal drive. Sir John Aird obviously willing his ball to go further in front of Ex-King Leopold of the Belgians, his wife Princess de Rethy and two caddies somewhere in the south of France.*

Le duc de Windsor fait un de ses nombreux « swings de pratique » avant le coup. Pieds joints, suivant conseils reçus.

the Japanese Ambassador. Knowing how crowded the courses were in Japan, de Rothschild thought it would be a particular treat for him to play Swinley's typically empty fairways. 'The day in question was a gloomy Saturday in November', Agius recalled, 'and so misty that it was impossible to see beyond the brook from the first tee.'[28]

The Ambassador was quietly excited by the occasion. 'He took a mighty swipe at his ball from the tee, almost falling over backwards in the effort.' His ball flew off into the fog and soon disappeared from sight. The Ambassador was perplexed. Turning to Agius, he said: 'Hah! Did not see where ball went. Did it go *reft* or *light*?' It actually went *reft* as he had 'hooked it something rotten'. It was all Agius could do not to double up with laughter. Fortunately His Excellency's golf and the weather both improved after that, and they had an excellent morning, capped by one of Swinley's famous lunches.

The same privileges were also extended to all High Commissioners. Lord Alvingham remembers seeing one High Commissioner from Pakistan, Lieutenant General Muhammad Yusuf, in the early 1960s wandering down to the first tee with a partner in the pouring rain. As Alvingham was on his own the High Commissioner waved him through, whereupon the second baron took out his Dai Rees driver and drove off. Unfortunately he had just polished the old leather grip with beeswax, and his hands were wet. At the end of his swing the ball remained on the tee and

76 *The longest serving member of Swinley, Major General The Lord Alvingham in his fine Oxfordshire garden.*

the club went sailing up in the air, to be caught in a branch of an old Scots pine. Yusuf watched the whole episode in total amazement and turned to his companion and declared: 'Oh my God. Never have I seen that shot before lunch!' Alvingham took out another club from his bag and drove the second ball 240 yards down the fairway. 'That's better,' he muttered as he walked off, leaving his club in the tree to be collected later.

In a similar vein, John McCall (who has killed more swallows on the wing than scored holes-in-one) was playing one December as a guest of Simon Negretti, who had taken a day at Swinley to celebrate his birthday. 'There was thunder and lightning and furious flurries of snow, but in true Swinley fashion, we played on undeterred by such rude weather.' It was McCall's turn to drive off at the 13th in his fourball. As he struck the ball there was a mighty crash of thunder. 'The club went significantly further than the ball which was easily found having dribbled a few yards along the fairway. The club less so. It had landed in a clump of old rhododendrons some 50 yards to the left, and took a devil of a long time to find!'[29]

At the beginning of 1960 staff changes came rapidly at Swinley. Colonel Snatt had resigned—he had become somewhat irascible and distant as one of his entries in the minutes shows:

> The committee was informed that *one* [author's italics] of our greenkeepers had been presented with the [Royal] Humane Society's parchment for saving the life of a man in the lake at Windsor Park in January 1960.

The hero green-keeper is still unnamed. Snatt died shortly after his resignation.

The Colonel was replaced by Group Captain Arthur King-Lewis, known as Dick. He had been secretary at Camberley Heath Golf Club, where he appears to have been a reasonably proficient golfer with a few 'captains and club secretaries' tournaments to his name. He, too, married late in life, having wooed Mrs Margot Brill on the golf course. As Miss Cains, she was at the top of her game, once captaining the Scottish ladies' team. King-Lewis clearly did not have the measure of Swinley when he proposed that a fruit machine be installed in the hall to generate extra income and a television set be placed in the sitting room. Naturally, both were strongly condemned by the committee as 'not Swinley'. In the end, Air Commodore Macdonald donated a small screen television which was placed discreetly in the alcove of the sitting room.

What King-Lewis did do was to update the changing room from a dark, Victorian hell-hole, somewhat reminiscent of the traditional private schools that smelt of Mansion Polish, old socks and cabbage, into a relatively civilised place. Club legend has it that two members met in the urinal. One remarked that it was all very smart, to which his friend replied, 'Yes it is. But it does make one's cock look most awfully shabby!'

Towards the end of his tenure King-Lewis spent more and more time away through ill health. When Dick Bateman, a fellow RAF officer who knew him from his Camberley Heath days, heard of it, he offered to cover for him as secretary while King-Lewis was in hospital. Bateman went for what passed for an interview with the chairman, Sir John Aird, yet another Swinley member with an Eton, Grenadier, Royal Household background (he was a former Equerry to the Prince of Wales, George VI and the Queen) and Brigadier Ronnie Senior. Bateman proudly declared that he was 'fully conversant with the rules of golf', which, as Mrs Bateman recalled, 'was barmy because the rules of golf didn't come into Swinley—the first hole was a Mulligan so if you went into the ditch, you could have another shot. They certainly didn't have handicaps then [or now]'.[30] Nor were the committee interested in taking up his references from the North Hants Golf Club, merely asking him for 'a spot of luncheon', then to join them in a fourball in the afternoon. When they returned, Kirk was waiting to say that King-Lewis had died that very morning. The next day, Bateman was invited to take over 'as soon as possible'. Tall and distinguished, he proved to be popular and efficient. Although he had had no experience as a golf club secretary before, he was admirably qualified, having run his family milling business and had a Service career in the Royal Air Force. Both he and his wife Kitty were good competition golfers. Mrs Bateman, who celebrated her 100th birthday in January 2007, declared: 'I don't want to brag, but I really think my bridge is as good now as ever it has been!'[31] The Batemans' time at Swinley was made even more enjoyable by the staff, particularly the Kirks, who shielded him on Fridays, his only day off in the week.

It was an especially happy time at Swinley, with everyone pulling together for the mutual enjoyment of the members. Bateman was everywhere—in the scrap yard with Joe Woodley to find spare parts for the machinery, behind the bar on the Kirks' day off or selling golf balls when Murrant was away. There were only two society days a week—Tuesdays and Thursdays. Bateman would watch them play and if they were 'hacking the course about' they would not be asked back. The secretary's bungalow was built for them.

At nearly 72, Dick Bateman finally decided 'that the time had come when he should lead a more leisurely life without the responsibilities he has carried for the last twelve years'.[32] He was remembered with affection by both members and staff, but not missed nearly as much as Ben, his Border collie dog. Just as Breeze, the present course manager Lawson Bingham's Border collie, is seen as the harbinger of his master, so too was Ben a familiar sight over the whole course. 'Ben was a particularly charming dog.'[33] If anyone was playing in a four-ball with Bateman, Ben would 'lie flat, totally motionless, under the trolley of whoever was playing the shot. He would watch the ball and mark the line and, if necessary, would wait for Dick to instruct him to find the ball. Ben would never pick it up, but gently nudge it, looking up as if to say "here it is, you fool".'[34]

77 *Dick Bateman, secretary of Swinley from 1965-77, on the practice green, shadowed by Ben, his faithful collie dog. A great favourite among all the members, no one ever lost a ball when Ben was around.*

78 *Ben 'Bateman' was greatly admired by Walter Annenberg, former United States Ambassador and member of Swinley. He had a special coat made for him with his name embroidered on the side. He hoped that he would maintain 'the form that has won him endless admirers'.*

Ben was adored by his master and greatly loved by all the members, not least Walter Annenberg, the United States Ambassador, who, Mrs Bateman recalled, had a coat made for him with 'Ben' embroidered on the side. One day we saw the Annenbergs coming up towards the 18th, so Dick rushed in to put the coat on Ben. He stood like an angel as he was strapped in, then both walked down to meet the Ambassador and his wife. Walter said 'I don't expect he likes it, but it's given me great pleasure to give it to him!'[35] In a letter to his master the ex-Ambassador hoped that Ben 'maintains the form that has won him endless admirers'.[36] Nobody ever lost a ball at Swinley, 'as the dear boy would always find them!' Ben was even written up in a United States broadsheet:

> Ben sits quietly while his master tees up and drives off … and he is off, streaming down the fairway, his fur flying in the breeze. Two feet from the ball, he 'points' at it, absolutely stationary, his whole body stiff, his nose in line with the ball, his tail down and his back quarters humped.
>
> He stays in this position, utterly concentrated, until the player arrives to play his second shot … If the ball is badly hit and lands in the rough … Ben can still find it if the general location is indicated to him … then unerringly he points towards it.
>
> Ben genuinely understands the game. Once when another player was about to drive, Ben's master, not noticing, began to walk ahead. Ben placed himself in front of the cart so it could not [be] moved.[37]

Ben had only one less endearing trait and that was his drinking habits: he would eschew all the dog bowls around the place in preference to the lavatory bowl.

Much in keeping with the feel of Swinley as a private golf course, dogs have always been a particular feature of the Club. When Lieutenant Colonel Sir John Johnston, a black Labrador at heel, arrived at Swinley for the first time in 1948, he 'knew he had joined a gentleman's club'[38] when he saw the two dog bowls at the front door. Dogs are well accommodated on the course—the three drinking fountains at the 8th, 12th and 16th greens all have dog bowls, the water being as much for them as the players. Consistent with the membership, their dogs roam free—perish the thought of them on leads at Swinley. They are mostly shooting dogs, Labradors and springer spaniels, all adept at retrieving golf balls. Stories abound and there is much rivalry as to which dog holds the record number of balls found on any given hole. The dogs are usually well behaved, but not always.

Very little seems to ruffle the quiet, ordered life of Swinley, where it has carried on in its quiet, unruffled way for decades. So when something untoward happens to disrupt that tranquillity, the event takes on epic proportions. And so it was when a member, Tim Pilkington, and his dogs, a golden retriever named Splash and two West Highland terriers, met Wooster, a yellow Labrador belonging to Roger Wellesley-

Smith. Wooster, whose main claim to fame was finding 43 balls in a single round, mostly at the 9th, was an 'out-of-hand field-trial champion'.[39] On that fateful day Pilkington was playing with his brother-in-law, James Norman, and arrived at Swinley at the same time as Wellesley-Smith and Sir Roger Gibbs. Both parties remember the events with wildly differing but crystal-clear, 20:20 hindsight vision. The two singles met at the first tee. Pilkington admits that he knew his golden retriever to be 'not very sociable, particularly towards Labradors',[40] so it came as no surprise to any of them when a serious dog-fight followed. A snarling Splash went for Wooster. The Westies joined in. It was a re-run of some years before at the Royal Wimbledon when Wellesley-Smith's bull terrier attacked a terrier called Bonnie (well-known for his ability to clear every grouse before a drive). The Splash affray ended with victory to the 'Pilkington three' with a savaged Wooster and Wellesley-Smith bitten badly in the hand. Blood was everywhere. 'My mistake was to put down my Callaway driver', Wellesley-Smith admitted. His hand had gone into spasm and he could not see one of his fingers in all the blood. He was 'sure that it was in one of the unmentionable dog's tummies trotting triumphantly down the fairway with its master in glorious weather!' He was rushed to Ascot hospital where his hand, mercifully still with finger, was stitched up, while Wooster went to the vet. When Gibbs and Wellesley-Smith finally returned to the clubhouse there was a £5 note waiting for them on the bar with a message, 'Sorry about this morning's little problem. Have a drink on me'—Pilkington insists that it was a bottle of iced champagne. Either way, the gesture was not appreciated.

But the retriever's behaviour was all too well known at Swinley, with no fewer than four recorded accounts of his aggression. The committee (which included Roger Gibbs who had had his birthday spoiled) and the chairman took an exceedingly dim view of the affair, even though Pilkington had written tending 'Splash's

79 *The quiet, unruffled life at Swinley was once shattered by a serious dogfight. In the yellow corner was Wooster, a Labrador and an inveterate finder of golf balls. In the other corner was a golden retriever, Splash, and two West Highland Terriers. By sheer weight of numbers, Wooster ended up with the vet, his owner in casualty.*

resignation'. The two 'contaminated' terriers were held to be accomplices and all three dogs were banned from the course. Eventually, when the more aggressive Westie had died, the other was allowed back in old age. But the ASBO on Splash remained to his dying day. The final word goes to Pilkington. Had his family not lost their estates in Lancashire and Cheshire to the Stanleys after the Battle of Bosworth then they, not the Derbys, might have 'founded' Swinley and Tim Pilkington would be revered as President of the Club today.

It was the owner and not the dog that was at fault, as is so often the case. Major Keith Barlow MC (Recorder of the Match Club 1959-63) was once playing at Swinley after some bracken had been sprayed with some deadly chemical. Barlow's Labrador went into the dying bracken to retrieve a lost ball, came out and was violently sick. Barlow was convinced that his dog had been poisoned and parcelled up a sample of the vomit to be sent to a laboratory for analysis. He complained vociferously to anyone who would listen to him or not. When the results came back it was found that the Labrador had been turning over the dustbins and had eaten some very choice smoked cod. Barlow's letter of apology to the committee was instant and grovelling.

It has often been said of English clubs that either the staff are nicer than the members or the members are more genial than the staff. Swinley has a careful balance of both, and the ideals and criteria of membership of the 17th Lord Derby are as strong today as they were in the 1920s when a member wrote: 'at Swinley Forest the atmosphere of privacy is carefully preserved. This does not mean stuffiness— rather the opposite: but the fun is private.' It is equally true today. This is hard for many outsiders to understand—even *The Times* wrote that Swinley members to a man (or woman) shout 'Phwoar!' for 'Fore!'[41] Others mock those who still refer to their clubs as 'golf sticks'. At Swinley, even if the members do not know each other personally, they are at least *known* to each other. As the *Sunday Times* had it: 'Swinley is the quintessential Establishment establishment; nouveaux riches are as rare as a hole-in-one at a par four … [it] boasts a membership list like no other. It is as if someone has ripped a few pages from Debrett's and shuffled them with a sprinkling of names from *Who's Who* in The City.'[42]

Before the renovations, societies used the only locker room so members were hugger-mugger with the visitors. Murrough O'Brien (who famously maintained that 'Swinley was a gentleman's club for gentle people') was once dressing next to some society visitor who was boasting that he had a very broad cross-section of members in his club, drawn from all walks of life. 'How interesting', O'Brien replied. 'That's certainly not a problem we have here.'

Unlike practically every other golf club in the world, Swinley is not a place where people join to make friends. Members go there to play golf with their *own* friends, never on the off-chance that they will meet a member hanging around the bar hoping to pick up a game. When Gervase Thomas and a female friend could not play at Sunningdale, she suggested that they pick another couple in the bar at Swinley for a fourball. 'Don't be daft', Thomas replied. 'You could wait for ten years and still not find anyone to play with.'[43] When one secretary in the 1970s took over from another he was given just one piece of advice: never interfere with the members. Soon after he arrived at Swinley he saw two senior members drinking at opposite ends of the room, and introduced one to the other. Later the chairman, Ronnie Senior, rebuked him, saying that at Swinley, 'if members wished to talk to one other, they would do so on their own account'.[44]

At around the same time, a visitor turned up to play with a member who was late. He helped himself to a cup of coffee and sat at the other end of the sitting room from a senior member who was reading *The Times*. After half an hour the bored visitor sauntered over to the member and remarked that it was a lovely day. The older man ignored him, turned in his chair and pressed the bell. When the steward arrived, he dropped his paper a fraction and barked: 'There is a gentleman here who wants to talk about the weather!'[45]

So rigid was the friendship code that it was virtually the only criterion for membership during the chairmanship of the Hon. Roger Frankland. Years before, a current member had been approached by an elderly bondholder and asked if he would like to join Swinley. Delighted at the prospect, he had his name put down, but heard nothing for ten years until the telephone rang one Friday evening and a voice asked if he was still interested in becoming a member. On hearing that he was, the voice continued, 'Well, come to the club at lunchtime on Sunday to meet some people.' The line then went dead. So he went to Swinley as suggested and was introduced to two or three of the committee in the bar before being summoned to meet the chairman in the hall.

'So, you would like to be a member of Swinley?', he began. On hearing that he would, the chairman continued, 'Well, you must understand that at Swinley we all play with our friends.' The prospective member confirmed that he had understood the point. Again the chairman fixed him with his eye: 'Good, I'll say it again. At Swinley we play with our friends. Got that?'

'Yes, I quite understand you,' the candidate confirmed.

'Good, you can be a member then.' With that the interview closed and he was duly elected.

Years later a comparatively new member was sitting quietly on his own on the terrace, within earshot of a very senior pair discussing the identity of the two players coming up the 18th. They finally agreed who one of the players was, but both puzzled over the other. When they were nearly on the green, the one with the better eyesight declared: 'It's his wife. I'm pretty sure the man's playing with his wife.'

'Good grief', cried his astonished companion. 'Hasn't the fellow got any friends?'

80   *Elected a member of Swinley in 1991, HRH The Duke of York, KG, KCVO, ADC, was Captain of The Royal and Ancient Golf Club of St Andrews during its 250th Anniversary in 2004. Here he is dressed in the red tailcoat of all captains of the R & A, which is worn at all official occasions and when representing them. On his lapel is the miniature of The Queen Adelaide Medal that was presented to the club in 1838 by William IV's widow, and since 1856 has been the symbol of captaincy.*

Living so close to Swinley the Duke of York plays there, often on his own in the early morning or later on in the day. In the very beginning he would arrive in the evening hoping to pick up a game, but invariably ended up playing with the then secretary Ian Pearce or a member of staff. The professional Parker, who should have been on hand to play with him, famously denied him thrice. The first time he said he was tired after a long day and wanted to go home, the second that he had an urgent appointment, while the third time he left to chair his local Freemason's Lodge meeting as Master. His Royal Highness never asked him again. But when the Duke was making a habit of teeing off too early in the morning, the secretary sent a note reminding him of the rules. The letter was studiously ignored, so the matter was brought to the attention of the chairman, Ted Baillieu, who consulted one of the Queen's Private Secretaries. 'Don't worry', he said. 'I'll have a word with his mother!'

Once the Duke of York was playing at Swinley with Bernard Gallacher, member of eight Ryder Cup sides, three of them as Captain. They were coming up the 18th fairway together when they were spied by a visitor who had just teed off at the first. He came bounding over, put his hand on the Duke's shoulder and whispered excitedly, 'I say, is that *really* Bernard Gallacher over there?'[46]

At the present time the Duke of York's handicap is 4.4, although there are no handicaps at Swinley. According to Mike Merritt, who partners the Duke when they occasionally play together at Stornoway on the Isle of Lewis, 'Golf is a huge part of his life, and in it he has found a release from his problems. But he also happens to be good at the game as well. He is a natural golfer with a beautiful swing.'[47] The Duke of York began playing when a naval colleague took him to a driving range at Weymouth when they were stationed at Portland in 1989. After hitting a few balls he suddenly felt that there might be something in the game of golf after all, so dug out a set of clubs that the Duchess had won in a raffle some years before and began to practise at Windsor. He then went to Doug McLelland, the teaching professional at Tilgate Forest near Crawley, who shaped his swing. 'When I first asked him to come to Windsor to give me a lesson', the Duke told John Hopkins of *The Times*, 'I think he thought it was a joke. He was told to go to Shaw Farm Gate and only when someone met him there did he believe that his assignment was serious.'[48] Soon after, the Duke telephoned McClelland at home, where one of the professional's children answered and asked who was calling. On hearing that it was the Duke of York she screamed 'Dad, the pub's on the 'phone.'[49]

The Duke of Edinburgh used to compete with Prince Andrew for the same piece of ground at Windsor Castle, the Duke to perfect his carriage driving and Prince Andrew to practise his golf. Once, in his early days, Prince Andrew was chipping away on the ground when his father called out from the box of the carriage to say that he had some golf clubs for him. The Prince thanked him for his gift, but was puzzled as he did not remember his father ever playing golf. After a moment, he realised that it was the patronage of several Royal Clubs that his father was passing on to him.

The Duke of York is the latest of many members of the extended Royal Family to play at Swinley. Soon after they married, Princess Elizabeth and The Duke of Edinburgh took Windlesham Moor, a commodious house on the Sunninghill Road that is now the home of Sheikh Hamden Al Maktoum, Deputy Ruler of the United Arab Emirates. A former owner had laid out a private 9-hole golf course on the 58 acres, but it is unlikely that either occupant ever played it in the two years they lived there in the late 1940s. As Windlesham Moor marches with Swinley (the western boundary of the land runs alongside the beginning of the 6th hole) Princess Elizabeth and The Duke of Edinburgh were given honorary membership, but again, it is certain that neither he nor The Queen ever played there.

In the early 1950s there were five other Royal honorary members, together with Stuart Fitz-James, the 17th Duque de Alba, the Spanish Ambassador to the Court of St James's throughout the whole of the Second World War. Although appointed by General Franco, de Alba had always been loyal to his fellow Swinley member, HM Queen Victoria Eugenie of Spain. Always known as Ena, she was daughter of Princess Beatrice and Prince Henry of Battenberg. As Queen Victoria would not think of allowing Beatrice, her youngest child, companion and confidential secretary ever to leave her side, and as Prince Henry was somewhat impecunious, Ena followed

the Queen with her parents to all the Royal residences. So it was at Windsor and Balmoral (where she was born) that she learned and played golf with her first cousins, Prince Arthur and Princess Patricia of Connaught. In 1905 Victoria Eugenie attended a dinner party given by her uncle, Edward VII, in honour of King Alfonso XIII of Spain. The King had just been rebuffed by Princess Pat, the 'object of his marital expedition', so set his sights on the pretty 18-year-old Ena whom he married the next year among great controversy. Alfonso was

81 *Stuart Fitz-James, 17th Duque of Alba, was descended from a long line of distinguished generals. He was the Spanish Ambassador throughout the Second World War and an honorary member of Swinley. Although appointed by General Franco, he equally served the deposed Queen Ena, another honorary member of Swinley.*

82 *Queen Ena was a spirited sportswoman, hunting and playing golf in England and the south of France after her husband Alfonso XIII of Spain was deposed, when she left Madrid in a train driven by the Hereditary Engine Driver, the Duque of Zaragossa.*

finally deposed in 1931, his Queen Ena leaving by the royal train driven by the Duque de Zaragossa, the Hereditary Engine Driver to the Spanish Royal Family. The ex-Queen went to live in Lausanne. At last she was able to devote time to golf courses in Switzerland, the south of France, Rome and at Swinley, where she had been an honorary member since 1932.

At that time the Duke of Windsor, his brother the Duke of Gloucester, and sister The Princess Royal were also honorary members. 'On 18 April 1936 the Earl of Derby wrote asking if Edward VIII would become "Patron [of Swinley] as he had been an Honorary Member for many years and had often played at the course, and was informed that the King would." '[50] Soon after the Abdication of his brother, George VI was invited on 1 February 1937 to become Patron of Swinley Forest Golf Club, and immediately accepted. He, too, had played there regularly as an honorary member throughout the 1920s and '30s. But the Duke of York did not have the temperament, or the passion, to be as good a golfer as his elder brother. In addition, in his early days he was:

> prone to depression in the face of minor difficulties, though he had learned to confront major problems, as, for instance, those of his health and speech, with a fine courage. In the sports in which he was proficient, such as golf and tennis, he was easily discouraged by defeat or by his own poor performance on an 'off day'; even to the extent of abandoning the match.[51]

83 *Prince Edward, later Prince of Wales, Edward VIII and Duke of Windsor, was passionate about golf. His father George V maintained that a 'game that could make a man unaccountably mad at himself ought not to be encouraged', and actively discouraged his children from taking up golf, yet most of them played and were honorary members of Swinley.*

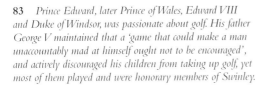

Sadly, after his accession the difficulties of the first years of his reign and the war put paid to the King's golf at Swinley, although he remained Patron of the Club. Queen Elizabeth The Queen Mother often visited Swinley when still Duchess of York in the early years of their marriage, both as a spectator and a player—she was to become the President of the Sunningdale Ladies Golf Club. In later life she had many friends who were members of Swinley, not least 'that consummate courtier',[52] Lieutenant Colonel Sir John Johnston GCVO, MC.

The Colonel was invariably known as 'Johnnie', sometimes 'Stopwatch Johnnie' in his position as Comptroller of the Lord Chamberlain's Office. As such he masterminded every royal ceremonial event, arranged weddings (most notably for the Prince and Princess of Wales and the Duke and Duchess of York), funerals including those of the Duke and Duchess of Windsor and Sir Winston Churchill, garden parties, investitures and State Visits, all executed with style and panache. Notwithstanding his distinguished military career in the Grenadier Guards, where he served throughout the war (his citation for his Military Cross described his 'complete fearlessness and brilliant leadership' during the final advance through Germany to the Elbe in 1945), it is the photograph of him in his uniform, standing beside The Queen on Horse Guards' Parade, holding her handbag, that is the

84 *Living so close in Windsor Great Park, Lt Colonel Sir John Johnston and his pair of flat-coated retrievers were a familiar sight at Swinley. When he was Comptroller of the Lord Chamberlain's Office, he organised many Royal Household days at Swinley. He knew it was time to retire when he heard himself described as 'old grumpy chops', a far cry from the 'golden delicious' on his arrival.*

85   *The Duchess of York chipping a ball around Polesden Lacey in Surrey, April 1923. Such was the public's fascination with her that she and The Duke allowed the press to intrude on their honeymoon. The Duke of York was a keen golfer but he did not have the temperament to become a really good player.*

lasting memory. His charm and 'ineffable British style' made him a great favourite among all the Royal Family and the Household, but, as he famously recalled, he knew it was time to leave when he heard himself described as 'old grumpy chops', as opposed to the 'golden delicious' on his arrival 23 years earlier.

Johnnie Johnston was married to Elizabeth Hardinge, the granddaughter of the 1st Baron Hardinge of Penshurst, an original bondholder of Swinley (see page 50). They lived at Adelaide Cottage, close to Royal Lodge in the Home Park at Windsor, the residence of Queen Elizabeth The Queen Mother and now the home of the present Duke of York. After church one Sunday, Queen Elizabeth was talking to the Colonel and asked if 'they still have that splendid cold buffet [at Swinley] they had when I played there in the 1920s?'[53] He replied that they were 'even better, and why did she not come and see for herself'.[54] So Sir John arranged for a lunch party on Monday 3 June 1996. Unfortunately he had forgotten that it was a Bank Holiday and the dining room was very full, 'not that that mattered'. Naturally the chef had made an extra-special effort to lay on a spectacular cold buffet, only for Queen Elizabeth to choose the hot steak and kidney pie. It was a very successful party, and the lunch 'every bit as good as she remembered it'. Afterwards a member

86 *Queen Elizabeth The Queen Mother recalled the splendid cold buffets she had had in the 1920s and '30s at Swinley, so Sir John Johnston and his daughter Joanna took her to lunch on 3 June 1996. It was all a great success. Less successful was her putting. When she left, she told her host, 'You do realise that if the green had been flat, that last putt of mine would have gone in!'*

produced a putter for her to recall her golfing days on the putting green. Try as she might, the balls remained obstinately on top, assiduously avoiding each hole as she sent them scudding across the green. The clubhouse emptied as members and their guests congregated to wave her off. As the car drew level with her host, Queen Elizabeth lowered the window, leant forward, and said to him: 'You do realise that had the green been flat, that last putt of mine would have gone in!'

★   ★   ★

To many, to become a member of Swinley is a long-held dream. Years of waiting in hope go by from the first proposal to the invitation to join. To one comparatively recent member, that euphoric day was clouded by his dread realisation that his golf was not good enough to play there, and he decided to put in some serious practice before taking up his membership.

The prospective member arrived at 6 o'clock one morning at his local golf course, which was near a reservoir, and made for the first tee. He was about to drive off when he saw a swan's head poking up over the ladies' tee some way below. Thinking that even he could hit the ball over the bird's head he drove off with gusto. In less than a second there was a dull thud, a strangled cry, and a lone feather floating in the still air. A dead swan lay on the fairway.

CHAPTER 8

Napoleonic in stature and temperament, Wing Commander Thomas Ingham had found his niche at last. To be secretary of Swinley Forest Golf Club suited him very well, but as it turned out he did not suit Swinley well enough. His road to Swinley, too, had been chequered. He cut his teeth at the Ashridge Golf Club near Berkhamsted, which had been carved out of the park of Ashridge House after the 3rd and last Earl Brownlow died. He was not there for long before he moved to Northern Ireland and the Royal Portrush Golf Club. This Harry Colt course is what 'most people will probably think … his masterpiece, a magnificent natural course which he almost entirely reconstructed and lived to see chosen for The Open Championship'.[1] The Wing Commander was soon on the move again as Mrs Ingham could not settle in Northern Ireland, and after just 11 months he accepted the post of secretary at another fine Colt-designed course, St George's Hill. His two-year tenure there was unmemorable, although it was the time of the three-day week and flagging membership. When they changed direction and encouraged societies, Ingham felt he would be more at home at Swinley, and accepted their offer to go there in 1977.

As at St George's Hill he is remembered by the Swinley membership, if at all, as being uninspiring at best. The Kirks were uncomfortable with his autocratic style and eventually left. From the start of his tenure matters began to slide, and the clubhouse and course suffered through neglect. Ingham's last years in office were dogged by ill-health, and he coped even less well than before with the running of the Club. Towards the end, for example, in October 1987 the great golf course architect Fred Hawtree had contacted Ingham over his biography of Harry Colt. Ingham replied nine weeks later:

> Regarding your Mr. Gilbert Hanse's visit here to Swinley, I may be able to accommodate him next April 1988, but this depends on how I feel at the time …
>
> For your information Swinley Forest are in the process of finding a replacement for me as Secretary in July next year, which is of course too late for the visit of your Mr. Hanse.[2]

87 *As secretary to the Royal Portrush, St George's Hill and finally Swinley, Wing Commander Ingham had plenty of experience of Harry Colt's courses, yet in his 11-year tenure he made no innovative changes to the course or clubhouse.*

The Wing Commander did indeed leave by July and donated a barograph, while his generous pay-off was received without acknowledgement. His replacement was Lieutenant Colonel Ian Pearce, late of the Royal Anglian Regiment and the Army Catering Corps. He had been tipped off about the vacancy by Parker, his Vice-Captain of the British Army of the Rhine golf team. Although he had no experience of running a golf club, Pearce was exactly the right man for the job at that time. He was a fine player with an impressive golf history. As a schoolboy of 16 with a handicap of three he had played for Essex. As a scratch, one- and two-handicap player he had won the Army championship at every rank, and had captained both the Army and the Combined Services sides. While serving in Aden he was once enrolled on a mythical 'Army sanitation course' in England so that he could play in a crucial Army match. He hitched a lift home with the legendary air ace, Air Vice Marshal Sir 'Johnnie' Johnson, a flight that took five days. He was to play for seven English county teams, often as Captain. Pearce once had a trial for England, but two years in Aden without even lifting a club put paid to higher things.

There were 80 applicants for the post of secretary, and it was Pearce's golfing prowess that won him the position. Pearce worked closely with the chairman, the Hon. Edward (Ted) Baillieu. It was a good combination, where Baillieu was devoted to Swinley and, living so near, was always there to 'jolly things along with the members', while Pearce beavered away in the background. The chairman had his own way of managing both the committee and the Club, and left the secretary very much to his own devices.

Pearce began by assessing the state of Swinley after years of neglect. The secretary's bungalow was virtually uninhabitable, while the interior of the clubhouse could have been described as 'tired'. Although the greens under the care of Bill Barrie and his staff were adequate, the rest of the course was somewhat unkempt—a definite advantage to a large faction of the membership. A gardener as opposed to a golfer, Barrie had made no innovative changes to the course, which suited some, while Ingham had made no improvements to the clubhouse, or to the course either. The machinery was antiquated, many of the green-keepers and clubhouse staff were disaffected, and the Club's finances were far from healthy. Pearce felt that 'the whole place was slipping away',[3] which was something of an exaggerated view.

88 *A former lieutenant colonel and an outstanding golfer in the Catering Corps, Ian Pearce was an obvious choice to take over as secretary in 1988. In his 17 years at Swinley, he was instrumental in repairing the fabric of the clubhouse and many changes to the course. Pearce standing beside the half-man-sized Colt Cup when Swinley were runners up in 1994.*

The new secretary began slowly, writing a paper on the state of Swinley as he found it and what needed to be done, and then working through the resulting list over the years. In his first winter's work he enlarged the 3rd green and built a new 18th tee 'nearer the 17th green to overcome the drainage problem in that area',[4] while the 16th green was remodelled to create a flatter surface. Another significant improvement made in those early Pearce years was to have the course measured properly in order to change it from bogey to par.

When Colt had completed Swinley he believed his course to be 6,185 yards long, which rated it a bogie 74. There is an undated score card (possibly from the 1940s) which shows the course to be just 6,001 yards, but every subsequent attempt in the past to have the course measured was instantly vetoed as being too professional and therefore 'not Swinley'. It is possible that the members did not want to know the true yardage, as it had long been suspected that it was shorter than the official distance, which would thus undermine their golfing skills. For some unexplained reason, it was proposed that 'Eton College would be approached to attempt to obtain an accurate measurement for each hole', but they 'were unable to assist'.[5] Finally, Strokesaver were called in to measure the course with a laser EDM (Electronic Distance Meter), accurate to 1 cm. To everyone's surprise it turned out to be just 5,920 yards, 31 yards short of an SSS 69 (and 265 yards short of Colt's original measurement). When it was suggested that the SSS (standard scratch score) of 69, par 68, should be maintained, Pearce said that it could be achieved by adding 26 yards to the 1st hole and six yards to the 5th. The additional bunkering around the surrounds of the 5th green to tighten the approach meant that the 5th would become a par 5 and the 12th became a par 4. Later it was agreed that the course should be an SSS 70 (par 69) so the 15th hole was lengthened by a massive 54 yards to bring the course up to 6,005 yards. Over the years the course has been stretched and today it measures 6,062 yards, the extra 57 yards being divided between the 3rd, 6th and 14th holes.

The local county Golf Union is normally responsible for determining the par of a course, usually by deducting just one stroke from the SSS, but Swinley has never been a member of the Berkshire, Buckinghamshire and Oxford Golf Union so they merely deducted a stroke on their own. Swinley has always been a law unto itself. As it is not a member of the English Golf Union—under whose rules their members would have to compete in medal competitions, an anathema to Swinley—they cannot allocate official handicaps. So, in true Swinley fashion,

PLAYER'S NAME AND HANDICAP   **DATE**

M'ker's Score	Hole	Yards	Bogey	Stroke Index	Player's Score	Won + Lost − H'ved 0	M'ker's Score	Hole	Yards	Bogey	Stroke Index	Player's Score	Won + Lost − H'ved 0
	1	370	4					10	210	3			
	2	350	4					11	286	4			
	3	305	4					12	480	5			
	4	165	3					13	160	3			
	5	465	5					14	375	4			
	6	437	5					15	433	5			
	7	410	5					16	430	5			
	8	155	3					17	180	3			
	9	430	5					18	360	4			
	Out	3087	38					In	2914	36			
								Out	3087	38			
								Total	6001	74			

Marker's Signature...................................

Player's Signature ....

Holes Won ....   Gross Score ....

Holes Lost ....   Handicap   ....

RESULT   NET SCORE

Handicap

Net Score

Bogey Result

89 *The old score card before the course was electronically measured.*

if a member needs a handicap certificate, he or she merely hands in three score cards to the secretary, who works it out on the spot. Many a member remembers telephoning the secretary when a handicap was needed to play elsewhere, only to be asked, 'And what handicap would you like?'.[6] There are no handicaps for the in-house singles and foursome competitions, a comparatively recent event. When Timothy Steel won the first singles competition he asked Peter Wilmot-Sitwell if he should present a cup to the Club. Wilmot-Sitwell, who was on the committee at the time, shook his head and, to the great disappointment of Steel, replied that 'such a thing was definitely not Swinley'. Instead a golf ball with a discreet silver shield, engraved with the names of the winners of the singles and doubles competitions, is strung on two old hickory-shafted clubs, a putter and a mashie niblick, both made by Angus Macdonald (see page 92), over the fireplace in the sitting room.

Swinley have two comparatively recent annual fixtures, when they play Sunningdale and the Seniors. They will also sometimes turn out a side for some commemoration or pertinent tournament, such as the Colt Cup held at Stoke Poges for teams from Colt courses. They were the runners-up in 1994, the inaugural year. The Club will also field a side for like-minded groups such as the Nibblick Golf Society, made up of members from Augusta and Pine Valley. Swinley is often the chosen venue (along with such clubs as Sunningdale, The Berkshire, New Zealand, St George's, Rye and Worplesdon) for the Golf Match Club.

The Match Club was founded in 1896 'for the purpose of enabling members to dine together, and to make and play matches'.[7] Today there are around 80 members who meet for a black-tie dinner, usually at a club such as White's or Boodle's, on the third Thursday of the month between October and April, at which anything between 20 and 40 members turn up. The matches are made before dinner and the slip placed in Robin's Bowl, named after a former recorder Robin Ingram. After dinner the Recorder (at the time of writing George Pope) reads out the names, and those in the now smoke-free room bet on the outcome. The players themselves put in £50 each, while the other members' wagers can be for any amount. The matches have to be played before the next dinner, when the results are read out.

Since the 1920s the Swinley membership has not been noted for its great golfing prowess, with only a handful of handicaps in single figures at any one time (if they had handicaps at all). There have, however, been a few exceptions. Francis Ricardo was

> statistically the most successful member [of the Match Club] of those who played at least ten matches. He also took part in the largest post-1945 win, by 14 and 13, at Swinley with an unfortunate guest as one of the opponents. He won fifteen and lost three, an 83% success ratio.[8]

AMATEUR GOLF CHAMPIONSHIP.—Mr. E. F. Storey (Cambridge University) beat Mr. Roger Wethered (Worplesdon) yesterday in the semi-final round of the Amateur Golf Championship. A photograph of Mr Storey driving.

90 *Swinley members have rarely been noted for exceptional prowess on the golf course, but there has been the odd exception. When still a Cambridge undergraduate, Edward Storey played for Great Britain in the Walker Cup and was narrowly beaten in the final of the Amateur Golf Championship of 1922.*

Ricardo won the Belgian Amateur Championship in 1934, beating F. Francis at the Golf Club de Fagnes. Not surprisingly, he cited Addington as his club, not Swinley. Mr Toad, the true hero of Kenneth Grahame's *Wind in the Willows*, was based on his uncle and namesake, Colonel Francis Ricardo.

Undoubtedly the most proficient member of Swinley was Edward Francis Storey, who joined in 1932 and was created an honorary member in 1964. One of Storey's greatest triumphs in a long and successful playing career came in 1924. While still at Cambridge and Captain of the University side, he played for Great Britain in the Walker Cup at Garden City, Long Island, and competed in the British Amateur Golf Championship held at St Andrews. Although beaten in the Walker Cup, he made it easily to the semi-finals of the Amateur Golf Championship, where he beat Roger Wethered, the reigning champion. On the final the following day a cold wind blew a steady rain against Storey and Sir Ernest Holderness, the 1922 champion who had beaten Robert Harris of the Royal and Ancient 2 and 1 the day before. 'At the end of the first nine holes Storey was three up; and at the end of the first round Storey still led by one hole.'[9] The second round proved fatal to Storey, when Holderness beat him 3 and 2 to become 'Amateur Champion of all Britain'.

The same semi-finalists were all united in the British Walker Cup team of 1926, that year played at St Andrews. 'Storey had taken the measure of the U.S. *enfant terrible*, Roland Mackenzie' to level the scores. At the last hole of the last match Harris needed to hole out with the final putt, but the ball stopped two inches short and Britain was denied victory. Storey was again in the British team for the 1928 Walker Cup in Chicago, playing in the foursomes with T.A. Torrance, but yet again they lost to the Americans and Storey was subsequently dropped from the side. That same year he stayed on in the United States to play in the American Amateur Championships.

E.F. Storey continued to play competition golf for the rest of his life, quite often on the international circuit. He represented England between 1924 and 1936, sometimes as Captain, seven times against Scotland, and once each against Ireland and Wales. He was the leading amateur in the 1938 Open. Storey was distinguished as much by his sartorial style as by his golfing prowess—his amateur status was once threatened when a golf clothing manufacturer used a photograph of him in an advertisement without his permission. He died aged 89 in 1990. Throughout his long and successful golfing career Storey played variously as a member of Cambridge University, West Hill, Royal Worlington and Sunningdale, but never Swinley, which he reserved for his fun and less competitive golf.

Towards the end of January 1936 Edward Storey was playing at Swinley in the teeth of a gale. He went out in 33, and by the time he drove off from the 15th he was 6 under. With the strong wind behind him a massive drive brought him to the bottom of the hill. It was there he made his first mistake of a near-perfect round. Taking out a long iron into the green he seriously over-hit the shot. He cursed his mistake as he watched it soar into the air with the gale behind it. But luck was on his side. The ball struck the top of the pin, and the linen flag wrapped around it and then released it onto the green a few inches from the hole. With this eagle at the 15th, and a birdie at the 17th, he came back in 31. This magnificent score of 64 is still a course record; the card is on display at the bottom of the back stairs, beside the rainfall details.

E.F. Storey.   Before starting insert Handicap Strokes (thus :   in Bogey Column.   Date. 26/1/36

Length in Yards	No.	BOGEY	Strokes	Won X Lost — Halved O	Length in Yards	No.	BOGEY	Strokes	Won X Lost — Halved O
370	1	4	4		210	10	3	3	
350	2	4	4		250	11	4	3	
305	3	4	3		480	12	5	5	
165	4	3	3		160	13	3	3	
465	5	5	4		375	14	4	4	
390	6	5	4		430	15	5	3	
395	7	5	4		430	16	5	4	
155	8	3	2		180	17	3	2	
430	9	5	5		360	18	4	4	
3025		38	33		2875		36	31	

BOGEY RESULT

HOLES UP.......... or HOLES DOWN.........

Marker's Sig. L. Garnett.

TOTAL............... IN 33

H'CAP ....

OUT 64.

S.S.S. 70

91   *Edward Storey's remarkable score card, January 1936. Storey over-hit on the 15th with a gale behind him but the ball was caught in the flag and dropped a few inches from the hole.*

In Pearce's early years there were many changes among the green-staff. After 40 years' service (where he never missed a day through illness), the assistant green-keeper Stan Baker retired. Strong and silent, and a familiar figure in his black beret, he had perfected the art of top-dressing a green with a shovel, the sand falling evenly in exactly the right amount over the whole green. Bill Barrie, the head green-keeper, also retired after just 18 years and was replaced by Gordon Smith, formerly of Liphook Golf Club. He began by shaving the greens to make them faster, as had been the custom at his erstwhile Hampshire course. The cut was followed by seven weeks of blistering heat and six greens were out of action, the worst being the 16th which looked as if it would never recover. But recover it did with the arrival of Lawson Bingham as course manager. The damage to the 16th is still spoken of in hushed tones.

Lawson Bingham began his career by caddying for the secretary of Prestwick Golf Club every Sunday, and it was he who suggested that at the age of 16 Bingham should work one summer holiday with the green-staff. He loved it so much that he left school to work there full-time. Bingham could not have had a better grounding, serving under the head green-keeper, David Wright, formerly of Muirfield and Gullane. A man of exacting standards and great knowledge, Wright was a true traditionalist, one 'of the old school'—he had Bingham mowing the greens by hand. Four years later Wright announced his retirement and his job was offered to Bingham, although there were others more senior to him with greater experience. He took over the next

year and spent '21 very happy years' there. He would have stayed there forever had Sunningdale not offered him a massive increase in salary, and so he came south in 1994. Bingham was later approached by an executive from the Trust House Forte Group who were sponsoring the Seniors Championship at Sunningdale. They asked him initially to look at their new course at the Penina Hotel in the Algarve, and again he was lured there by 'a substantial rise in salary'. When Trust House Forte was taken over everything changed, and the Algarve became unbearable for Bingham and his family. Soon

92 *It is not difficult to find Lawson Bingham on the course at Swinley as his harbinger, his collie dog Breeze, is invariably there before him. Bingham is a natural for Swinley, being of the 'old school'. He was head green-keeper at Prestwick aged 21, then Sunningdale followed by a blip in the Algarve before his appointment as course manager at Swinley.*

after, Bingham was telephoned by Gordon Smith, asking about green-keeping jobs abroad. So the ball was set in motion, and came to rest with Ian Pearce asking him to come for an interview. Sir Roger Gibbs and a full committee offered him the job immediately, and Lawson Bingham started in May 1996. He was fortunate to work with Peter Hill-Wood, chairman of Arsenal Football Club and the member of the committee responsible for the course.

While Swinley is fortunate to have Lawson Bingham as course manager, he is equally lucky to be at Swinley. They complement each other perfectly, as both hold with traditional values and the old-fashioned ways. It could be any season of the year, at any time of the day, in any weather, and the course can be guaranteed to be looking marvellous, although in the words of Mrs Stanley Baldwin, 'there are always those who have disapproval in their eyes eternally looking for somewhere to place it'.

The improvements and alterations to the course came hard on the heels of the much-needed renovations and improvements to the clubhouse. When Pearce was entertaining his Sunningdale counterpart Stewart Zuill in the sitting room, they began their drinks by the window, but the cold air coming through the ill-fitting windows was so 'fresh' that they moved further and further away until they found themselves huddling in the back of the hall. Clearly, in the words of the Prince of Wales addressing the plight of the Welsh miners, 'something had to be done'.

In 1993 the chairman, the Hon. Edward Baillieu (always known as Ted), supported by the secretary Ian Pearce and a strong and experienced committee with a wide range of expertise, was in an ideal position to tackle the much-needed renovations and proposed alterations. After the chairman, the longest-serving member of the committee was Malcolm Pearson, later Lord Pearson of Rannoch. He was once playing a singles, followed all too closely by two big-hitters from Sunningdale. Thrice the Sunningdale members hit into them: thrice they retreated. When they were all in the bar afterwards Pearson launched into one of them, a close friend since pre-prep school days. The tirade went on and on. Pearson expressed the hope that they would never come to Swinley again, but that if they did they would show some manners. Two members of the committee witnessed the outburst and then looked at each other, each with the same thought—this young man of 33 should be on the committee. Pearson accepted the invitation, being no stranger to controversy. Gerald Bristowe, Andrew Martin Smith, Roger Gibbs and Fergus Hughes-Onslow were the other members.

The fabric of the clubhouse had been let go during years of neglect by the previous secretary, Tom Ingham, but it was only when Health and Safety visited the clubhouse and found that there was no fire escape for the housekeeper that the committee was forced into action. It was then that the whole of the front of the building, in the teeth of the prevailing wind, was found to be riddled with wet rot (*Merulius lacrymans*)—19 gallons of water were removed from around the main beam—with dry rot (*Serpula lacrymans*) in the sitting room. Moreover, the kitchens were antiquated.

93 *Being in the teeth of the prevailing south-west wind, the façade of Swinley clubhouse suffered badly. Much of the membership were opposed to any kind of restoration, but when completed they barely noticed the difference.*

While it was obvious that the repairs were essential and had to be done as quickly as possible, it made sense that any alterations thought necessary should be carried out at the same time. But with an institution as conservative as Swinley it came as no surprise that the proposals attracted a wide variety of opinions from all sections of the membership. Most welcomed the proposals, but change (the word is hardly synonymous with Swinley) in any form was to be resisted by a certain faction. Fergus Hughes-Onslow drew a parallel between the Swinley plans and the installation of central heating to replace individual fireplaces in the Boys' Houses at Eton that had been 'wildly deplored' some 30 years before. The secretary, who could not understand this opposition, looked for some common factor among the objectors and deduced that a proportion were also members of the Royal West Norfolk Golf Club at Brancaster. When he went there one weekend he found 'it more in need of a face-lift than Swinley'.[10]

The dissent was loud and vociferous. Certain elements of the membership resented the autocratic way in which the proposals were being foisted on them, particularly after the Annual General Meeting where those attending were outraged to hear from the chairman that 'strictly interpreting the Club's Rules, the committee was not obliged to consult the Membership about [the] large planned expenditure'.[11]

Letters pointing out that 'the Chairman and committee … are dealing with a Membership of above average intelligence who will not respond favourably to being told what to do' flooded in and there was 'a <u>deep</u> groundswell of dissatisfaction about certain attitudes shown [at the AGM]'.[12] Most telling was the question: 'Who actually owns the Club?'

Nor were all the committee entirely happy about how the proposed changes were sold to the membership—after the AGM Andrew Martin Smith wrote 'that there was a cry for more open government'.[13] The same went for the works themselves. To the irritation of the chairman, the committee would not rubber-stamp his proposals. There were endless discussions as to how much should be done, and when. But the principle that 'if something was questioned, it did not necessarily mean that it was not agreed upon'[14] was not always appreciated by the chairman, who took opposition to his plans as dissent.

Again, it was Andrew Martin Smith who voiced his concern that the 'past ideals' of Swinley were being 'subordinated to the economic realities' that faced the Club. 'The consequence of this has been that we cater more and more for the non-member, visiting society because it is they who are using the club and paying the bills and not the club.' Further, he was concerned that the rebuilding of the Club's finances and taking the course in hand was

94 *Nearly back after a Sunday morning round. It is the dream of many a golfer to play at Swinley.*

having too material an influence on the direction we are taking the club for the longer term. Swinley is a special place for many different reasons but most of all because it has a character which is both exclusive and unpretentious. We do not differentiate between visiting societies, non-member visitors and members. The course and clubhouse does not lend itself to large parties and Swinley has an atmosphere in which, rather like a family Sunday lunch, everyone is there by connection and invitation. In the interests of the club's finances, and because it is under-utilised, we have made Swinley more accessible. This policy, while financially successful, may be damaging the fabric of the place and is not necessarily the only route for preserving the club for the future. [15]

Another area for discussion was whether it was necessary to have two changing rooms, as in the view of some of the committee it would create an 'unwanted distinction'. To them, if visiting societies' money was good enough for them to play at Swinley (and so subsidise the members' subscriptions) then they should be treated as day members and so share their facilities.

After much discussion and a great deal of angst all the works were put in hand, to be done simultaneously with the repairs to the fabric of the building. It was a triumph, with most of the credit being due to Fergus Hughes-Onslow, the prime mover of the whole scheme. Peter Bedford wrote of him: 'To persuade the

members to accept this large spend required skilful advocacy'; that he and the architect 'obtained unanimous agreement to go ahead with these plans [was] quite an achievement where Swinley members are concerned!' [16] Sadly Fergus Hughes-Onslow did not see the results of his great contribution, as he died before the works were completed.

As nothing had been done for such a long time the proposals appeared far more drastic and more expensive than if they had been done piecemeal. Apart from the basics of rewiring, plumbing and eradicating the wet and dry rot, the new works could hardly have been described as radical. The bar was

95 *On the first day of the cricket season, Fergus Hughes-Onslow holds a copy of* Wisden Cricketers' Almanack. *He was a prime mover in 'selling' the improvements and renovation of the clubhouse to the members, likening their opposition to the Swinley proposals to the decision to replace the individual fires with central heating in the Boys' Houses at Eton.*

extended into what had been the ladies' changing room so that two people could work together at busy times. The ladies' changing room was in turn moved upstairs into part of what had been a small staff flat, a vast improvement on the past when they had had to sidle through the bar to change. The men's changing room was enlarged and generally upgraded and the secretary's office was extended. Finally, a balustrade was added to the parapet off the dining room.

At what was probably the right time Baillieu stood down as chairman, his 'reforms' well in hand. In a letter to Ian Pearce, Lord Pearson of Rannoch wrote:

> … could I record my admiration for the truly excellent job you [Pearce] and Ted [Baillieu] have done as Secretary and Chairman over recent years? I think that you have proved beyond doubt that Swinley is best run on a day-to-day basis by an active chairman and a first-class Secretary, supported and occasionally guided by a non-executive committee of broad experience and interest.[17]

And so Sir Roger Gibbs was thrust into the role of chairman, which he agreed to take on for no more than three years. His style was totally different from that of his predecessor—his first committee meeting lasted four hours. He was a good choice, being a fine communicator with long experience of running committees and raising large sums of money—he is credited with turning around the bleak fortunes of the St Moritz Tobogganing Club (which operates the Cresta Run) with its multifarious, multinational membership. Tall, debonair and modest, Sir Roger is said to be 'the only man to have written more books [1] than he has read: [and] the only man who has more honorary degrees [4] than O levels'.[18] Notwithstanding his poor showing at Eton (where he, Peter Hill-Wood and Edward Cazalet had an all-too-close association with the local bookmaker), he went on to a glittering career in the City, finishing as chairman of the Wellcome Trust, the massive independent charity, which funds research to improve human and animal health.

Sir Roger was the proverbial new broom. Unlike many of his predecessors, he was kept in line by the members of his committee, in particular:

> Peter Wilmot-Sitwell (a natural stirrer of the highest quality), Hugh Stevenson (immensely able) [the present chairman of Swinley], and the treasurer, Peter Bedford who was damned good. You couldn't get away with anything as chairman on that committee—almost entirely due to Sitwell. Old friends are there to keep you on your toes.[19]

He had also had the advantage of serving on Baillieu's committee, where he held the watching brief over the building works, and fielding the complaints of the membership—nearly 80 letters that ranged from 'voicing suspicion' to 'roundly condemning the scheme'.

96 *All-round action man and chairman of Swinley and the Wellcome Trust, Sir Roger Gibbs steered the committee through the financing of the renovations and improvements. He was President of the St Moritz Tobogganing Club and ran the London Marathon aged 55, raising nearly £½ million for a new body-scanner for Guy's Hospital in London.*

The funding, started in the reign of Ted Baillieu, was finally agreed upon under Roger Gibbs. They began by selling life memberships to those over 65 on a sliding scale, and allowing in one new member for each life membership sold. The subscription was nearly doubled to £600, and the membership increased from 225 to 300. The ladies side, traditionally one tenth of the male membership, was increased from 25 to 30. The entry fee, ridiculously below that of all the neighbouring clubs, was increased from £1,000 to £3,000. As at that time the average age was well over 60, there was also a real push to introduce younger members, starting at age 27—the chairman was ribbed as he had several nephews of that age on the waiting list, although only one did in fact become a member.

Loans, linked to discounted membership dues, were raised from members and the rates for societies were dramatically increased.

And so work started on the renovation of the clubhouse, which remained open despite the builders' mess. 'The membership was incredibly patient— they took it on the chin. The societies too, although they knew if they ever cancelled their day they would never get back.'[20] Just when the building subcommittee were priding themselves on bringing the project in on budget, it was found that the whole roof had to be replaced, thus throwing their finances out. But it had to be done, and the money was found. In the end the

clubhouse was reopened to the general approval of the membership. It looked exactly the same as before—rather like at Balmoral, where worn-out fabrics are replaced with exactly the same material and rooms repainted in the same colours, suitably aged so that nobody notices any difference. But the 'new broom' did not stop with the building and finance.

Peter Wilmot-Sitwell was a sub-committee of one, responsible for the management of the house, including the catering. Not long after he had taken over, an American visitor came up to him and asked how often he changed the menu. Wilmot-Sitwell scratched his head and said, 'I don't really know, I think it was some time around 1892!' Nothing changed after the Hon. Michael Spring Rice took over, save that the vegetables became rather more *al dente* (which prompted one member to complain that he could not 'squash his Brussels sprouts!') and the tinned apricots were replaced with tinned peaches at the chairman's request. Rice pudding is still a permanent fixture at Swinley, ever since the Prince

97 *Peter Wilmot-Sitwell, stalwart committee member of Swinley and, according to the chairman, 'a natural stirrer of the highest quality' who kept him on his toes and very much in line.*

of Wales brought James Braid into the clubhouse. The Prince had been playing with the professional at the nearby Royal Berkshire Golf Club and took him for lunch after their game. The secretary reminded him of the rules that professionals could not even enter the clubhouse and that Braid was therefore not welcome. The Prince of Wales was incensed. He removed their Royal status and drove straight to Swinley for lunch, where Braid tucked in happily to the rice pudding.

After the equipment in the kitchen had been completely renewed and stringent hygiene practices introduced, it was all the more surprising that there was an outbreak of food poisoning among the guests of the Jockey Club who had taken a day. It was very serious, and one of the caddies nearly died. Ministry food inspectors were called in and exhaustive checks were carried out. In the end Swinley was given a clean bill of health, and the virus was traced to the Jockey Club's egg, chicken, tomato and mayonnaise sandwiches that had spent the night in the boot of a senior steward's car.

Through careful management the bank loans for all the renovations and improvements were all paid off within three years, mostly through increased society days and subscriptions, with the members' loans being redeemed by 2002. As promised, Roger Gibbs, described as 'brilliant in this role', resigned as chairman of his supportive committee, his job well done.

There was then the question of a successor. Peter Wilmot-Sitwell was the obvious candidate and initially accepted the post, but in the end had to turn it down as it suddenly conflicted with his business commitments. But it was up to him to provide a replacement. He had in fact been playing with Jo Floyd and Sir John Milne (chairmen of Christie's and Blue Circle Industries respectively) a few days before, and recalled that they had done nothing but complain the whole way round about the state of Swinley. With this in mind he felt that either of them would make an admirable chairman, even though neither of them had ever served on the committee. Sir John had retired from Blue Circle Cement (where he was

98 *Sir John 'Cement' Milne was delighted to take up the challenge as chairman of Swinley, as he felt that nobody ever asks anyone to do anything aged over seventy. Compared with the upheavals of his predecessor, his six-year tenure was 'happy, if undemanding'.*

known variously as 'Cement' Milne or 'Lord Cement') and was delighted to take it on—he once maintained that on reaching 70 nobody ever asked 'one to do anything'. He was an admirable choice. According to one of his committee: 'It would be hard to find a more affable and sporting fellow', adding that he was 'a most amusing story-teller'.[21] Compared with the vast changes that had been dealt with by his predecessor, Sir John Milne's tenure was 'a happy, if undemanding one'. What was more, he fitted the role perfectly. Swinley is unique in that there is no captain appointed annually, just a chairman who usually serves around five years, which tends to preserve a sense of continuity. But, given the kind of membership at Swinley, it is sometimes necessary to have a high-profile figure with the standing, on rare occasions, to deal with a recalcitrant member.

Societies have always been a particular feature of Swinley, opening the course to many thousands who might otherwise never play there. With its strong military background, they began with mostly Service golfing societies, notably the Brigade of Guards and the Green Jackets, London Clubs and Livery Companies, who traditionally played on Tuesdays and Thursdays. As late as the 1960s it was suggested that there should be only one society day, as it put too much work on the staff. But from the very outset these days have always been a contentious issue: income versus privacy. In 1983 J.R. Henderson, a member since 1947, spearheaded a move to cut down on non-member societies. Johnny Henderson had been serving in the 12th Royal Lancers in North Africa when he was sent to the 8th Army Headquarters in Cairo as a trial ADC to General Montgomery. By his own admission he was totally unsuited to the post, but when he had his hat eaten by an elephant at the zoo on a ceremonial occasion it 'seemed to convince Montgomery that he was worth a longer apprenticeship'.[22] The unlikely pair remained together for the rest of the war. Henderson left the Army to go into the City, where his directorships were legion—Cazenoves, Hendersons, Barclays Bank, Whitbread and more. A successful owner, his greatest contribution to racing was to set up the Racecourse Holdings Trust that was to save Cheltenham from the developers. Other provincial courses followed, famously including Aintree thus saving the Grand National. His younger son Harry is now a member.

Henderson was typical of the faction who tended to play during the week and so wished for fewer society days, as opposed to those who played mostly at the weekends, who positively relished the societies to keep the subscription down. But the societies continued very much as before, although all agreed that 'Swinley was a premium venue for corporate golf and the club's charges should be raised sharply to reflect this fact'.[23] There was a time when, 'in the light of the very favourable financial status', Hugh Stevenson, the present chairman, suggested 'creating Friday as a free day except for those Societies sponsored by a member'.[24] In true Swinley fashion, the secretary was to report back, and life continued exactly as before. But the subject would not go away; Rupert Hambro and Peter Wilmot-Sitwell proposed that 'all Societies on a Friday in July and August be cancelled and the course reserved for the exclusive use of Members'. Again it was thought that the 'suggestion … would lead to an unnecessary rise in subscriptions and probably a deserted golf course'. [25] The matter was finally laid to rest at the AGM, where it was agreed that 'the loss of income was not in the best interest of the membership', and there the matter rests.

As evidenced by the queue of societies wishing to take days, Swinley Forest Golf Club continues to be a victim of its own success. It is quite unique, although courses like the Royal West Norfolk come close. Swinley relies on the quality and beauty of the challenging course, rather than competitions hosted, for its undoubted fame. 'It is perhaps the finest example of the pleasure there is to be had from heathland golf', [26] Tony Jacklin wrote when voting Swinley his fourth most favourite course after Pebble Beach in Carmel, California, St Andrews and Portrush. It is unashamedly exclusive—'it simply smells of old money, just like stepping back in time', as one golf commentator has it. It is well known at Swinley that 'a dukedom doesn't impress people there much, and an earldom not in the slightest'. [27] It is unpretentious, too, 'with none of the glamour of its near neighbours Sunningdale and Wentworth'—it is said that 'members of The Berkshire Golf Club are all gentlemen and love to play golf; all the Sunningdale members love to play golf but not all are gentlemen; and all the Swinley Forest members are gentlemen but don't give a fig whether they play golf or not'. [28] Others have it that 'if joining The Berkshire and Sunningdale is golf's equivalent of being invited to Buckingham Palace, then becoming a member at Swinley Forest is like entering the Sovereign's bedroom'. [29] Paul Daniels, the television magician, tells the story of a man who is driven to suicide by golf. He is in the locker room of his club, wrists slashed, bleeding into the basin.

> 'So you have decided it's all too much then?', says his golfing partner of many years.
>
> 'Yes, it's all over. I hate this awful game,' the man replies. 'Goodbye. You can have the electric trolley; the Pings go to old Bert, and any spare balls in the locker, give them to the youngsters.'
>
> 'That's such a shame,' replies his friend. 'Because we're one short for Swinley Forest tomorrow.'
>
> Suddenly, banging his wrists together to stem the flow of blood, the would-be suicide looks up and says in a faltering voice: 'What time?' [30]

But Swinley is not to everyone's taste. Sir Sean Connery played there only once, with John Davies, the Walker Cup player, and declared: 'Quite frankly, I wasn't very impressed!' [31] His is a minority view, for Swinley has invariably featured prominently in the golfing league tables from the very beginning. It was rated variously the 10th best course in Great Britain by *Golfing Monthly* magazine, 36th in the world by

Golf World, while *Golf Digest* voted Swinley one of the hundred best courses outside the United States. It is no surprise that the list of prospective members grew and grew, to unmanageable proportions. With only eight or nine vacancies each year and over 300 prospective candidates, the whole process was clearly out of control. The Hon. Michael Spring Rice, formerly of the Irish Guards, agreed to look into the matter and come up with a proposal. Both Sunningdale and The Berkshire (who had recently overcome a similar problem) were consulted and, based on his findings, the system was finally brought under control.

After 18 years as secretary Ian Pearce took early retirement and went to live in Spain. By his own admission Pearce was somewhat introverted, and not a good communicator—'he could walk from his office to the front door on a Sunday when the place was humming with people and not say a word to a single member, their wife or guests'.[32] Nor was he universally popular with the membership, who generally disliked the number and background of the society days, which they attributed solely to him. In his undeniable defence, when he was secretary, 'Swinley has flourished as never before, so his contribution to its success is probably much underrated'.[33] His innovations on the course were generally seen as improvements and he had other good ideas. He instigated the Fun Day just before Christmas, when the course was played backwards. He put together the whole package, the stroke index and the card, but the chairman, Ted Baillieu, vetoed the idea. The committee over-ruled him and the competition went ahead. It was a great success, save for the chairman, who 'on purpose played the course by himself (with dog) the normal way and naturally messed everyone up'.[34] That day was won by Miles Maskell and Simon Bradley with a very low score.

After a general shake-up the professional Stuart Hill, who had come from The Berkshire in 2002, took over the organisation of the society days, while the house manager John Fribbance has the added responsibility for the catering. The one enduring link, who 'has kept the whole show on the rails'[35] over the last 16 years, is Mrs B. Martin, known to all as Annette. After much discussion the committee decided that they did not need a full-time secretary, and were fortunate to find Stewart Zuill to take on the post on a part-time basis. A softly spoken Scot and a fine player, Zuill had (like Harry Colt nearly a century before) been secretary of Sunningdale.

Late in 1909, when Harry Shapland Colt began thinking about a new course that was to become Swinley Forest Golf Club, he clearly felt that he could create something special with the land available, and was indeed fortunate that those acres lent themselves so well to his genius and visionary approach to golf course design. Colt was also fortunate to be joined at the outset by Sir Hubert Longman, with his experience in founding Sunningdale, and Lord Derby, with his vast wealth and influential circle of friends. Theirs was an unbeatable combination, one that saw the course built to Colt's exacting standards and set the tone of the membership and

99 *One of the greatest golf course designers of all time, Harry Shapland Colt died on 21 November 1951 aged 82. In his career, he participated in the design of more than 300 golf courses, 115 in his sole right. Long gone are the days when the sun never set on the British Empire, but today the sun still never sets on a Colt course.*

the understated style that has lasted, virtually unaltered, to the present day. As a club, part of its success can be attributed to the right staff being employed by a strong management team drawn from landowners, the armed forces and the City, which has engendered loyalty and unparalleled lengths of service. Today there is as good a team, if not better, as ever in the past.

Swinley is an anachronism, living in its Edwardian past. But it is an anachronism that works. Nearly one hundred years on, the membership is drawn from virtually the same families, with a few boasting an unbroken line from a founding member. All subscribe to the original ideals and criteria—'a quiet atmosphere, with agreeable colleagues and an old-fashioned lunch'.[36] The course, too, although stretched for modern play, would still be recognised by Colt, his legacy carefully preserved by the present course manager. It is undeniably true that Swinley 'packs more interesting shots and possesses more memorable holes'[37] than any 7,000-yard course built since the last war—no wonder Colt himself would talk about 'craving for my usual game around the Swinley Forest Course' after he had moved away to Oxfordshire. Harry Colt always maintained that the real test of a course was, 'Is it going to live?' By his own admission Swinley Forest Golf Club was Harry Colt's 'least bad course'. It is alive and well today as it looks forward to the next century and beyond, the enviable model of a course and club.

100 *Swinley has always been understated – even the signpost is barely visible from the road, as many a visitor will testify after having been up and down Coronation Road many times looking for the place.*

EPILOGUE

On a glorious Sunday in early June, one that P.G. Wodehouse's Oldest Member would have described as 'where all nature cried fore', a comparatively young member set out to impress his new girlfriend by taking her to Swinley. They had lunch in the clubhouse, and then went out to play the 18 holes in the cool of the afternoon on a completely deserted course. It was all a great success. When she returned to her home in Cornwall she mentioned the game to her father, himself a proficient golfer.

'I can't remember where we went, but it was a perfectly magical place outside London. It was incredibly beautiful,' she enthused. 'There was not a soul about, so we had the whole place to ourselves. Lunch was fantastic, with just the nicest staff imaginable. I came away thinking that I had been somewhere very special.'

'There is only one place in the whole world where that could be,' replied her father, stifling the envy in his voice, 'and that is Swinley Forest Golf Club.'

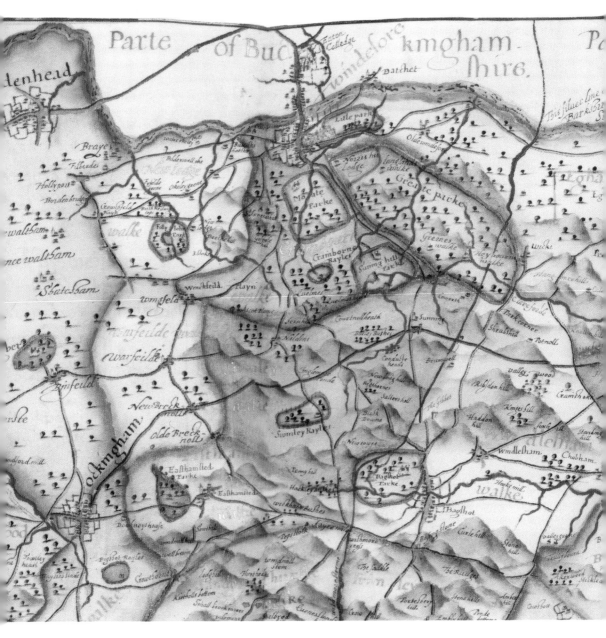

101 *Detail of John Norden's Survey of the Honor of Windsor, 1607. Swinely Forest Golf Club is just to the east of Swinley Rayles.*

Appendix i
Swinley Forest Golf Club
Hole by Hole

In the report in *The Times* of the 1999 US Open held at Pinehurst, North Carolina, the course was compared with Swinley with its 'glorious, sandy-based turf underfoot and fairways that are lined by trees that do not come into play'.[1] The comparison went further. Donald Ross, who had designed the course in the early years of the last century after emigrating from Dornoch, wanted players to experience 'the infinite variety of short-game options'. Like Colt at Swinley, Ross believed that the most desirable approach shots 'are those which take the ball over little knolls, undulations and hillocks, instead of absolutely flat and smooth country. Obviously, when such elements govern the approach to the green, the golfing merits of the course are infinitely superior'.[2] And when on the greens, 'errant balls roll off casually exploring nooks and crannies until settling on a spot where gravity can influence them no longer'. Harry Colt went even further; as those who are privileged to play at Swinley Forest Golf Club know, it is an incomparable course.

The First—par 4
Blue: 389 yards (Colt 380)
White: 364 yards
Yellow: 362 yards
Red: 342 yards

This medium-length par 4 plays longer than it appears through the gentle rise from 'the landing area to the green'.[3] From the elevated tee the expansive fairway is even more impressive than from Colt's original tee, which was tucked in to the left at the end of the trees. The fairway, with its grassed rough, lacks the ubiquitous heather that is to follow on the next hole, and is protected on the right by a flanking fairway bunker. In Colt's day the main fairway was slightly further to the left, as can be seen by the old, and typical, Colt cross-bunker immediately

102 *The 1st hole at Swinley Forest Golf Club was always played as a Mulligan: to a few, it still is today. The tee position has been modified twice since Colt's original to gain a few yards on the first hole.*

below what was Colt's original green (to the left of the present one). This too is 'classic Colt, one that displays gentle borrows and is ringed with drop-offs and mouldings that tie into, and off, the green'. It is here that a significant part of Swinley's greatness can first be appreciated—there are no straight putts to be had anywhere on the course. Colt strongly maintained that flat putting surfaces offered neither challenge nor pleasure, and would later design other courses, such as the original Eden Course (1913) at St Andrews, with boldly contoured green surfaces and surrounds.

The first hole was always played as a Mulligan, and to many a member it still is. It has been the scene of many a mishap, often caused by nervousness or lack of practice. John Brennan recalls his first visit to Swinley. It was the stuff dreams are made of, but in his case all too real at the time.

I was young, a bad golfer and extremely nervous. Walking towards the course I spotted Henry Cotton with Lord Forte on the putting green. There, on the first tee, was Sir Archibald Forbes, Chairman of the Midland Bank (where I had an unhealthy overdrawn account) practising his swing. He asked us to go ahead. With the usual first tee nerves, I struck the ball. Inevitably, I sliced it badly and watched in horror as it veered towards two players coming up the 18th fairway. 'Fore', I shouted, rehearsing my apologies as I sheepishly walked over to them.

As I approached, one of them, who was an American, said with a great smile on his face: 'Gee, that was a wild one!'

I took another look at him. It was Bing Crosby.[4]

In fact Sir Archibald would have been on the ladies tee, where he played against his friends on the men's tee. 'As he was so grand and important nobody liked to say that it was a bit rough.'[5] Nor was he alone. Sir John Aird (see page 126), the 3rd baronet and chairman in the 1960s, also played off the ladies' tee, while his wife, the Lady Priscilla (*née* Heathcote-Drummond-Willoughby), played off the men's tee. She was the daughter of the 26th Lord Willoughby de Eresby, an original bondholder of Swinley (see page 45). Their daughter Susie Aird is now a 5-day member. It was here that the last of a fourball to drive off hooked badly and sent his ball onto the railway line. The dreadful shot was followed by a loud expletive, 'F★★★ing son-in-law'. When asked to explain what his son-in-law had to do with his appalling golf, he replied, 'Not quite what one would have hoped for!'

The 1st hole tragically claimed the life of Fergus Hughes-Onslow, he who had done so much on the clubhouse improvements. On 23 November 1994 he was playing with Christopher Watson and Ronnie Taylor (and his dog Peppi).

C'est visible. Le colonel Aird est un débutant, dit Cotton. Ses tenues (vestimentaire et physique) sont d'un novice.

103 *Sir Archibald Forbes, chairman of the Midland Bank, and Sir John Aird, a great courtier and chairman of Swinley in the 1960s, both played off the forward ladies' tee. Although never a great golfer, Sir John (left) certainly did not deserve this harsh criticism from Cotton of his style shown in the south of France.*

He had teed off and nearly reached the green when he suddenly felt dizzy and sat down. He told his companions to go ahead. They would not abandon him, and he died soon after from a massive cardiac arrhythmia. Later, Peter Bedford said of him: 'I can think of few members who have made a greater contribution to the wellbeing of the club during my time as a member.'[6] His widow Minnie presented the bookcase in the sitting room to the Club in his memory.

A perennial topic brought up at the AGM by David Norman was the creation of a lake running across the 1st and 18th holes by the stream. The notion was finally laid to rest by Sir John Milne when chairman, who felt that 'along with the older members, he would not derive much enjoyment hitting balls into a lake at the beginning and the end of what could well have been a disappointing round'.[7]

The Second—par 4
Blue: 367 yards (Colt 370 yards)
White: 356 yards
Yellow: 334 yards
Red: 281 yards

This is the only recorded hole that was altered by Harry Colt in all the years that he was associated with Swinley, when he was 'instructed to make a grass fairway to the left of the carry bunker from the 2nd tee to enable short players to play round the bunker instead of short of it in the heather.[8] Colt's original green has crept back to its present position, hard against the heather ridge, in the very apex of the triangle of land owned by Swinley. The hole starts with a blind drive over a hill, with two gaping, heather-draped cross-bunkers placed at the top. Once in sight of the green, the fairway slopes from right to left to capture the errant, pulled drive. Playing downhill on the next shot, 'it is difficult to realise the extent to which the green surface falls away from the line of play, which is not apparent from the elevated position, so a carefully gauged shot is required to bounce short and right of the pin position'. A snaking, open ditch runs across the fairway some 40 yards short of the green. This originally led into a gully that wraps itself around the left side of the green, while a deep bunker at the rear traps those shots that are struck too boldly.

There is a close affinity between Swinley and the St James's Street Clubs, where discussing business is taboo but everyone does it so long as they are not seen or heard to be doing it and there are no papers involved. The golf course is a very different matter, where privacy and intimacy are guaranteed. It is an ideal place. 'One of the great things about golf,' declares Peter Wilmot-Sitwell, 'is that you have a captive audience. You have the man for 3½ hours. You don't look at him as you walk down the fairway, so there is no eye contact. If you bog it, you can always make sure your ball goes in one direction and his in another to give yourself a good five or six minutes to get your act together.'[9] A classic example at Swinley was a massive deal struck on the 2nd fairway. When it was announced that the Wellcome Trust was to sell its holdings in Wellcome Plc, Peter Wilmot-Sitwell's 'greedy colleagues' at Warburg Securities told him to contact his great friend, Sir Roger Gibbs, 'to get the business'. He telephoned the chairman in his office.

'Ha, ha, ha, Petesie, I know what you want,' Gibbs laughed. 'There is absolutely no chance of you being involved. We've got Cazenove, BZW, Flemings—there just isn't room for you.'

Wilmot-Sitwell said he quite understood, but added that they had just done a deal that was similar which might be helpful. They arranged to play at Swinley the following Saturday, and there, on the 2nd fairway, Gibbs reminded him of their telephone conversation and 'the clever way of doing the thing'. With that Gibbs invited Warburgs to pitch for the business, which they eventually secured. 'That was a prime example', Wilmot-Sitwell recalls, 'of what a wonderful business game golf is.' When it was all over and a great success, Gibbs wrote to his friend thanking him and the team for all their support. Then came the postscript: 'But you needn't have lost 2 and 1 in order to get the business!'

The 2nd green is closest to the railway line. Once a member was playing accompanied by a caddie called George Draper, always known as 'Dordy', as he could not pronounce his G's. When the member asked, 'What's the line, caddie?', Dordy replied smartly, 'Ascot to Camberley, Sir!'

The Third—par 4
Blue: 290 yards (Colt 325 yards)
White: 288 yards
Yellow: 280 yards
Red: 264 yards

This is another mystery Colt hole. Although the green today is in exactly the same position, Colt had his tee forward and far to the right of the present tee on the edge of the trees and just behind the path, yet his measurement is 35 yards longer. It is a short and slightly uphill par 4 dog-leg left that requires a precise positional drive to either side of the fairway (depending upon pin position), as the elevated green is pinched at both sides by flanking bunkers. The approach shot must be precise, as there are three distinctive subtle levels on the green's melded surface. 'It can be taken on from the tee, but the drive must finish on the fairway or green, otherwise the golfer is left with a testing recovery from thick rough or heather.'

It is thus quite remarkable that anyone should achieve a hole-in-one here, but it was managed by Joel Cadbury, playing as guest of his stepfather Robin d'Abo in April 1996. It was a unique shot that Ian Pearce put down to 'an extraordinary

104 *Swinley mechanised slowly, sometimes due to the munificence of Lord Derby as with this adapted 1925 Morris commercial van with a home-made pick-up back and spiked wheels.*

fluke; it's a long shot and a very difficult green to get into'.[10] There was a sharp intake of breath from some of the members (and great embarrassment from Cadbury) when his great feat appeared in Nigel Dempster's *Daily Mail* gossip column, they declaring that it was 'not Swinley'. A year later his father Peter Cadbury (the probable source of the leak to Dempster) also had a hole-in-one at Lyford Cay, going round in 78, two shots under his age. 'Last year my younger son Joel had a hole-in-one at Swinley', said Cadbury, 'and I didn't want to be outdone by him.'[11]

The Fourth—par 3
Blue: 184 yards (Colt 160 yards)
White: 171 yards
Yellow: 147 yards
Red: 109 yards

The first of the par 3s is one of immense beauty. Swathes of heather run 'from the front of the tee up to an elevated table-top green that in turn is supported to

105   *The course took a long time to recover from Colt's massive original felling.*

106   *Many claim that the 4th at Swinley is one of the finest holes of any course in the country.*

the right by a gorse and heather hillside with a pronounced drop-off to the left. The green, the smallest on the course, is mightily fortified with three bunkers: a large one flanks the left side, and the two to the right of the green capture any off-line shots that land short.' The deep bunker to the right is known as an 'Arrison after Colt's partner, C.H. Alison. It was named after him, except the Japanese pronounced his name 'Arrison, which has stuck.

This redan green,[*] set on a natural shelf, is considered by many as one of the finest inland(or otherwise) one-shotters in the British Isles. A savage front left bunker gathers indifferent shots with swift certainty. The distance is often difficult to gauge, 'as the player is sheltered from the wind by the pine trees at the green, and frequently underestimates just what an uphill shot this is. The proper club may be two more than the player first suspects'.[12] The green has a 'false front' and is swift from back to front.

The green has been remodelled in recent years. Every year a party of golf architecture students from the Edinburgh College of Art and Design come to view Swinley. In 2002 they were invited to submit their designs for the 4th green, which needed remodelling. Five years later, under the guidance of Martin Hawtree, the bunker on the left of the green has been redesigned to form two bunkers.

It is this 4th at Swinley that Ronan Rafferty (who famously said that he would swap a 'Chateau Lafitte '61 for a round of 61') claims as being the best individual hole in the British Isles, the lesser others being 'the 17th at Birkdale, the first at Machrihanish, the 14th at St Andrews, the fifth at Royal County Down, the 11th at Dornoch, the sixth at Brancaster, the 18th at Doonbeg, the 11th on the East course at Wentworth, and the 12th at Kingsbarns'.[13]

Sir Christopher Lever, a veteran player of over 60 years, has achieved only one hole-in-one and that was here on the 4th hole using a 5 iron. Today, he admits, it would take him 'something like a 5 wood to reach the green!'.[14] It is possible that this was also the place that Henry Tiarks 'on one celebrated occasion holed in one'.[15] Tiarks was still playing at Swinley aged 92, just three years before he died. This is also a memorable hole for two great friends of 30 years and former chairmen of Swinley, Sir Roger Gibbs and Peter Hill-Wood. They have probably played together 150 times, Gibbs receiving six or eight shots. As Roger Gibbs wrote:

---

[*] A redan hole is usually a par 3 where the green is longer than it is wide, angles diagonally away from the tee, and generally slopes front to back and right to left. It is often guarded by a deep bunker fronting the middle part of the green, and/or bunkers on the right and left fronts, exactly as at Swinley. Bernard Darwin described it as 'a beautiful one-shot hole on top of a plateau, with a bunker short of the green to the left and another further to the right, and we must vary our mode of attack according to the wind, playing a shot to come in from the right or making a direct frontal attack'.

Its origins lie in the Crimean War when British forces captured a Russian-held stronghold at Sebastopol. The fort, known as a *redan* in the local dialect, was 'one having two parapets whose faces unite so as to form a salient angle toward the enemy'. John White-Melville, an officer who was present at the assault, compared the occasion with the old 6th green (now the 15th) on the West Links at North Berwick and the name has stuck. All other redans are modelled on the original.

107 *A former chairman of Swinley, Peter Hill-Wood is one of its leading players. He is the current chairman of Arsenal Football Club, whose new Emirates Stadium was opened by HRH The Duke of Edinburgh standing in for The Queen. The Duke is an honorary member of Swinley.*

I must have beaten him five times, but we always enjoyed the incredibly one-sided battles. One day we were playing the fourth and I took out my six iron and hit it as hard as I could. For once I had timed it and it went straight as an arrow towards the pin, finishing eight inches from the hole. Hill-Wood, totally unmoved and unimpressed, hit a most relaxed five iron straight onto the green and into the hole. I, of course, then completely folded and lost six and five![16]

On Peter Hill-Wood's 60th birthday, he went round in 65.

The Fifth—par 5
Blue: 497 yards (Colt 490 yards)
White: 480 yards
Yellow: 474 yards
Red: 427 yards

This hole was elevated to a par 5 when it was stretched by 17 yards by moving the tee to behind the 4th green and adding more bunkering around the surrounds of the green to tighten the approach. It was Hugh Stevenson who originally suggested a pond on the 5th and, fully established today, it is deemed a success. It is there to penalise as well as being an amenity feature, as are the man-made ridges halfway down the fairway.

In the early 1970s Paul Harker, who had resigned from Swinley when he went to live in Mallorca, was playing with his brother Matthew who was still a member. A caddie was duly engaged for Paul Harker, who turned out to be 'of a certain age and clearly had plenty of experience'.[17] After four holes of very indifferent golf the brothers were walking down the fairway chatting to the caddie, who informed them that he had been at Swinley since before the war. Hearing that, Paul Harker asked if he remembered their father, Lieutenant Colonel Tom Harker, a bondholder from the 1920s who played regularly with an eminent gynaecologist. The caddie remembered them both well, having often caddied for the surgeon. When the brothers told him that they had both been 'brought into the world' by the gynaecologist, the caddie replied:

'Really sir? Bloody waste of time that was, wasn't it?'

The brothers were dumbfounded. Family legend does not include the size of the tip at the end of the round. There have been three generations of Harkers at Swinley, Jamie and Simon Harker being current members, with a fourth in the wings.

One fine, sunny day in June William Sanders was playing with his wife Rowena, a Lady in Waiting to Princess Michael of Kent. Mrs Sanders was playing well above her form, which she partially attributed to using her favourite ball. But her luck ran out at the 5th hole. She sliced the shot and the ball landed in the middle of the pond. Undaunted, she took off her shoes, socks and shorts and went into the water to retrieve her ball. Unfortunately the water rendered her Agent Provocateur knickers completely transparent. To her horror she heard two balls land to the left of the fairway, and then saw two members advancing towards her. She appealed to her

108 *Trying to retrieve her favourite, lucky ball in the pond on the 5th, Rowena Sanders emulated the Lady of the Lake by squatting in the water when two male members advanced down the fairway.*

husband for help, to which William replied she should squat in the water like the character in Sir Walter Scott's *Lady of the Lake* (she baulked at emulating Millais' *Ophelia*) while he hid in the wood. She remained undetected, her honour intact, but played the rest of the round with totally black legs.

The Sixth—par 4
Blue: 424 yards (Colt 460 yards)
White: 394 yards
Yellow: 380 yards
Red: 340 yards

Once again, Colt's measurements are well out for this hole as, although his tee and today's yellow tee are in exactly the same place, he is 80 yards long in his measurement. But notwithstanding this discrepancy in yardage, the uninterrupted vista (and that at the 7th) epitomise the spaciousness of heathland golf. Compared with the first five holes, this is open country, where the heather surrounds make the player drive the ball long and accurately for a good angle into the green. Some 40 yards short of the green lies a diagonal ridge. This is flanked on either side by large bunkers that partially hide the green's surface and appear to foreshorten the actual distance of the green from the fairway.

This is a big-hitter's hole—Retief Goosen, the South African winner of the US Open (among other trophies), hit a 390-yard drive here, the ball landing just short of the ridges. The professionals love to play at Swinley as 'it is all about the terrain'.[18]

It was here, too, that Jo Durie (winner of the 1987 Wimbledon mixed doubles with Jeremy Bates) was once rebuked by a guest for playing off the white tee. So enraged was she that she promptly hit the ball almost to the green.

Marching with the sixth are Brian Gubby's gallops. This owner-trainer originally made his fortune in the motor trade and hotel business, but now trains only his own flat horses (usually about 10 to 12) on his 88 acres that border Swinley and Windlesham Moor. Here he has a one-and-a-quarter-mile all-weather gallop, and another mile on turf that he calls his 'little bit of paradise'.[19] The quiet, silver-haired Gubby is the son of an Epsom-based jockey who 'took to handling horses after he had finished with his previous love',[20] racing saloon and sports cars and graduating briefly to Formula One. He has won at least four Group races and scored major successes with his best horse, the sprinter Gabitat.

Not surprisingly, Gubby took a dim view of Swinley members' dogs straying onto his land to collect lost balls. Sir John Wrixon-Becher claims the record when his dog Whitney retrieved 11 golf balls going up the 6th, which he believes instigated the sign 'This is a horse racing gallop and do not stray beyond the OB'.[21] The gallops are now fenced off.

Over the years Swinley has suffered from many forest fires, most usually at the far end of the course. One June afternoon in 1957 Mike Sandham, his son Christopher and his godfather Sidney Beckwith arrived at the 6th tee. There they saw a fire engine parked beside the fairway with the firemen stretched out snoozing in the afternoon sunshine after their exertions in putting out a heath fire. Sandham senior teed off, sliced the shot, and watched with horror as the ball hit the side of the fire engine full toss with an almighty bang. The firemen leapt to their feet. Helmets tumbling, they sought sanctuary behind their vehicle. As Sandham arrived to play his second shot he wished the firemen a good afternoon, and offered his profuse apologies for the large dent in the side of the vehicle. The firemen's exact response has not been recorded, but was said to be 'choice'.[22]

It is here too that Sir Christopher Lever achieved the longest shot he has ever holed—a brassie (2 wood) for a par 4. 'You can imagine the preceding three shots', he added.[23]

During the tenure of one chairman (who not unnaturally remains anonymous), a rare and mature *Cupressus* was moved from beside the cottages by the clubhouse and replanted between the 6th green and the 7th tee. As it was such a handsome tree it was agreed that this was worth the expense and the risk of its not surviving. The result was greeted with howls of derision by the members. Club legend has it that it was his wife who gave it the soubriquet 'The Chairman's last erection'.[24] The more charitable dubbed it 'Lawson's Folly', as it was Bingham's idea and execution.

The Seventh—par 4
Blue: 400 yards (Colt 400 yards)
White: 393 yards
Yellow: 345 yards
Red: 340 yards

How typical of Colt to utilise the ridges two-thirds of the way up the fairway, and then use a large bunker, short of the green, to deceive the player as to the length of the approach into the green on the crest of the hill. It is an interesting uphill hole, where a shot to the left results in a tricky chip to a green that falls away. The hill has a pronounced slope to the right, with two recently constructed greenside bunkers.

Those playing on a Monday morning along these two back holes might hear an eerie siren filling the air. At any other time this would signify a prison break from the nearby high-security prison, but at 10 o'clock the authorities are merely testing their equipment. At least those at Swinley are not subjected to the taunts of the inmates, as tends to happen at the Trump International Golf Club, West Palm Beach, where players are barracked by the prisoners for poor shots or given unwanted advice from behind bars.

The Eighth—par 3
Blue: 146 yards (Colt 160 yards)
White: 141 yards
Yellow: 123 yards
Red: 123 yards

Here Colt changes the pace with his penchant for the one-shot hole, this being the shortest hole on the course. It follows the same direction as the preceding two holes, yet the tee-shot is very slightly downhill over swathes of heather to a long, narrow green that is resolutely defended by two features. As if the distinctive green contours were not enough to challenge the player, there is a gaping 15-foot drop to the immediate right that runs by the side of the green. Equally, the putting surface possesses some sporty movement on the left half. Standing on the tee there can be few who are not overcome by the 'sheer beauty and the terror of this fine short hole'.

   In the match against the Artisans, Peter Hill-Wood had a hole-in-one here. There was wild whooping from the opposition in excitement, but the former chairman 'showed no reaction, almost as if it had never happened'. The celebration in the bar afterwards, at his expense, went on long into the night.

109   *The shortest hole on the course, the par 3, 8th, is typical of Colt—difficult enough to be interesting and where any error is punished.*

110   *This glorious dog-leg was made out of the original Fernhill Allotment, which provided firewood for the poor of Winkfield. Later the land was absorbed into the Royal hunting preserve of Swinley Forest.*

The Ninth—par 4
Blue: 434 yards (Colt 445 yards)
White: 407 yards
Yellow: 366 yards
Red: 361 yards

This is classic Colt at his best. As a heathland hole there are no better examples than this 9th fairway. Colt has used the natural sweeping hillside contours to produce a difficult, full-blooded par 4. From the elevated tee behind the 8th green, the hard dog-legged left is protected on the inside by a mass of rhododendrons running the length of the hole, while the outside is bordered by heather and ridges guarding the corner of the dog-leg. Colt demanded a long, controlled draw from his tee (just above the present red tee) to gain distance to better see the elevated green, but here he used the man-made ridges that divided the Fernhill Allotments into strips as natural hazards. The play from the new elevated back tees is challenging, as the ground drops away abruptly in front and then gradually rises. If the shot is not executed correctly the ball can run through the dog-leg into the heather ridges: if over-drawn, it will find deep rough or rhododendron. Here 'you pays your money and you takes your choice'.[25] The safe and less risky drive is straight and short of the dog-leg corner, but this leaves a monumental, uphill second shot to an ample, yet subtly contoured, bunkerless green with sharp falls on either side and to the rear.

It was here that Robert Abel-Smith lost Bodger, his egotistical terrier. Entreaties for his return fell on selectively deaf ears, and the search was temporarily abandoned. It was only when Abel-Smith returned to the clubhouse that he found Bodger sitting on Sir Denis Thatcher's knee. Another regular terrier is Peter Wilmot-Sitwell's Jack Russell Zita, who adores Swinley.

> She knows the course better than I do—she takes all the short cuts from hole to hole. There is that charming fellow Tony who takes the drinks out on the course in a buggy with 'a fringe on top'. As soon as Zita sees the fringe waving in the breeze she's off like a rocket as she knows he always has dog biscuits on board!

The Tenth—par 3
Blue: 205 yards (Colt 230 yards)
White: 195 yards
Yellow: 170 yards
Red: 152 yards

111 *Dappled afternoon winter sun by the 10th. The beauty of the heather and Scots pine are part of the infinite charm of Swinley.*

Again Colt is far out in his measurement. Although he placed his tee well behind those of today, that is, behind the hut, his green was well forward, just in front of the first bunker. Here a par is a welcome score. The third and longest of Colt's par 3s, it 'is split into a left and right section with the dividing line being a slight ridge that meanders sinuously up the middle of the green'. Those attacking the pin will be forced to produce a finely controlled draw to reach pin positions on the upper-left half of the green, yet the preferred route to the lower right is a well-hit fade. There is a large, gaping bunker front left that catches slightly overcooked draws when the hole is cut left, and there are two bunkers short left and right of the green to collect any weak fades. If navigated to the correct portion of the green, the putt is easier, albeit with a deceptive borrow to negotiate.

The Eleventh—par 4
Blue: 278 yards (Colt 275 yards)
White: 277 yards
Yellow: 249 yards
Red: 229 yards

The back tee of this short par 4 dog-leg is off-set from the fairway and unaltered since Colt's original plan, although his two cross-bunkers to the left have long been obsolete. Heather guards the entire left side of the fairway, while a series of fairway bunkers and more heather line the somewhat blind right side of the hole. 'Flirting

with the right fairway bunkers is preferred, as a fearsome bunker guards the left-front half of the narrow green. The longer, and more right-handed, the drive, the better the angle to make the green.'

It had long been thought that those going to the 12th tee should have some method of warning those playing towards the 14th. In the end the committee decided on a bell, and it was left to Lawson Bingham to come up with something suitable. He had long been friends with the Royal Armourer at Windsor Castle, who had recently repaired a fine ship's bell and, through Lieutenant Colonel Sir John Johnston's Household connections, The Queen personally agreed to the permanent loan of the bell to Swinley.

112 *The replica ship's bell of USS* Ranger *given to The Queen on her visit to San Diego and later lent to Swinley.*

113 *Commissioned in 1957, USS* Ranger *was the first aircraft carrier in the world with an angled flight deck. She had a long and distinguished service record around the world, including Vietnam where she was awarded 13 Battle Stars. The* Ranger *appeared in many films including* Top Gun *and* Star Trek.

The replica bell had been presented to Her Majesty by the officers and men of the USS *Ranger* on 26 February 1983. At the invitation of President Reagan she and The Duke of Edinburgh made a nine-day visit to California that began with a review of the 83 ships of the United States Pacific Fleet in San Diego. It was 'a symbolic gesture for the American assistance to Britain during the Falklands conflict'.[26] The royal party had lunched aboard the aircraft carrier, where The Queen also 'inspected fighters on board and was amused to be introduced to an aircraftsman called Groucho Marks'. The next day The Queen had lunch with her old friend Walter Annenberg on his ranch near Palm Springs.

At 56,000 tons and over 1,000 feet long, USS *Ranger* was commissioned in 1957 and was the first aircraft carrier in the world to be built with an angled flight deck. She joined the Atlantic Fleet for sea trials, and then the Pacific Fleet where she was used for extensive training. In May 1964 *Ranger* monitored the French nuclear tests on Mururoa Atoll using the Lockheed U-2, the then top-secret spy-plane. She had four extensive tours in North Vietnam, where her aircraft 'hit a wide variety of targets, including ferries, bridges, airfields and military installations. Truck parks, rail facilities, anti-aircraft guns and SAM sites were also treated to doses of Air Wing 2's firepower'.[27] With *Kitty Hawk*, she held the record for 233 sorties in a day. *Ranger* was awarded 13 battle stars for her service in Vietnam.

In the decades after Vietnam she was deployed in trouble spots all around the world, including Kenya and Yemen. After a series of extensive refits, some as the result of sabotage by terrorists, she was deployed in Operation Desert Storm, the liberation of Kuwait in 1991. *Ranger* was finally decommissioned in 1993 and is now laid up as a museum in Bremerton, Washington State. Her film career was no less impressive, doubling for the USS *Enterprise* in *Top Gun* and *Star Trek IV*, and as USS *Nimitz* for the scenes in Pearl Harbour in *The Final Countdown*.

The Twelfth—par 4
Blue: 455 yards (Colt 490 yards)
White: 430 yards
Yellow: 412 yards
Red: 395 yards

Many skills are needed to negotiate this long fairway that resembles an elongated S, so the drive must be drawn to reach a point as close as possible to the left-hand edge of the fairway so as to have a better view of the green. Within striking range of very long-hitters are two bunkers that give good directional help to the somewhat blind first half of the hole. As the back tee is offset to the fairway it is a tricky decision as to how much of that fairway to take on, for playing safely out to the right side 'brings into play a series of huge pine trees in the middle point of the S'. Some of the most undulating ground on the course, starting 60 yards short of the green, leads onto the elevated putting surface itself. This is a convoluted green, where 'a hard running shot that chases up onto the green is a delight to watch'. It is an impressive green, too, particularly in May with its violet wall of rhododendrons, but it is also 'the most severely contoured one on the course ... so walking to the next tee with a par will surely feel like a birdie'.

In the mid-1960s there was a tramp named Archie living in the middle of the rhododendrons. He was a charming fellow who always wore an army greatcoat, winter and summer, regardless of the weather. He occasionally caddied for members but made his money by collecting golf balls and selling them to the professional, Murrant, at a shilling a ball. One morning Archie was cooking his breakfast when his open fire set light to his 'quarters' and the rhododendrons were burned to the ground. Archie fortunately escaped unhurt.

It was here that David Naylor-Leyland was playing a fourball with his two sons and brother-in-law when he pushed his 'drive right across the fairway just short of the rhododendrons. 'My second shot', he recalled, was blocked so I decided to play a Seve shot and told the boys I would bend it round the trees. As at the time my handicap was 14, it was to be expected that 99 times in a 100 the result would be 'reload'. This time, as soon as I made contact with a three wood, I knew it was as good a shot as I can hit, but naturally I could not see where it landed. When we reached the green, there was no sign of the ball. It was only when the others putted out that we found my ball in the hole for an eagle two (or even an albatross on the old bogey card).

Naylor-Leyland has 'never even got close to a hole-in-one', but that amazing shot 'will do for now'.[28]

On a glorious morning in early June 2006 David Carlton-Paget sat in his wheelchair, bathed in dappled sunlight in his room overlooking a pretty garden. He was in the advanced stages of motor neurone disease, and had just three months to live. Yet despite the awful death sentence hanging over him he was controlled and fully focused. Nor was the Trinity Hospice in the least forbidding, but a truly cheerful place.

At the mention of Swinley, Carlton-Paget, a member since 1996, smiled involuntarily. 'Some of my happiest times were spent there with my friends. I used to take a day for them, some were fellow members, some not.' It was on one of those days at the 12th green, with its backdrop of rhododendrons in full flower, that the idea of a conversation piece of himself putting, watched by his two daughters, Zoë and Thalia, along with his favourite caddie, Hughie O'Meara, came to him. Carlton-Paget had long admired Richard Foster as an artist, having seen his works at an exhibition at Raphael Vall's Gallery in London, where he bought a view of the hillside above the Arno looking towards Pisa. It was an instant decision to commission him for his Swinley conversation piece.

After Harrow, a spawning ground for artists, Richard Foster studied at Studio Simi in Florence and the City and Guilds Art School. Tall and urbane, he is the original of London's 'pin-stripe painters' and a former Vice-President of the Royal Society of Portrait Painters. A native of Norfolk, he painted his erstwhile neighbour, the Princess of Wales, besides a host of other luminaries over the years that includes the partners of C. Hoare and Company. For Foster, the Carlton-Paget commission was not without its difficulties. He began by taking photographs of the composition, not to copy but the better to judge the scale of the four subjects: Carlton-Paget flanked by two deliberately bored-looking daughters and the caddie. He then made two sketches of his proposed picture, one with the rhododendrons in the background and the other with the rhododendrons as a complete backdrop. To Foster's disappointment Carlton-Paget chose the former. The next step was to paint the green. On some afternoons the course was quiet, and Foster could paint relatively undisturbed. But more often they were society days, with balls dropping around him like outsized hailstones. Both artist and canvas remained

114   *Richard Foster, the archetypal 'pinstripe' artist, painted the late David Carlton-Paget with his two daughters, Zoë and Thalia, with his caddie, Hughie O'Meira, on the 12th at Swinley against a backdrop of rhododendrons. It was a dangerous assignment to capture the background, hence Foster had his subjects sit for him singly elsewhere. The composition was Carlton-Paget's idea, having seen one similar by Sir John Lavery. (Reproduced by kind permission of Mrs D. Carlton-Paget.)*

intact, although there were several close encounters—'for those in peril on the tee' as P.G. Wodehouse's Oldest Member would have it.

Obviously Foster could not capture his subjects *in situ*, so instead he painted Carlton-Paget and Zoë in Hyde Park, standing each in turn on an orange box to give them the same height in relation to his position slightly below the 12th green. It was a bizarre sight for walkers in Hyde Park, many of them mutual friends, to see a man hunched over a putter a foot above the ground one day, then a girl, holding a club and scowling, the next. Thalia was painted in comparative comfort in a room in Oxfordshire, while O'Meara posed in the car park outside the Artisans' hut. Unlike many a caddie he is the eternal optimist—'having hit a perfectly dreadful shot into the trees, Hughie will say "Oh, it's not too bad, Sir. Get a nine iron onto it!" '[29]

The painting was finished by July 2003 and Carlton-Paget went to Foster's studio to collect it. He was a little later than planned, for that morning he had been diagnosed with motor neurone disease. David Carlton-Paget died on

23 September 2006. More than 800 family and friends attended his memorial service in the Guards Chapel. Rupert Hambro now organises The Paget Masters at Woburn in aid of MNDA (the Motor Neurone Disease Association). Having raised well in excess of £60,000 in 2006 and the same in 2007, it is hoped to make it an annual event. A photograph of the conversation piece is to be presented to Swinley in his memory.

The Thirteenth—par 3
Blue: 174 yards (Colt 160 yards)
White: 167 yards
Yellow: 149 yards
Red: 131 yards

This fourth par 3 is so typical of Swinley. Where its predecessors have somewhat open greens, this is enveloped on three sides by towering pine trees, rhododendrons and silver birch, with the open front a sea of heather. It runs diagonally from right to left, and two heather-covered bunkers partially hide the green's front surface from the elevated tee. Colt's tee was where the yellow one is today, so positioned as to allow for a controlled draw to land just over the heather, but short of the green, to roll on 'with the risk of overdrawing into the frontal bunkers, or fading over the bunkers to land more softly on the side-sloping green'.

The 13th was the favourite of Sidney Beckwith, a member in the 1960s, for here he had a hole-in-one on his birthday. 'He hit a fine 6 iron, one bounce and into the hole.'[30] When he died a bench with a suitably engraved plaque was placed behind the tee. It has long since gone, although the bench to the immortal memory of Jimmy Carlton Harrison is still there, sited by his widow Hazel. It has been better preserved, as today all the wooden tee-markers and benches are polished daily when the greens are cut.

It was here, too, that a member, playing on his own some time before the Second World War, had a hole-in-one. Delighted with his performance, but disappointed that there was no one to witness it, he returned to the clubhouse and the bar. Like the course it was deserted, so he left a £5 note with the steward to buy drinks for members in celebrations of his great feat. Three months later the steward handed him back his change, £2 12s. 6d.

Leopold Hirsch, a member since 1997, was playing in some 'geriatric' competition and took his new love along with him. 'I can hardly bear to be parted from her.' He was referring to his whippet, Marble. Notwithstanding the sharpness of her nails, Marble sleeps in his bed, to the chagrin of many a hostess who is left bewailing the torn sheets and muddy eiderdowns.

On that day, 'Marble was her usual perfect self, anyway in my eyes', Hirsch continued. 'You probably know, though I had not appreciated it, that whippets are Arab hunting dogs from the desert. In Marble's case her Arab background shows itself most forcefully in her love of sand which I find charming.' Hirsch and his partner approached the short 13th that is more or less 'surrounded by the stuff—sand I mean'. It was then that 'Marble clearly felt the call of the desert and in a fit of exuberance starting racing round the green, in the bunkers, at absolutely full tilt—always, I have thought, a particularly entrancing sight. My ball was, unusually, on the green, so maybe I was less aware than I should have been that my opponent was having a disappointing hole and that his second shot had got him only as far as the front bunker. Doubtless the ground staff and the players in front of us had left it in perfect condition, but by the time my poor opponent got to it it looked as much like a ploughed field as a bunker can, and Marble was still flashing through it every eleven seconds or so! I only realised that something was amiss when I heard my opponent say, "I was always brought up to believe that, above all things, one should never criticise anyone's children or their dogs …" His voice trailed off.' Marble continued the rest of the round on a lead.

The Fourteenth—par 4
Blue: 366 yards (Colt 360 yards)
White: 354 yards
Yellow: 332 yards
Red: 295 yards

What is so remarkable about Harry Colt at Swinley is that his course and design can be 'tweaked' sympathetically to give extra length without remotely altering the character or charm of a hole. The 14th is a prime example of this, where the green has been moved back some 25 yards to great advantage. So on this glorious fairway the heather-covered hummocks put in by Colt to guard the green now partially conceal the new green on this slightly uphill hole. Thus, the farther the drive up the fairway, the better it is to see over these heather-hummocks into a green that has no special backdrop and falls slightly away from the line of play.

The Fifteenth—par 4
Blue: 450 yards (Colt 480 yards)
White: 433 yards
Yellow: 412 yards
Red: 290 yards

Colt can only have been delighted to have been able to use both sides of Fernhill to such advantage, but nowhere more so than here at the 15th. From the back tee, 'it is now a long par 4 that rises gradually, then more sharply as the fairway approaches the green'. The left-hand side of the fairway is flanked by three bunkers,

115 *The incline up to the 15th green was named 'New Members' Hill' by the Earl of Hardwicke. The bunker originally put in by Colt was later abandoned, but has subsequently been reinstated. The maestro knew best.*

one stepping above the next, the last being some 20 yards short of the green, while a solitary bunker guards the right side of the fairway some 40 yards out. This was an original Colt bunker that was later abandoned, but now reinstated.

The steep incline was named 'New Members' Hill' by the 9th Earl of Hardwicke (Eton, the Life Guards and the Special Air Service) as it was thought steep enough to kill off older members so that their spiked, brogue golfing shoes could be filled by younger candidates. The Earl was a great friend of Bob Hope and together they organised hugely enjoyable charity days. But Hardwicke was a total stranger to the changing room, declaring it to be a 'filthy, smelly place', and preferred to change his shoes in the car park.

This was the site of the famous exchange between Boyer, an ancient caddie, and the Rajmata of Jaipur. Boyer, who invariably wore his cap over his ear, was something of a legend at Swinley. He had a junk shop in Sunninghill, but, although a huge man, he was terrified of his wife, so caddying at Swinley came as a great relief. That day he was with the Rajmata, who had made a spectacularly bad second shot that landed far into the rough. Boyer was ordered in to find it. As he left, he shook his head, fixed her with his eye and pronounced: 'If Mrs Gandhi saw you play that shot, she'd put you back in prison.'[31] The Rajmata comes to England during the polo season and has always been keen on her golf. Once she went to take her second shot on the 1st with what she thought was her ball. When she holed out

she was puzzled by its size—the larger American ball that is now standard. It turned out that the ball belonged to either Bob Hope or Bing Crosby, who were following on behind. Both Crosby and Hope (who famously declared 'Golf is my profession. Show business is just to pay the green fees.') were charm itself over the incident.

In Colt's day there were several wooden sheds dotted around the course for the green-keepers and their machines. The last one was here at the 15th green and was only pulled down in the mid-1990s, much to the chagrin of the tramps who regularly slept there during the summer. A few of them had even been employed as caddies in the past, but the last intake was mostly winos from Ireland. When not being rude to members or societies on the course, they went for breakfast at St Mary's Ascot (when it was a convent), then a spot of luncheon at the Marist Convent in Sunningdale, back to St Mary's for tea, and then the sheds at Swinley with their hooch in time to barrack the Artisans playing in the evening.

It was here at the 15th that Alistair Buchanan scattered his father's ashes in 1983. John J. Buchanan was an amateur player of some note before the war, playing in the English Amateur Championship and turning out for such sides as the Old Harrovians and the Lucifer Golf Society. Although never a member, he had always enjoyed playing at Swinley, particularly in the Household Brigade matches and the White's competitions. The first time father and son played together at Swinley was in 1961 at the invitation of a bondholder, Major General Sir John Marriott, KCVO, CB, DSO, MC, a distinguished Scots Guardsman who had commanded the Brigade of Guards and was G.O.C. London District from 1947 to 1950.

The two Buchanans, both Coldstream Guardsmen and both bill brokers with Allen Harvey and Ross, had been staying in Wiltshire one weekend in August and decided to take up the General's offer to play on their way back to London. When they arrived at Swinley, the clubhouse was closed and the professional's office shut up. As there was no one around they helped themselves to the course, changing their shoes in the car park. There were no pins, which made the 'judgement of the distance to the green difficult'.[32] Undeterred by this obvious setback, they played an enjoyable round together. On their return to the car park a rather surprised secretary, Dick King-Lewis, asked them what they were doing there. They explained they were playing on the General's bond. When they inquired why the place was deserted, the incredulous secretary replied with a lofty air: 'The members? Oh, they're in Scotland!' Of course they were: it was the 13th of August. Not long after that the age-old practice of closing down for the whole month of August was abandoned.

It was also here at the 15th, in the 1978 match against the Artisans, that the legendary E.F. Storey told his partner, Alistair Buchanan, about his amazing good fortune in his record-breaking round of 1936 (see page 145). During that match Storey, renowned as a great putter, divulged the secret of his success to his partner: every morning before breakfast he would stand six feet away from a spindly, wooden chair leg and hit 50 balls at it. If he missed just once, he would start again from the beginning.

The Sixteenth—par 4
Blue: 415 yards (Colt 430 yards)
White: 400 yards
Yellow: 382 yards
Red: 359 yards

In Colt's day, the tee was further back and to the left, and the fairway was much wider and not 'pinched' in the driving area as it is today. The two bunkers guarding the right, and the one to the left, are both Colt's, as is the lone flanking bunker. A third bunker has been grassed over. Playing this hole, the preferred line is to take on the fairway where it is flat, giving the opportunity to drive the ball further and leaving a more lofted club for the second shot to a long, narrow two-tiered green with typical Colt-design fall-offs to both sides and the rear. At 41 yards it is the deepest green on the course.

Beside the 16th and 5th tees is one of the best (of many) views at Swinley where eight holes can be seen at once. During a match against the Artisans one fourball with Richard Goodhew stopped off at the drinks cart for a sharpener. The steward remarked that this was his favourite spot on the whole course, to which Goodhew replied, 'Mine too, which is why we chose it to scatter my father's ashes on the blue tee of the 5th'. In fact his father Gordon Goodhew had considered two options for his ashes: either there at Swinley or by the bookies' rail at Ascot. He made the right decision, as the other spot would have been lost when the racecourse was redeveloped. Living in Swinley Forest House (next to Boden's Ride), Gordon Goodhew was devoted to Swinley. Once in the mid-1960s he had a hole-in-one, and was so delighted that he told the club steward that he would stand every member who came in that week a drink: it cost him all of £8. The ashes of Rodney Holmes, Richard Goodhew's step-father, are also scattered to the left of the 5th tee 'as he used to always hook there into the woods'.

117 *A total of eight holes can be seen between the 5th and 16th tees, the ideal spot for the drinks cart on match days.*

The Seventeenth—par 3
Blue: 170 yards (Colt 195)
White: 170 yards
Yellow: 161 yards
Red: 127 yards

This penultimate hole is Colt's final par 3 and his *pièce de résistance*, requiring both mental strength and finesse to negotiate its considerable defences. From the elevated tee the target appears small and formidable, requiring a full carry to reach the safe haven. A stray shot off the left, right, or the back of the green will require the most fortuitous recovery shot even to get onto the putting surface. The green is set upon a high, conical mound that rises sharply to the front edge and falls away on the other three sides, while the green itself, in typical Colt fashion, slopes very much towards the front. The combination of a valley in front, a gully to the right and back, several mean bunkers (one of which is the deepest bunker on the course) abutting the green to the left to gather many a tee shot, coupled with an

118 *The 17th, where Colonel Snatt, the secretary, would give odds of 7-1 on anyone hitting the green from the tee.*

119   *The 17th. Oil on board by Chris Osborne, assistant caddie master at The Berkshire. This is the final par 3 of the course where mental strength and finesse are required to overcome all manner of hazards surrounding the knob-like green. (Reproduced by kind permission of Rod Stevenson.)*

undulating green that is none too big (and also difficult to putt), all makes for a testing hole. Yet because of its length the hole remains within the capability of most: a two to a five awaits.

Not noted as a betting man (and quite against the moral code of the Club), Colonel Snatt, secretary between 1949 and 1960, would sit in a folding chair beside the tee and give odds of 7-1 on anyone hitting the green. It is said that he 'made good money'[33] from his wagers.

As the Air Marshals that made up their own exclusive golfing society faded away, the remainder decided to abandon their annual fixture at Swinley, and their day was given to Richards Longstaff Insurance Brokers. In their first year (1987) one of their guests, Dennis Johnson, not only made the 17th green, but holed in one. Johnson—who was part of the firm who famously insured a German actress's breasts for $500,000 (excluding 'scratching and biting') that were 'warranted surveyed by Leading Lloyd's underwriter'—was naturally delighted, and the great feat cost him dear in the bar afterwards. The next year, when Richards Longstaff decided to offer a decent prize of £5,000 for a repeat performance, Duncan Pearson was deputed to insure the sum in the Contingency Market. He secured a premium of £250. On the morning of the day no one even hit the green in one shot. To make matters worse, Pearson was told that 1p would have been a more appropriate premium.

When Eric Sermon was caddying for Henry Cotton the legendary golfer asked him what club he should use on the 17th. Sermon produced a 4 iron, to which Cotton replied that it was indeed exactly the right club, then added 'but give me the 2 iron and I'll show you how to stop a ball'. With that he struck his shot onto the green, the ball stopping dead in its tracks.

The Eighteenth—par 4
Blue: 368 yards (Colt 375 yards)
White: 341 yards
Yellow: 306 yards
Red: 280 yards

Like the neighbouring 1st there is no heather on this hole, as this was originally agricultural land rather than heath or forestry. This 368-yard par 4 calls for the drive

120 *The final putt now in full view of the clubhouse, although in Colt's original plan there was no terrace and the 18th green was screened by a hedge.*

to negotiate a meandering stream a little short of the landing area while avoiding the bunkers on the left and the heather mound on the right. This is followed by a mid- to short-iron approach uphill to a well-guarded and angled green that slopes swiftly from back to front. Finishing above the hole will require a good nerve to putt down the slope, and the over-hit shot will be out of bounds once it crosses the road at the back of the green.

The Nineteenth

And when the round is over there is the clubhouse and the bar. There is the famous Swinley Special (the formula is a closely guarded secret) created by a previous steward, William Henry. Always known as Hopalong Jim since his motorbike accident when a young man, he was popular among some of the members for his cheery disposition. Others found him, and particularly his whistling, profoundly irritating. Not only did he eavesdrop on members' conversations at the bar, but he often joined in as well. His 'alarming "always a pleasure to serve a gentleman!" was never uttered to non-members'.[34] His wife Frieda still works in the kitchens.

The last word surely goes to Sir John Wrixon-Becher (1989):

> I think we all know the charm of the place: the Saturday morning atmosphere is simply unique. And after the game, it's even more satisfying when the proverbial smart, low-handicap, long-hitter from Sunningdale has been caught out by our beloved course's subtleties, and he broods over his drink at the bar, whinging about the lack of caddies and all those badly behaved dogs …

Appendix II
In the Beginning

When Harry Colt was tramping through the scrub, heath and woodland on the edge of Swinley Forest to create his new golf course at the back end of 1909, neither he (nor indeed the hundreds of thousands who have enjoyed his creation over the last century) could possibly have had any idea that this former wasteland could have held such a rich and varied history.

When the Romans were setting out the Devil's Highway (that marches alongside the 6th, 7th and 8th holes), Swinley Forest was barren, open country—the term 'forest' being much like a Scottish deer forest today, or as the great 18th-century naturalist the Reverend Gilbert White described it, the land was mostly 'moss and muir, heath and fern, with few trees'.[1] It was a desolate place in 942, when the Saxon king Edmund the Magnificent (940-6) gave the lands about 'Swinleie to a most religious woman called Saethrithe'. She in turn soon bestowed it on the Abbot of the Benedictine abbey, dedicated to the Virgin Mary, at Abingdon. Not long after that, in 1025, Lady Elfleda, possibly a daughter of Edmund the Younger, bequeathed the remaining portion of Swinley Forest to the same abbey. By the time of the Norman Conquest and the subsequent Domesday Book, Swinley Forest was described as a place of 'pannage for pigs' (the practice of turning out domestic swine in a wood or forest to feed on fallen acorns and beechmast) which means that, by then, parts of the forest must have been heavily wooded with deciduous hardwoods. The Normans continued to afforest the open heathland under the king's chief verderer at Windsor, Sir Richard de Battaille. At the beginning of the 13th century the Abbot of the day took out a suit against Geoffrey de Bagshot who 'successfully claimed the right of pannage there'.[2]

Despite the indisputable rights of the Abbots of Abingdon to the lands at Swinley, successive Great Foresters encroached on the woodlands under the direct orders of their monarch to enlarge Windsor Great Park for hunting. In return, the monastery was still permitted to 'enjoy the land and woods without molestation'. But in the latter half of the 15th century Henry VII annexed 'the Grove of Swinley along with a hunting lodge', part of the 191 acres that had by that time been bequeathed to the Church of St Mary de Stratford at Westham by the Abbot of Abingdon.

121 *'Gathering Acorns', November, on vellum from a calendar by Master Ermengaut (d.1322). Large tracts of Swinley Forest were used for pannage, as here where a swineherd is beating acorns out of an oak tree to feed his pigs. Biblioteca Monasterio del Escorial, Madrid.*

It was still a wild, barren place when the young Princes Arthur and Henry tried 'their hands at hawking for a heron over the swamps and pools of the Great Park and Swinley … He [Arthur] was then about 14 years of age, his brother Henry ten; the elder boy was too delicate to excel in athletic pursuits, but the younger was especially strong and robust, and was thenceforth much in our [Swinley] forest, enjoying perhaps the happiest, at least the most innocent, years of his life'.[3]

A less innocent Henry, as King Henry VIII, hunted stag over precisely the same country with much enthusiasm, as did his daughter Queen Elizabeth I, who followed her deerhounds. She often killed the stag herself with a crossbow, or delivered the *coup de grace* with a knife—so much for the 'body of a feeble woman' that she always claimed.

By the time of John Norden's survey of 1607 a house, kennels and small paddock were recorded within an enclosure of 300 acres then called 'Swinley Walke'. This was 'environeth [fenced] on all sides by a rail of high hurdles, as were all walks of

The booke of Hunting.

that the Prince or chiefe (it so please them) doe aligyr and take assaye of the Deare with a sharpe knyfe, the whiche is done

L.iij.   iij

Windsor at that time' to contain '100 head of [red deer, of] which 30 were "antlers", 16 "stags" and the rest probably hinds'. The house was renamed Swinley Lodge (as opposed to Baird's Lodge after the under-keeper), and later became the official residence of the Master of the Royal Buckhounds (a slight misnomer as they hunted the red deer, not fallow deer, kept within 'Swinley Railes'). The first occupant of the Lodge was 'Sir Henrie Nevell, chiefe keper', with old Baird as kennel huntsman. Neville was a great favourite of James I, himself a passionate huntsman—he had ambled south from Edinburgh to claim his throne in 1603, hunting all the way with a draft of hounds from the Royal kennels given by Elizabeth I.

Charles I was a fine horseman and keen hunter—he kept a pack of harriers alongside the Buckhounds at Swinley. He is also recorded as shooting red squirrel in the woods. But during his reign the introduction of draconian forest laws led to a vast increase in deer numbers that caused genuine hardship to the peasant farmer through ruined crops. These forest laws were among the many causes of the

Civil War. During the Commonwealth much of the forest was destroyed and the deer stocks culled. At the Restoration of Charles II the forests (including Swinley) were replanted and restocked with deer, some requisitioned, some imported from Germany and others exchanged for baronetcies. Thereafter the hunting was legion. 'One stag being hunted, went away, and was taken at Lord Petre's seat in Essex: only five came in at the end of this seventy miles' run—the King's brother the Duke of York being one of them'.[4]

But Swinley Forest really came into its own as a hunting preserve with Queen Anne and her husband, Prince George of Denmark. Both were devoted to the chase. Later on, when the Queen could no longer ride, vast swathes of the forest were opened up with long, straight rides. Bogs were drained so that she could 'hunt in a chaise, which she drives herself, and drives furiously like Jehu, and is a mighty hunter like Nimrod'.[5] Nine of these rides converged on a point near Englemere House, one-and-a-half miles due north of the farthest holes of the Swinley course. There was certainly one ride that crossed the 15th fairway just below the crest of the hill, and another that clipped the 9th tee. Also at this time the Queen ordered that the 'grounds within and without Swinley Rails should be leveled and the rabbits therein exterminated'. Instructions were given 'to trench the burrows which must be at least three feet deep, fill them in again and ram them to make ye ground fit and safe for her Majesty's hunting'.[6]

George I did not care for hunting, and the Royal Buckhounds and Swinley Forest suffered from neglect. Matters improved slightly during the reign of George II, when the Lords of the Treasury voted £1,000 for 'increasing the game there for the King's Royal Sport and Diversion',[7] but it was George III who eclipsed all in the hunting field. He revived the Royal Buckhounds and re-installed the master in Swinley Lodge. New rides were opened up, and carted (as opposed to harboured) deer were hunted from Swinley. The meets were extremely popular—one in 1779 was attended by the King, the Prince of Wales, his brother the Prince of Osnaburgh, the Princess Royal, the Princess Sophia and some 300 followers, although fields of 150 to 200 were more the norm. The chosen stag, all with names like the '*Warfield Heavier*',[8] were taken from the paddock at Swinley Lodge usually to Tower Hill (about a mile to the north-west of the course and clearly visible from the 15th green) and released. After a wait of about five minutes, hounds were cast and the stag pursued. Quite often he just ran back and popped over the rails into his enclosure a few hundred yards away; more often the stag ran well, sometimes for hours. On one occasion in November 1781 'His Majesty rode above 80 miles' and on another occasion a 'fine run of six hours, at the end of which "the stag dropped down dead before the hounds ; not twenty of the horses out of 150 were in at the death." '[9] As often as not the stag would run to the south and east following the rides, the lie taking it over the present Berkshire and Swinley golf courses.

By 1782 George III had bought the Manor of Winkfield, which included the whole of Swinley, from Katherine Meeke and Grey Neville, and it is through this transaction that the Crown Estate now leases 179 acres to Swinley Forest Golf Club. At the turn of the century the King reviewed 32,000 of his troops that were camped in the area. 'Swinley was quite the rage. The Princesses [the six daughters of George III] appeared in white with "light village cloaks," and they and all the young ladies of fashion adopted "the Swinley slouch ornamented with a white military plume!" '[10] This is the first mention of the 'slouch', it being a felt hat with its wide brim pinned back, similar to a Gurkha hat today but worn sideways.

Like Queen Anne, when George III became too ill to follow mounted, he extended the rides so that he could be driven in a carriage. There is still an area of forest immediately to the north of Swinley Forest Golf Club called Kings Ride that dates from this time. After the death of George III the Royal Buckhounds were less active, the Master's duties being principally as the Sovereign's Representative at Ascot. The hunt servants were known as Yeoman Prickers, and they too are to be seen today in the Royal Enclosure at Ascot in their 18th-century green uniforms.

The Prince Consort bought the Duke of Gloucester's estate at Bagshot and annexed it to the Crown Lands at Swinley for forestry and shooting. There he experimented with

rearing blackcock or cock of the woods which is extremely plentiful in various parts of Scotland. The splendid live birds were presented to the Prince as a present from the Duke of Hamilton about 2 months ago … and were bred on his Grace's estate in the Isle of Arran.[11]

Her Majesty's Staghounds, as they became known on the accession of Queen Victoria, continued to exist in a minor way, and were revitalised in the 1860s. Although the Royal Kennels had moved to Ascot, and the master now lived elsewhere, stags were still kept in the Swinley enclosure and often hunted from there. These stags had been chosen by Prince Christian of Schleswig-Holstein, Ranger from

123 *The Ranger of Windsor Great Park, Prince Christian of Schleswig-Holstein, with a record head. It was he who chose the stags that were transported to the Swinley enclosure to be carted for the Royal Buckhounds.*

124   *A kennel meet of the Royal Buckhounds, 1898, with Lord Ribblesdale (second from the right) the last Master but one. His wife, Charlotte, née Tennant and sister of Margot Asquith, was a member of Swinley.*

1867 to 1917, from the considerable herds in Windsor Great Park. The Staghounds continued under various masters, many of them the forebears of Swinley members, the likes of the Lord Kinnaird (1841-2), the Earls of Rosslyn (1842-7), Grenville (1847-9), Hardwicke (1874-80) and Coventry (1886-92). The last Master but one, Lord Ribblesdale, was Master in 1892-5. He 'clung to old-fashioned dress and customs … His high, square hat, wide stock tie, eccentric manner of speaking, and inclination to use high sounding and sonorous words early stamped him as a man of personality'.[12] He married Charlotte Tennant, sister of Margot Asquith, who died, and then Mrs John Astor, a lady member in the 1920s. There is no record of him having been a member of Swinley, but he was a golfer and Captain of the Royal Ascot Golf Club in 1892-5.

The office of Master was abolished with the hunt in 1901 after the 'wire in Middlesex, the villa in Berkshire, the pheasant in Buckinghamshire, and all the apparatus of population and residential amenity'.[13] One of the last of the Swinley stags was taken in Weston's Yard 'before a large assembly of Eton boys and maidservants. It was stag-hunting at its very worst.'[14] Even in the late 19th century stag-hunting had its detractors—a petition was signed, mostly by the workers of Huntley and Palmer's Biscuit Factory in Reading. After the demise of the Royal Buckhounds the Swinley paddocks were used to rear pheasants at the instigation of the Deputy Ranger, Captain Sir Walter Campbell. On the few shooting days the guns were 'almost exclusively confined to the royal party, and five guns are usually engaged. In the morning, pheasants are shot and in the afternoon rabbits.'[15]

When Colt was constructing his course, materials and fertilisers were brought the short distance from the Swinley Brickworks on the branch line from Ascot. The brickworks, founded in the 1860s, produced specialised 'rubber' bricks (those that can be easily shaped by rubbing) that were used for facing in the construction of such buildings as Westminster Cathedral, Madame Tussaud's and Harrow School. During the First World War it became the headquarters of the Aeroplane Group of the Royal Air Corps, where a large number of aircraft were assembled. The empty buildings were taken over by the Bertram Mills Circus in the 1930s as their winter quarters, until the Second World War when the animals were exchanged for internees, most notable among them the Blackshirts, the supporters of Sir Oswald Mosley, leader of the British Union of Fascists, although he himself was kept in Brixton Prison. They in turn were later replaced by Italian prisoners of war.

Being on the edge of the forest, and an extension of Bagshot Heath, the original 50 acres that were bought by Swinley Forest Golf Club (see page 14) were very different from the rest of the forest. The land had been enclosed in 1817 and transferred to the Reverend Arthur Godley and his wife Elizabeth, and was later tenanted. It eventually formed part of the Earlywood estate that was sold to Alexander Rutland Davey. The rest is the history of Swinley Forest Golf Club.

References

Introduction

1. Seth-Smith, Michael, *The Friendship of the Earl of Derby and the Hon. George Lampton 1893-1945*, London, 1983, p.37.
2. Sheridan, James, *Sheridan of Sunningdale, My Fifty-Six Years as Caddie-Master,* London, 1967, p.29.
3. Churchill, Randolph S., *Lord Derby, King of Lancashire*, London, 1959, pp.31, 32.
4. *The Times*, Saturday 29 March 1890, p.5, Issue 32972, col. B.
5. Minutes 1901, Sunningdale Golf Club, p.8.
6. Whitfield, John, *Sunningdale Golf Club*, Abertilley, 2000, Appendix 5.
7. Programme Publications, *The Sunningdale Centenary*, Epsom, 2000, p.17.

Chapter 1

1. The Sunningdale Golf Club Minutes, Vol. 1, p.64.
2. *Golf Illustrated*, 26 July 1901, p.36.
3. *The Times*, 15 July 1882, p.1.
4. Swinley Forest Golf Club Minutes, Vol. 1, 15 October 1909, p.1.
5. *Ibid.*, p.3.
6. *Ibid.*, pp.4, 5.

Chapter 2

1. *Golf Illustrated*, 16 July 1909, p.95.
2. Duncan, George and Darwin, Bernard, *Present Day Golf*, London, 1921, p.252.
3. Colt, H.S. and Alison, C.H., *Some Essays on Golf-Course Architecture*, Worcestershire, 1993 edition, p.50.
4. *Ibid.*, p.17.
5. Hawtree, Fred, *Colt & Co.,* Woodstock, 1991, p.197.
6. Duncan and Darwin, p.252.
7. Hartley, George, *A History of St George's Hill Golf Club, 1913-1983*, 1983, p.12.
8. *Ibid.*, p.250.
9. Swinley Forest Golf Club Minutes, Vol. 1, p.6.
10. *The Times*, 19 June 1914.
11. Swinley Forest Golf Club Minutes, Vol. 1, p.9.
12. Sutton, Martin H.F. (ed.), *The Book of the Links*, London, p.20.
13. *Ibid.*
14. *Ibid.*, p.9.
15. Personal comment, Martin Hawtree to author.

16. Colt and Alison, p.13.
17. Hawtree, p.198.
18. Sutton (ed.), p.34.
19. *The Times*, 28 November 1911, p.15, col. A.
20. Sutton (ed.), p.26.
21. *Country Life*, 29 November 1913, p.760.
22. *The Times*, 9 August 1927, p.12.
23. Swinley Forest Golf Club Minutes, Vol. 1, p.20.
24. Sutton (ed.), p.12.
25. *Ibid.*, p.13.
26. *Ibid.*, pp.28, 29.
27. Hawtree, p.201.
28. *Ibid.*, p.114.
29. Huxley, L., *The Life and Letters of Joseph Dalton Hooker O.M.*, London, 1918, Vol. 2, p.257.
30. Allan, Mea, *The Hookers of Kew*, London, 1967, p.225.

CHAPTER 3
1. Churchill, Randolph S., *Lord Derby, King of Lancashire*, London, 1959, p.177.
2. Magnus, Philip, *King Edward the Seventh*, London, 1964, p.170.
3. Quoted in Courtney, Nicholas, *Sporting Royals*, London, 1983, p.162.
4. Hawtree, Fred, *Colt & Co*, Woodstock, 1991, p.40.
5. Personal comment to author.
6. *The Times*, 8 August 1920.
7. Swinley Forest Golf Club Minutes, Vol. 1, p.25.
8. *The Times*, 21 November 1941, p.7, col. E.
9. *Country Life*, 3 June 1922, p.53.
10. Balfour, Arthur James, *Chapters of Autobiography*, London, 1930, p.223.
11. *Ibid.*, p.228.
12. *The Times*, 3 November 1941, p.6, col. D.
13. Bagley, J.J., *The Earls of Derby 1485-1985*, London, 1985, p.213.
14. Waugh, Evelyn, *Vile Bodies*, London, 1930, p.50.
15. Raison, John (ed.), *Golf Match Club 1896-1996*, London, 1996, p.xxxi.
16. *Ibid.*, 22 May 1922.
17. Swinley Forest Golf Club Minutes, Vol. II, p.54.
18. *The Times*, 4 October 1942, p.19, col. B.
19. Churchill, Randolph, *Lord Derby, King of Lancashire*, London, 1959, p.73.
20. Frankland, Noble, *Witness of a Century, the Life and Times of Prince Arthur of Connaught, 1815-1942*, London, 1993, p.375.
21. Swinley Forest Golf Club Minutes, Vol. II, p.39.
22. Bagley, p.231.
23. Churchill, p.73.
24. www.richardworth.co.nz/quotations.htm
25. Hawtree, Martin, personal comment to author.
26. *Swinley Forest Golf Club Minutes*, Vol. II, p.23.
27. Hutchinson, Horace (gen. ed.), *Golf* (The Badminton Library), London, 1890, p.381.
28. *The Times*, 20 October 1881, p.6, col. E.
29. Churchill, p.107.

30. *Ibid.*
31. Swinley Forest Golf Club Minutes, Vol. I, p.62.
32. *Golf Illustrated*, 8 October 1911, p.38.

CHAPTER 4

1. Personal commment, Archie Baird to author.
2.   Sheridan, James, *Sheridan of Sunningdale: My Fifty-Six Years as Caddie-Master*, London, 1967, p.42.
3. *Ibid.*, p.41.
4. The Agenda Club, *The Rough and the Fairway, and enquiry by the Agenda Club into the golf caddie problem*, London, 1912, p.1.
5. *The Times*, 5 January, p.13, col. B.
6. Swinley Forest Golf Club Minutes, Vol. I, p.92.
7. *Ibid.*, p.85.
8. Hutchinson, Horace, *Golf* (Badminton Library), London, 1890, p.304.
9. *The Times*, 5 January, p.13, col. B.
10. Swinley Forest Golf Club Minutes, Vol. I, p.90.
11. Concannon, Dale, *Bullets, Bombs and Birdies, Golf in the Time of War*, Ann Arbour, MI, 2003, p.22.
12. McCrone, Kathleen E., *Sport and Physical Emancipation of Women 1870-1914*, London, 1988, p.277.
13. *The Times*, 1 March 1913, p.8, col. A.
14. *Votes for Women*, 21 February 1913, p.3, col. 2.
15. *Ibid.*, col. 3.
16. *Votes for Women*, 23 February 1913, p.1, col. 4.
17. *Golfing Illustrated*, Vol. 3, No. 1 (1913), p.46.
18. *The Manchester Guardian*, 17 February 1913, p.5, col. A.
19. *The Times*, 19 February 1913, p.12, Issue 40139, col. F.
20. House of Lords Record Office, Correspondence ref. LG/C/7/2/2.
21. *The Eye-Witness*, quoted in Adelman, Paul, *The Decline of the Liberal Party, 1910-31*, London, 1995, p.48.
22. David, E.,(ed.), *Inside Asquith's Cabinet: from the diaries of Charles Hobhouse*, London, 1977, p.139.
23. Hutchinson, p.294.
24. The Swinley Forest Golf Club Minutes, Vol. I, p.56.
25. *The Times*, 1 November 1902, p.11, col. F.
26. Melford, Michael, *Denham Described, A History of Denham Golf Club 1910-1992*, Droitwich, 1992, p.9.
27. Swinley Forest Golf Club Minutes, Vol. I, p.95.

CHAPTER 5

1. Sheridan, James, *Sheridan of Sunningdale, My Fifty-Six Years as Caddie-Master*, London, 1967, p.45.
2. Raison, John (ed.), *Golf Match Club 1896-1996*, London, 1996, p.xxvii.
3. *Golf Monthly*, quoted in Concannon, Dale, *Bullets, Bombs and Birdies, Golf in the Time of War*, Ann Arbor, MI, 2003, p.30.
4. *Ibid.*
5. Whitfield, John, *Sunningdale*, Abertilley, 2000, p.15.

6. Marie Louise, HH Princess, *My Memoirs of Six Reigns*, London, 1956, p.181.
7. *Ibid.*
8. Whitfield, p.16.
9. Personal comment, Lord Glenconner to author.
10. Swinley Forest Golf Club Minutes, Vol. I, p.107.
11. *Ibid.*
12. Hutchins, Victoria, *Messrs Hoare Bankers: A History of the Hoare Banking Dynasty*, London, 2005, p.18.
13. Swinley Forest Golf Club Minutes, Vol. I, p.108.
14. *The Times*, 10 May 1916, col. E, p.5.
15. Swinley Forest Golf Club Minutes, Vol. I, p.128.
16. *Ibid.*, p.115.
17. *Golf Illustrated*, 12 October 1916, p.23.
18. Swinley Forest Golf Club Minutes, Vol. I, p.113.
19. *Ibid.*, p.121.
20. Windsor, Duke of, *A Family Album*, London, 1960, p.130.
21. *Ibid.*, p.131.
22. Collis, Maurice, *Nancy Astor*, London, 1960, p.177.
23. Swinley Forest Golf Club Minutes, Vol. I, p.124.
24. *Country Life*, 1 May 1928, p.42.
25. Swinley Forest Golf Club Minutes, Vol. I, p.37.
26. Personal comment, the Hon. Michael Spring Rice to author.
27. Swinley Forest Golf Club Minutes, Vol. I, p.133.
28. Personal comment, Rupert Hambro to author.
29. Swinley Forest Golf Club Minutes, Vol. I, p.130.
30. *Ibid.*, p.133.
31. Cousins, Geoffrey, *Golf in Britain, A Social History from the beginning to the present day*, London 1975, p.127.
32. Fernhill Workmen's Golf Club, Swinley, List of General Members, Rules and General Information, 1924, p.4.
33. *Ibid.*, p.14.
34. Darwin, Bernard, *Golf Between the Wars*, London, 1944, p.17.
35. James, Robert Rhodes (ed.), *Chips, The Diaries of Sir Henry Channon*, London, 1967, p.202.
36. *The Times*, 20 May 1929, col. E, p.10.
37. Darwin, p.206.
38. Swinley Forest Golf Club Minutes, Vol. II, 3 February 1932, p.36.
39. *Ibid.*, p.41.
40. *Ibid.*, p.47.
41. Colt, H.S., testimonial for Angus Macdonald, 20 October 1932.
42. Fernhill Artisans' Minutes, 1 April 1938.
43. Colt, testimonial.
44. *Ibid.*
45. Swinley Forest Golf Club circular letter to members dated December 1938.
46. Swinley Forest Golf Club Minutes, Vol. I, 10 September 1939, p.89.
47. Personal comment, Mrs Sheena Boreham (*née* Macdonald) to author.
48. Quoted in Weightman, Christine, *Remembering Wartime Ascot, Sunningdale and Sunninghill 1939-1945*, Ascot, 2006.

49. Swinley Forest Golf Club Minutes, Vol. III, 15 July 1945, p.17.
50. *Ibid.*, p.58.

CHAPTER 6
1. *The Times*, Tuesday 20 November 1962, p.15, col. A.
2. *Single or Return—The official history of the Transport Salaried Staffs' Association*, ch. 22, No. 5.
3. *The Times*, Tuesday, 20 November 1962, p.15, col. A.
4. *Ibid.*
5. Fleming, Ian, *Goldfinger*, London, 1959, p.58.
6. Donaldson, Frances, *Edward VIII*, London, 1974, p.275.
7. Monckton Papers, quoted in Donaldson, p.283.
8. Hyde, H. Montgomery, *Baldwin the unexpected Prime Minister*, London, 1973, p.458.
9. *Ibid.*
10. Donaldson, p.283.
11. Hyde, p.517.
12. *Ibid.*
13. Swinley Forest Golf Club Minutes, Vol. III, p.135.
14. Personal comment, Lord Alvingham to author.
15. *Ibid.*
16. Swinley Forest Golf Club Minutes, Vol. III, 20 February 1949, p.87.
17. *Ibid.*, p.96.
18. *PGA Profile* magazine, February 1950, p.2.
19. Swinley Forest Golf Club Minutes Vol. IV, circular letter, 12 May 1954, p.47.
20. Swinley Forest Golf Club Rules, 27 April 1997, p.6.
21. Personal comment, Lord Alvingham to author.
22. Personal comment, Mrs James Harrison to author.
23. Personal comment, Lord Alvingham to author.

CHAPTER 7
1. Personal comment, Mrs Dick Bateman to author.
2. *Ibid.*
3. Personal comment, anon to author.
4. Personal comment, Mrs Dick Bateman to author.
5. Personal comment, Lord Alvingham to author.
6. Personal comment, The Hon. Anthony Warrender to author.
7. Letter from Henrietta, Duchess of Bedford, to author, 16 July 2007.
8. Personal comment, Jamie Illingworth to author.
9. Personal comment, Andrew Martin Smith to author.
10. Personal comment, Sir Roger Gibbs to author.
11. *Foremost Newsletter*, September 2001, Issue No. 65, p.4.
12. de St Jorre, John, *Legendary Golf Clubs of Scotland, England, Wales and Ireland*, Florida, 1998, p.195.
13. Sir John Wrixon-Becher Bt, email to author.
14. Swinley Forest Golf Club Minutes, Vol. IV, 9 July 1950, p.135.
15. Personal comment, Lt Col Sir John Johnston to author.
16. *Ibid.*

17. Personal comment, Robert Buxton to author.
18. Cousins, Geoffrey, *Golf in Britain, A social history from the beginnings to the present day*, London, 1975.
19. Personal comment, Lady Brabazon of Tara to author.
20. Quoted in Cousins, p.103.
21. Papazian, Gib, *San Mateo County Times*, p.10
22. Swinley Forest Golf Club Minutes, Vol. VI, 12 July 1987, p.8.
23. *Ibid.*, Vol. IV, 3 March 1989, p.39.
24. *Ibid.*, 22 January 1989, p.61.
25. *The Daily Telegraph*, 9 June 2002, p.36.
26. Letter from Roger Harman to Sir Roger Gibbs, 28 February 1995.
27. Swinley Forest Golf Club Minutes (supplementary), Vol. VI, 14 January 1990, p.86.
28. Letter from Marcus Agius to author, 6 July 2007.
29. Personal comment, John S. McCall to author.
30. Personal comment, Mrs Dick Bateman to author.
31. *Ibid.*
32. Swinley Forest Golf Club Minutes, Vol. V, 24 October 1976, p.70.
33. Personal comment, Mrs Hazel Harrison to author.
34. Letter from Chris Sandham to author.
35. Personal comment, Bateman to author.
36. Letter from Walter Annenberg to R.F. Bateman, 12 November 1971.
37. *Christian Science Monitor*, 2 August 1971, p.13.
38. Personal comment, Lt Col Sir John Johnston to author, 29 June 2007.
39. Personal comment, Roger Wellesley-Smith to author.
40. Personal comment, Tim C. Pilkington to author.
41. *The Times*, 2 June 2001, p.8.
42. *Sunday Times*, 19 September 1993, p.11.
43. Personal comment, Gervase Thomas to author.
44. Personal comment, Lt Col Ian Pearce to author.
45. Personal comment, Colin Frizzel to author
46. *The Daily Mail*, 29 March 1997, p.6.
47. *The Daily Mail,* 28 March 1996, p.39.
48. *The Times*, 2 October 2001, p.6.
49. *Ibid.*
50. Letter from Miss Allison Derrett, Assistant Registrar, The Royal Archives, Windsor Castle to author.
51. Wheeler-Bennett, Sir John W., *King George VI, His Life and Reign*, London, 1958, p.131.
52. *The Times,* 14 September 2006, p.69.
53. Duke of York to John Hopkins, *The Times,* 2 October 2001, p.6.
54. Personal comment, Lt Col Sir John Johnston to author.

CHAPTER 8

1. *The Times*, Saturday, 24 November 1951, p.8, col. E.
2. Letter from T.W. Ingham to F.W. Hawtree, 15 December 1987.
3. Letter from Lt Col Ian Pearce to author.
4. Swinley Forest Golf Club Minutes, Vol. VI, 10 July 1988, p.40.

5. *Ibid.*
6. Personal comment, Roderick Bullough to author.
7. The Golf Match Club rule book, p.43.
8. *Golf Match Club 1896-1996*, London, p.xxxvii.
9. *Time Magazine*, 9 June 1924, p.42.
10. Personal comment, Lt Col Ian Pearce to author.
11. Letter to the Hon. E. Baillieu, 5 November 1993.
12. *Ibid.*
13. Letter from Andrew Martin Smith to the Hon. E. Baillieu, 6 September 1993.
14. Personal comment, Andrew Martin Smith to author.
15. Letter from Andrew Martin Smith to the Hon. E. Baillieu, undated.
16. Letter from Peter Bedford to author, 5 July 2007.
17. Letter from Lord Pearson of Rannoch to Lt Col Ian Pearce, 10 September 1993.
18. Julian Jack, farewell speech to Sir Roger Gibbs as chairman of the Wellcome Trust, February 2000.
19. Personal comment, Sir Roger Gibbs to author.
20. *Ibid.*
21. Personal comment, anon.
22. *The Times*, 9 January 2004, p.48.
23. Swinley Forest Golf Club Minutes, Vol. IX, 2 April 2005, p.20.
24. *Ibid.*, Vol. IX, 7 November 2005, p.2.
25. *Ibid.*, Vol. IX, 4 September 2005, p.1.
26. *The Daily Mail*, 17 July 2004, p.20.
27. *The Financial Times,* 4 December 2004, p.14.
28. *The Times,* 5 September 1998, p.36.
29. *Sunday Times*, 19 September 1993, p.11.
30. *The Times*, 1 September 1990.
31. Personal comment, Sir Sean Connery to author.
32. Personal comment, Sir John Milne to author.
33. Personal comment, Sir Roger Gibbs to author.
34. Letter from Miles Maskell to author.
35. Personal comment, Sir Roger Gibbs to author.
36. *Sunday Times*, 19 September 1993, p.11.
37. Swinley Forest Golf Club entry on Golf Club Access, http://www.golfclubatlas.com/swinley000134.html

APPENDIX 1
1. *The Times,* 16 June 1999, p.41.
2. *Ibid.*
3. Tally, Russel, *passim.*
4. Letter from John Brennan to author.
5. Personal comment, Peter Wilmot-Sitwell to author.
6. Letter from Peter Bedford to author, 5 July 2007.
7. Personal comment, Sir John Milne to author.
8. Swinley Forest Golf Club Minutes, Vol. II, 3 June 1949, p.65.
9. Personal comment, Peter Wilmot-Sitwell to author.
10. *The Daily Mail*, 10 April 1996, p.29.

11. *Ibid.*, 4 March 1998, p.37.
12. *Ibid.*
13. *The Independent*, 7 June 2004, p.36.
14. Letter from Sir Christopher Lever to author, 3 July 2007.
15. *The Times*, 11 July 1995, p.19.
16. Letter from Sir Roger Gibbs to author, 16 August 2007.
17. Letter from James Harker to author, 9 July 2007.
18. Personal comment, Lawson Bingham to author.
19. Oakley, Robin, *The Spectator*, 17 May 1997, p.78.
20. *Ibid.*
21. Personal comment, Sir John Wrixon-Becher to author.
22. Letter from Christopher Sandham to author, 29 June 2007.
23. Letter from Sir Christopher Lever to author, 2 July 2007.
24. Letter from anon to author.
25. Quoted in Lean, V.S., *Collections*, 1902.
26. *The Times*, 28 February 1983, p.6, col. D.
27. www.uss-ranger.org
28. Letter from David Naylor-Leyland to author.
29. Personal comment, Richard Goodhew to author.
30. Letter from Chris Sandham to author, 6 July 2007.
31. de St Jorre, John, *Legendary Golf Clubs of Scotland, England, Wales and Ireland*, Wellington, Florida, 1998, p.179.
32. Diary entry, 13 August 1964, Alistair Buchanan.
33. Letter from John Shipton to author, 9 July 2007.
34. Letter from Sir John Wrixon-Becher to author, 6 June 2007.

APPENDIX II

1. Hughes, G.M., *History of Windsor Forest, Sunninghill and the Great Park*, London, 1890, p.26.
2. Maitland, Frederick W., *(Henry de) Bracton's Note Book*, Vol. iii, London, 1987, p.42.
3. *Ibid.*, p.41.
4. *Ibid.*, p.77.
5. Swift, quoted in Hughes, G.M., p.72.
6. Maitland, p.61.
7. Hore, J.P., *The History of the Royal Buckhounds*, London, 1893, p.385.
8. *The Times*, 10 October 1797, Issue 4010, p.3, col. D.
9. Hughes, p.78.
10. *Reading Mercury*, 18 July 1800, p.1.
11. *The Times*, 17 October 1843, p.4, col. E.
12. *New York Times*, 22 October 1925, p.8.
13. Ribblesdale, Lord, *The Royal Buckhounds*, London, 1897, p.85.
14. *Ibid.*, p.175.
15. Ditchfield, the Rev. P.H. and Page, William, *The History of the County of Berkshire*, London, 1907, p.301.

INDEX

Compiled by Auriol Griffith-Jones

Page numbers in *italics* refer to illustration captions.

Parte of Buc.

Maydenhead

Braye

Filbrdes

New Lodge

Bildewell the

Hollyport

okely greene

Bordenbridge

Crowfeild

walke

Wynckfeild

Flayn

White waltham

Wyngfeld

Laurence waltham

Shatessam

wynfeilde wal

Warseilde

Russcombe

Billmghey

Twyforde

Brinfeild

New Brook

olde Breck-noll

Sun

Hurste

Ockingham

Easthamsted Parke

Easthamsted

walke

Noddenbridge

Sandford mil

Deery hill

Bearewood

Domey house

Towsley heath

Crowthorne

Brgbot Rayles

wellbotom

Hertledge

...that the walke
...yly walk is for
...inclosed ground
...un to be stored w
...Deere by Sir
...C keeper of the
...tance

YLI-

WIKE